Spinoza and the Stoics

For many years, philosophers and other scholars have commented on the remarkable similarity between Spinoza and the Stoics, with some even going so far as to speak of 'Spinoza the Stoic'. Until now, however, no one has systematically examined the relationship between the two systems. In *Spinoza and the Stoics* Jon Miller takes on this task, showing how key elements of Spinoza's metaphysics, epistemology, philosophical psychology, and ethics relate to their Stoic counterparts. Drawing on a wide range of secondary literature including the most up-to-date scholarship and a close examination of the textual evidence, Jon Miller not only reveals the sense in which Spinoza was, and was not, a Stoic, but also offers new insights into how each system should be understood in itself. His book will be of great interest to scholars and students of ancient philosophy, early modern philosophy, Spinoza, and the philosophy of the Stoics.

Jon Miller is Associate Professor of Philosophy at Queen's University, Ontario. His many publications include *Hellenistic and Early Modern Philosophy* (Cambridge, 2003), *Aristotle's Nicomachean Ethics: A Critical Guide* (Cambridge, 2011), and *The Reception of Aristotle's Ethics* (Cambridge, 2012).

Spinoza and the Stoics

By
Jon Miller

CAMBRIDGE
UNIVERSITY PRESS

CAMBRIDGE
UNIVERSITY PRESS

University Printing House, Cambridge CB2 8BS, United Kingdom

One Liberty Plaza, 20th Floor, New York, NY 10006, USA

477 Williamstown Road, Port Melbourne, VIC 3207, Australia

314-321, 3rd Floor, Plot 3, Splendor Forum, Jasola District Centre, New Delhi-110025, India

79 Anson Road, #06-04/06, Singapore 079906

Cambridge University Press is part of the University of Cambridge.

It furthers the University's mission by disseminating knowledge in the pursuit of education, learning and research at the highest international levels of excellence.

www.cambridge.org
Information on this title: www.cambridge.org/9781108456043

First published 2015
First paperback edition 2018

A catalogue record for this publication is available from the British Library

Library of Congress Cataloging in Publication data
Miller, Jon, 1969–
Spinoza and the stoics / by Jon Miller.
  pages   cm
Includes bibliographical references and index.
ISBN 978-1-107-00070-4
1. Spinoza, Benedictus de, 1632–1677.   2. Stoics.   I. Title.
B3998.M49   2015
199′.492–dc23
                                        2014042935

ISBN 978-1-107-00070-4 Hardback
ISBN 978-1-108-45604-3 Paperback

Contents

Acknowledgements   vii
List of abbreviations   ix

Introduction   1

1 The apparent similarities between Spinozism
   and Stoicism   3
2 Why study Spinoza and the Stoics?   6
3 Methodological notes   8
4 Overview of the chapters   11
5 What is not covered in this book   15
6 Historical background: Stoicism in Spinoza's day and what
   he knew of it   16

1 Monism   24

1.1 Monism in general   26
1.2 Stoic and Spinozistic monisms   29
1.3 Arguments for monism   47
1.4 Conclusion: teleology   53

2 *Phantasia* and ideas   61

2.1 Externalism versus internalism   62
2.2 Typology   74
2.3 Contextualizing impressions/ideas   85
2.4 Conclusion   98

3 *Conatus* and *oikeiosis*   100

3.1 *Oikeiosis*, not *horme*   101
3.2 Self-preservation   103
3.3 From self-preservation to . . .?   119
3.4 Conclusion   137
Appendix: on the (in)coherency of Spinozism   137

4 Value   144

4.1 Value theory   145
4.2 Three categories of value   147
4.3 On the normativity of the good   150
4.4 Relativism versus absolutism   156

4.5 The factualness of values 164
4.6 Conclusion: what counts as good 167

5 Happiness 170
5.1 The language of happiness 173
5.2 The form and content of happiness 182
5.3 Eudaimonic form and content in Stoicism 183
5.4 Cartesian innovations 187
5.5 Spinoza's eudaimonic form 189
5.6 Spinoza's eudaimonic content 195
5.7 Conclusion: life according to nature 202

Conclusion: Spinoza and the Stoics? 207

Bibliography 211
Index of names 231
General index 236

Acknowledgements

Research and writing can bring me great pleasure. The greatest ones may be those associated with the learning and discovery. Close behind, however, are those connected to all the interactions that I am able to have with fellow citizens in the republic of letters. Because this particular venture has been years in the making, I am not able to remember everybody who has contributed to it in some way. For those who I am omitting, I must ask their forbearance.

As I think about whom to acknowledge, I must start with Brad Inwood, Calvin Normore, and Phillip Mitsis. Brad's skills as a philosopher and scholar are only surpassed by his skills as a teacher; I consider myself fortunate to have spent so much time learning from him. Calvin may not be as organized as Brad, but when I was able to attract his attention, I was sure that there were not many people on the planet (and maybe in the universe(s)) who could provide better guidance. Phillip is one of the rare few (in my experience, at least) who can take philosophy and scholarship seriously, while also keeping it in perspective. As an added bonus, all three men make what we're doing fun.

Besides those three, there are many others to whom I find myself in the right kind of debt. High on this list would be the friendly folk from the Nordic countries, especially Lilli Alanen, Eyjólfur K. Emilsson and Olli Koistinen. Equally high would be the equally friendly (if occasionally quirky) folk from the land of the early moderns, especially John Carriero, Alan Gabbey, André Gombay, Fabrizio Mondadori, and Steve Nadler.

Beyond the aforementioned, I have benefitted enormously from discussions and correspondence with Hans Blom, Deborah Brown, Ed Curley, Michael Della Rocca, Aaron Garrett, Don Garrett, Louis-Philippe Hodgson, Terry Irwin, Susan James, Charlie Jarrett, Richard Kraut, Henrik Lagerlund, Mike LeBuffe, Tony Long, Frédéric Manzini, Stephen Menn, Don Rutherford, Chris Shields, Justin Steinberg, Valterri Viljanen, and Catherine Wilson. Here at my university, I want and need to thank my colleagues Rahul Kumar and Steve Leighton, as well as my students in various classes (especially Torin Doppelt, Elyse Platt, and Erich Schaeffer).

Hilary Gaskin of Cambridge University Press has been an excellent editor, at times patient, at other times prodding, depending on what the circumstances required. Her assistants Anna Lowe and Rosemary Crawley always provided timely and helpful advice. The excellence of Gaskin and her team shows, inter alia, in their choice of anonymous referees to vet my manuscript. The reports which they produced were thorough, critical, tough – and extremely helpful. I am greatly obliged to them for their hard work.

Financial assistance of various kinds was provided by Queen's University and SSHRC at different stages during the work on this manuscript. I am grateful for their support.

Finally, I come to my immediate family. Our three finite modes Magnolia, Gus, and Poppy are endless sources of infinite joy for me. I only hope that I have been able to give them some knowledge, however inadequate, of how much they mean to me. The same is true for my wife, Sabra.

Many thanks, to all.

Now I must offer a different kind of acknowledgement. While the great majority of this volume is new, I have occasionally incorporated ideas and passages from previously printed publications. I am pleased to acknowledge those instances here:

- Chapter 1 has drawn upon material from Jon Miller, 'Spinoza and the Stoics on substance monism': 99–117, in *The Cambridge Companion to Spinoza's Ethics*, edited by Olli Koistinen, © Cambridge University Press 2009. Reprinted with permission.
- Chapter 4 has drawn upon material from Jon Miller, 'Spinoza's axiology', *Oxford Studies in Early Modern Philosophy*, edited by Daniel Garber and Steven Nadler, vol. II: 149–172.
- Chapter 5 has drawn upon material originally published as 'A distinction regarding happiness in ancient philosophy', in *Social Research: An International Quarterly of the Social Sciences*, Volume 77, Number 2 (Summer, 2010): 595–624. Used with permission of *Social Research* <www.socres.org>.
- Chapter 5 has also drawn upon some material published as 'Spinoza on the life according to nature', in *Essays on Spinoza's Ethical Theory*, edited by Andrew Youpa and Matthew Kisner, Oxford University Press 2014.

Finally, the epigraphs for Chapters 1–5 are drawn from either Long and Sedley (1987) or Curley's translation of Spinoza (Spinoza (1985)). The Long and Sedley epigraphs are reproduced with permission of Cambridge University Press. The Spinoza ones are reproduced with permission of Princeton University Press.

Abbreviations

Standard abbreviations are used when referring to passages in Spinoza's *Ethics*. A Roman numeral refers to the part number, 'D' for 'Definition', 'A' for 'Axiom', 'P' plus an Arabic numeral for a Proposition, 'Cor' for 'Corollary' (with an Arabic numeral where required), 'Dem' for 'Demonstration' (with an Arabic numeral where required), 'S' for 'Scholium' (with an Arabic numeral where required), 'App' for Appendix, and so on. For example, 'IIP7' refers to Proposition 7 of Part II, and 'IIIP40Cor2Sch' refers to the Scholium of the second Corollary to Proposition 40 of Part III.

Acad.	Cicero, *Academica*
Aet. mundi	Philo, *On the Eternity of the World*
AM	Sextus Empiricus, *Against the Mathematicians*
A-T	*Oeuvres de Descartes*, Charles Adam and Paul Tannery (1897–1913)
CSM	*The Philosophical Writings of Descartes*, vols. I–II (Descartes 1984–91)
CSMK	*The Philosophical Writings of Descartes*, vol. III (Descartes 1991)
Curley	*The Collected Works of Spinoza*, vol. 1 (1985)
De ben.	Seneca, *On Benefits*
De comm. not.	Plutarch, *On Common Opinions Against the Stoics*
De fin.	Cicero, *On Ends*
De mix.	Alexander of Aphrodisias, *On mixture*
De off.	Cicero, *On Duties*
DK	Diels and Kranz, *Die Fragmente der Vorsokratiker* (1903–)
DL	Diogenes Laertius' *Lives of Eminent Philosophers*
Ecl.	Stobaeus, *Eclogues*
G	*Benedict de Spinoza Opera*, ed. Carl Gebhardt, 1925
I-G	Inwood and Gerson (1997)

L-S	Long and Sedley (1987)
In Ar. An. Pr.	Alexander of Aphrodisias, *On Aristotle's Prior Analytics*
In Ar. Top.	Alexander of Aphrodisias, *On Aristotle's Topics*
ND	Cicero, *On the Nature of the Gods*
NE	Aristotle, *Nicomachean Ethics*
Noct. Att.	Gellius, *Attic Nights*
PH	Sextus Empiricus, *Outlines of Pyrrhonism*
PHP	Galen, *On the Opinions of Hippocrates and Plato*
Stoic. Rep.	Plutarch, *On Stoic Self-Contradictions*
SVF	*Stoicorum Veterum Fragmenta*, ed. Hans von Arnim, 1903–5
TD	Cicero, *Tusculan Disputations*
TdIE	Spinoza, *Treatise on the Emendation of the Intellect*
TP	Spinoza, *Tractatus Politicus*
TTP	Spinoza, *Theological–Political Treatise*

Introduction

From his day to ours, commentators have talked about the remarkable similarities between Spinoza and the Stoics. Possibly writing while Spinoza was still alive, Leibniz branded him a leader of a 'sect of new Stoics' which held that 'things act because of [the universe's] power and not due to a rational choice'.[1] Much later in his life he said,

> Certain ancient and more recent thinkers have asserted ... that God is a spirit diffuse throughout the whole universe, which animates organic bodies wherever it meets them, just as the wind produces music in organ pipes. The Stoics were probably not averse to this opinion ... In another way Spinoza tends towards the same view.[2]

This particular commonality also impressed Pierre Bayle, who attached even more importance to it than Leibniz. Bayle said in his *Dictionary*, 'The doctrine of the world-soul, which was ... the principal part of the system of the Stoics, is at bottom the same as Spinoza's.'[3]

Around the same time, the Lutheran theologian–philosopher Johann Franz Buddeus (1667–1729) wrote a dissertation called 'Spinozism before Spinoza'.[4] In this treatise and elsewhere, he closely linked Spinozism with Stoicism. For him as for Leibniz and Bayle, what makes the two systems so similar is that both make God immanent in the world.[5] The same is true for Giambattista Vico. In the third edition of his *New Science*, he said that because they made 'God an infinite mind, subject to fate, in an infinite body', the Stoics were 'the Spinozists of their day'.[6]

During the nineteenth century Hegel argued that, although they belonged to different dialectical stages in the 'progress of Philosophy',

---

[1] The excerpt comes from an untitled paper thought to be written by Leibniz between 1677 and 1680 (trans. Arlew and Garber, in Leibniz (1989), 281 ff.).
[2] Leibniz to Hansch, 25 July 1707 (trans. Loemker, in Leibniz (1969), 594).
[3] Bayle (1740), article on Spinoza, entry 'A' (my translation).   [4] Buddeus (1701).
[5] For more on Buddeus' interpretation of the Stoics as proto-Spinozists, see the excellent discussion in Brooke (2012), 141 ff.
[6] Vico (1948), §335 (p. 87).

1

2Introduction

Stoics and Spinoza should be seen as contributing in their own ways to the articulation of an idealistic metaphysics, one which dogmatically asserts what he called the metaphysics of the understanding.[7] A few generations later, Wilhelm Dilthey expressed an analogous thesis, holding that 'rigorous Stoicism' and Spinozism marked successive phases in the unfolding of 'objective idealism', one of the three principle types of worldview that have been articulated through the course of history.[8]

In our own day, many commentators have argued that Spinozism matched or even surpassed the Stoicism of the ancient Stoics in all respects: metaphysically/physically, methodologically/logically, and normatively/ethically. Thus Susan James has published an article called 'Spinoza the Stoic'[9] while Amélie Oksenberg Rorty asserts, without argument, that Spinoza's 'indebtedness to ancient Stoicism is apparent'.[10] Even those who are more cautious see profound connections between Spinoza and the Stoics. For example, even as he acknowledges other 'influences', Andreas Graeser says that Stoicism plays 'a special role' in the formulation of Spinoza's thought.[11] Similarly, A. A. Long writes, 'Spinoza's striking affinity to Stoicism coexists with striking differences between them.'[12]

Augustine often marvelled on the congruence of Plato's views with those of his devoted follower Plotinus. At one point he went so far as to write, 'one might think them contemporaries if the length of time between them did not compel us to say that in Plotinus Plato was reborn'.[13] For all differences between the two cases, it seems that much the same could be said of Spinoza and the Stoics. Or could it?[14]

[7] Hegel (1896), vol. III, 358–9.
[8] Dilthey (1924), 402 (my translation). See also Dilthey (1957), ch. 5.
[9] James (1993).
[10] Rorty (1996), 338. To be fair to Rorty, she surely could muster an argument if pressed. My point is rather that she does not feel the need to advance one, since she takes Spinoza's borrowings from the Stoics to be totally obvious.
[11] Graeser (1991), 336 (my translation).
[12] Long (2003), 10. Bidney (1962), Matheron (1994), and Lloyd (2008), 200–14, are others who see Spinoza as arguing for Stoical ideas without identifying him as a Stoic.
[13] *Contra academicos* III.18.41.
[14] As is appropriate for a philosophical work, I will deal with apparent similarities in the ideas and arguments put forward by Spinoza and the Stoics. For what it is worth, however, I would note that Spinoza was also said to have a Stoic personality in what is regarded as the earliest known biography of Spinoza, that by Johannes Colerus. Towards the end of his book, where he is describing how Spinoza endured his last days, Colerus says that Spinoza 'always exprest, in all his sufferings, a truly *Stoical* constancy' (Colerus (1706), 87).

1   The apparent similarities between Spinozism and Stoicism

To decide the answer to that question, at least provisionally, let me offer a survey of many core philosophical beliefs held by Spinoza and the Stoics. Both identified God and Nature, taking God/Nature to be eternal and the immanent cause of all things.[15] They contended that God/Nature is the only true substance, relegating all other members of the universe to the status of non-substances.[16] They held that all beings belong to a causal network in which causes are necessarily connected to their effects. In Stoicism, 'nothing exists in the world or happens causelessly';[17] in Spinozism,[18] 'nothing exists from whose nature some effect does not follow'.[19] They both based this causal network on God/Nature. As the Stoics argued, 'the world would be wrenched apart and divided, and no longer remain a unity, for ever governed in accordance with a single order and management, if an uncaused motion were introduced'.[20] In Spinoza's words, 'In nature there is nothing contingent, but all things have been determined from the necessity of the divine nature to exist and produce an effect in a certain way.'[21]

Regarding the relation of human beings to God/Nature and the eternal exceptionless causal series which it instantiates, Stoics and Spinoza both stressed that we are just as much a part of, and governed by, the world-system as all other discrete individuals. Stoics were reported to hold that 'Our natures are parts of the nature of the universe',[22] while Spinoza flatly stated, 'It is impossible that a man should not be a part of Nature.'[23] Free will in the sense of choosing between two (or more) equally available options is ruled out by the causal series: 'for they [the Stoics] deny that man has the freedom to choose between opposite actions',[24] and 'The will cannot be called a free cause, but only a necessary one.'[25] The ideal human condition is found by melding with the determinations of God/Nature. For Stoics,

---

[15] For Stoics, see *ND* 1.39 and *AM* IX.75–6. For Spinoza, IP15 and IP18. I will address the difference between 'Nature' and 'nature' on p. 28.

[16] For Stoics, see DL VII.148. For Spinoza, IP16.

[17] Alexander of Aphrodisias, *De fato* 192 (L-S 55N2).

[18] Here and throughout I use 'Spinozism' (and its cognates) because it is the only unstrained pairing of 'Stoicism'. It should be understood, however, that 'Spinozism' refers to Spinoza's own thought and not that of his followers. In this respect, Spinozism differs from Cartesianism, which can invoke the ideas of Descartes' followers as much as it does the thought of Descartes himself.

[19] IP36.   [20] Alexander of Aphrodisias, *De fato* 192 (L-S 55N2).   [21] IP29.

[22] DL VII.88 (I-G 191).   [23] IVP4.

[24] Alexander of Aphrodisias, *De fato* 181 (L-S 62G1).   [25] IP32.

[T]he goal [of life] becomes 'to live consistently with nature', i.e., according to one's own nature and that of the universe ... And this itself is the virtue of the happy man and a smooth flow of life, whenever all things are done according to the harmony of the daimon in each of us with the will of the administrator of the universe.[26]

On Spinoza's view, 'perfect' human nature consists in 'the knowledge of the union that the mind has with the whole of Nature'.[27]

The list of overlapping commitments goes on and on. For example, the main features of each party's philosophical psychology are practically identical. *Pace* Plato, the mind has no parts but rather is comprised of a single entity with diverse powers.[28] The single entity comprising the mind, both parties agree, is reason.[29] Because they think of the matter of the mind as constituted by reason, Spinoza and the Stoics explained all mental conflicts as conflicts internal to reason and nothing else.[30] To cite a different example, this time from the moral domain, both parties defined virtue in terms of utility or benefit, so that some good is a virtue only in the case that it is necessarily useful or beneficial to its possessor.[31] Now, they thought that a good could be useful or beneficial to its possessor only insofar as it agrees with its possessor's nature.[32] Since our natures are essentially rational, they concluded that reason is the greatest virtue.[33] Or, to be more precise, reason is the *only* virtue.[34]

Even apparent differences of opinion seem to mask comity on a more basic level. For instance, Spinoza singled out the Stoics for criticism in the Preface to Part V of the *Ethics*: 'The mind does not have an absolute dominion over [the passions]. Nevertheless, the Stoics thought that they depend entirely on our will, and that we can command them absolutely.'[35] Now, even if Spinoza correctly read the Stoic position on whether and to

---

[26] DL VII.88 (I-G 191–2). Cf. Epictetus: '[The philosopher] should bring his own will into harmony with what happens, so that neither anything that happens happens against our will, nor anything that fails to happen fails to happen when we wish it to happen' (II.14.7, trans. Oldfather; Epictetus (1928)).

[27] *TdIE* §13. Cf. IVApp32.

[28] For Stoics, see Aetius 4.21 or Galen, *PHP*, V.6.37. Note that I am ignoring those Stoic dissidents, such as Posidonius, who partitioned the soul. An argument is required to clarify Spinoza's psychological monism but I think it is shown well-enough by IVP36Sch.

[29] For Stoics, see Stobaeus II.88 ff. For Spinoza, see VPref (at G II, 280: 22).

[30] For Stoics, see Plutarch, *On Moral Virtue*, 446 ff., together with discussion by Graver (2007), 69. For Spinoza, see his definition of 'vacillation of mind' in IIIP17Sch.

[31] For Stoics, Sextus Empiricus, *AM* 11.22 ff. For Spinoza, IVP18Sch (at G II, 222: 24–5).

[32] For Stoics, DL VII.101–2. For Spinoza, IVP31 and IVP31Cor.

[33] For Stoics, Seneca, *Ep.* 76.10. For Spinoza, IVApp4.

[34] For Stoics, Stobaeus II.77 or, more poetically, Epictetus, *Discourses* IV.8.12. For Spinoza, IVP26.

[35] G II, 277: 20 ff.

what extent we can control our emotions,[36] and even if there is a genuine difference here between his views and those of the Stoics,[37] the importance of the whole business becomes nugatory when other elements in each party's theory of emotions are factored in. Both Spinoza and the Stoics took the emotions to be cognitive – they thought that emotions have propositional contents which are believed or endorsed as true by those having the emotions.[38] However, the propositional content found in emotions is not actually veridical, for the states of affairs that they represent are not accurate.[39] And this leads to a problem. Given that emotions are false beliefs, they prevent us from reaching our ultimate objective of becoming fully rational beings.[40] Here we learn why both Spinoza and the Stoics regarded most[41] emotions as moral hazards that ought to be extirpated. Fortunately, the very feature of emotions that makes them morally repugnant also provides the means by which we may correct them. Once their falsity is recognized, Spinoza and the Stoics thought the emotions themselves would dissipate, leaving us more rational than before.[42]

So far I have spoken of places where Spinoza and the Stoics agree on major issues. But the remarkable similarity of the two systems is perhaps even better demonstrated by the many smaller points of convergence. These are present in many areas of the systems but since I have just been talking about the theory of emotions, let me cite a pair of examples from there. While Spinoza and the Stoics argue for the extirpation of negative emotions, they simultaneously identified a small set of positive emotions that could be part of the ideal life.[43] The Stoics called these 'good feelings'

---

[36] Long (2003), n. 14, argues that Spinoza conflates two Stoic theses: (1) passions are judgments of the rational mind; and (2) the will is free, at least in principle, from antecedent causation.

[37] Stoics were well-aware of the difficulty of controlling emotions (see Graver (2007), ch. 3 for discussion). For his part, Spinoza offered an argument only a few pages after the passage of VPref that I just quoted, to the effect that any passion whatsoever can be controlled by the mind (see VP3–4 together with the discussion in Pereboom (1994), 611–15).

[38] For Stoics, see Galen, *PHP*, IV.3.2 and V.2.49 ff. (SVF I.209 and II.841). For Spinoza, see especially the analysis on the origins of the passions in *Ethics* III, where they are shown to be ideas (especially IIIP9 and P11).

[39] For Stoics, see Stobaeus II.88 ff. (SVF 3.378 and III.389). For Spinoza, IIIP3.

[40] For Stoics, see Galen, *PHP*, IV.2.9–18 (SVF 3.462). For Spinoza, IVAppIV–V.

[41] The need for this qualification is given in the next paragraph.

[42] For Stoics, see Epictetus, *Enchiridion*, 5. For Spinoza, VP3.

[43] So Martha Nussbaum is mistaken when she writes, 'The Stoics and Spinoza dislike the emotions intensely' (Nussbaum (2000), 73). Stoics and Spinoza dislike emotions which interfere with our ability to lead a life according to nature. They like all emotions which augment the life according to nature. Nussbaum explores Spinoza's views more fully in Nussbaum (2001), 500–10.

(*eupatheiai*); Spinoza labelled them 'active affects'.[44] Additionally, Spinoza and the Stoics held similar views on specific emotions. To offer but one example,[45] Seneca wrote, '[H]ope and fear, dissimilar as they are, keep step together ... [T]he chief cause of both these ills is that we do not adapt ourselves to the present, but send our thoughts a long way ahead.'[46] Echoing this thesis almost verbatim, Spinoza argued that there is no hope without fear and neither will have any part in the healthy mind for they burden it with inconstancy.[47]

There is a passage in Spinoza that has understandably been called 'transparently and profoundly Stoic'.[48] To finish making the case for his Stoicalness, I can do no better than to quote it at length:

Human power is very limited and infinitely surpassed by the power of external causes. So we do not have an absolute power to adapt things outside us to our use. Nevertheless, we shall bear calmly those things which happen to us contrary to what the principle of our advantage demands, if we are conscious that we have done our duty, that the power we have could not have extended itself to the point where we could have avoided those things, and that we are a part of the whole of nature, whose order we follow. If we understand this clearly and distinctly, that part of us which is defined by understanding, i.e. the better part of us, will be entirely satisfied with this and will strive to persevere in that satisfaction. For insofar as we understand, we can want nothing except what is necessary, nor absolutely be satisfied with anything except what is true. Hence, insofar as we understand these things rightly, the striving of the better part of us agrees with the order of the whole of nature.[49]

2   Why study Spinoza and the Stoics?

As that survey suggests, there is much to be said for the scholarly tradition linking Spinoza and the Stoics. This makes all the more conspicuous the one thing that cannot be found in it: namely, there is not a single published book-length study that takes into account all of the main parts of

---

[44] For Stoics, see DL V.116 and Plutarch, *Stoic. Rep.* 1037f–38a, together with Graver (2007), 51–3. In Spinoza, the transition to active affects begins at the end of the Scholium to IIIP57.
[45] Others include anger (*orgê, ira*; compare Stobaeus *Ecl.* II.91.10 (SVF III.395) and Seneca *De ira* I.12.2–5 with IIIP40Cor2Sch), hatred (*misos, odium*; compare Cicero *TD* IV.21 and DL VII.113 with IIIP13Sc), and distress or grief (*lupê, tristitia*), which both parties omit from the mental life of the wise person (compare DL VII.116 with IIIP59).
[46] *Ep.* V.7–8 (trans. Gummere in Seneca (1925)).   [47] IIIP50 and IIIDefAffXIIIexp.
[48] Long (2003), 14. Others who have singled out this passage include Matheron (1994) and Rutherford (1999), 457.
[49] IVApp32.

the two systems.[50] For at least three reasons – one comparatively small and two larger – this gap in the scholarly literature is problematic. The small reason is that we cannot be sure how deep apparent similarities of the sort that I have just enumerated really run without the prolonged and meticulous study only possible in a monograph. A reply to this is that it is not clear whether we should attach any philosophical significance to whether those apparent similarities are real. As a matter of history, one might want to know whether Spinoza was truly a Stoic but what does that teach us about his system or that of the Stoics?

This leads me to the other reasons for my undertaking. I believe that much can be learned about the two systems, as well as larger philosophical issues, by methodically aligning Spinoza's views to those of the Stoics. Certain features of Spinoza's system are best discernible against the backdrop of Stoicism. In particular, we can see Spinoza's conceptions of value and happiness, and see them in a new way, by contrasting him to the Stoics. This emerges especially in Chapters 4–5 below.

The last reason for the importance of this project takes us beyond just Spinoza and the Stoics. Spinoza is a transitional figure who also retains important linkages to his ancient predecessors. Just which core commitments of the ancient Stoics can be maintained by Spinoza, and which ones must be dropped, and why they must be dropped – answers to these questions would illuminate not just Spinoza or the Stoics but also what is happening more broadly in early modern philosophy.

With the present volume, I aim to fill the gap in the scholarly literature that I just mentioned. By the end of my book, I hope to have provided convincing point-by-point comparisons of Spinoza's and the Stoics' views on major issues in metaphysics, epistemology, philosophical psychology, and ethics (both meta-ethics and normative ethics). To be sure, the ground that I cover will only be partially turned and much other terrain will be completely untouched. Nevertheless, I aspire to put us in a much better position to decide the exact extent of the similarities – and differences – between Spinoza and the Stoics.

---

[50] There is one – but so far as I am aware, only one – published monograph on Spinoza and the Stoics (see DeBrabander (2007)). While I shall have more to say about DeBrabander in the main part of my book, here I will just note that the scope of his project is much smaller than mine, for he focuses on ethics and political philosophy, completely ignoring metaphysics, epistemology, and philosophical psychology. Besides DeBrabander, I have found one unpublished book-length manuscript on Spinoza and the Stoics (Heller (1932)).

3   Methodological notes

There are many ways in which one could compare Spinoza and the Stoics. For the next few pages of my Introduction, I will explain how and why I have chosen to conduct my study. Let me start by describing my comparison in the broadest of terms. I have chosen to concentrate on the conceptual affinities – and lack thereof – between Spinoza's system and that of the Stoics. I will identify a number of important philosophical concepts in Spinozism, align them to their Stoic counterparts, and determine the ways in which they resemble each other. My overarching objective will be to state as fully and precisely as possible just how Spinoza's substantive philosophical theses – and the arguments that he provides for these theses – relate to analogous theses and arguments found in Stoicism.

As that may imply, neither *Rezeptionsgeschichte* nor *Quellenforschung* are part of my project. To be clear, it is not that I do not find *Rezeptionsgeschichte* and *Quellenforschung* interesting or important.[51] Rather, it is out of respect for them that I have decided they are best excluded from my project. Properly done, *Rezeptionsgeschichte* and *Quellenforschung* require painstaking study of the transmission and circulation of texts, thorough exploration of possible presence of the texts in the works of the individuals in question, and then careful application of the results of these investigations to illuminate the ideas of those individuals. I could not accomplish all of that while simultaneously striving towards my main goal of determining the conceptual affinity of Spinozism to Stoicism.

My decision to concentrate on conceptual affinity sets my approach apart from a number of others that can be found in the recent literature. For example, P. O. Kristeller has argued that Spinoza was 'strongly influenced by Stoic … concepts, either in their original ancient form, or in the transformation they had undergone during the Renaissance'.[52] Susan James goes even further, claiming that 'much of the substance and structure of the *Ethics* – its central doctrines and the connections between them – constitute … a reworking of Stoicism'.[53] Alexandre Matheron speculates about a different connection between Spinoza and the Stoics: '[W]hoever tries to establish a causal link [*parenté entre*] between the two doctrines runs

---

[51] Indeed, I have undertaken *Rezeptionsgeschichte* in Miller (2009), where I show how Stobaeus was received by Grotius.

[52] Kristeller (1984), 1–2.

[53] James (1993), 291. In defence of both Kristeller and James, they were reacting against the scholarly tendency at the time they were writing to emphasize other sources and 'influences' on Spinoza, including Descartes or various Scholastic and medieval Jewish philosophers, without simultaneously taking into account the Stoics. Given such a context, it is understandable that they should have stated so forcefully the importance of the Stoics for Spinoza.

the risk of facing an objector saying that his comparison is but superficial and covers a very deep opposition. But the objector in turn runs the risk of not having seen that this opposition covers up an even deeper causal connection, etc.'[54] For Matheron, the direction of causation runs not from the Stoics to Spinoza but from a single non-historical source to both parties. In any event, whatever the differences in how they theorize that bond, Kristeller, James, Matheron, and many others have posited that a causal bond ties Spinoza to the Stoics.

Not me, at least not in this book. Unlike Kristeller, James, and Matheron, I will generally not speak about any lines of influence between the Stoics and Spinoza.[55] It is true that I can find claims of Stoic influence on Spinoza to be problematic. If we want to look for influences on Spinoza, it seems to me that we should start with more proximate figures such as Descartes or medieval Jewish philosophers, whom we know played major roles in his intellectual development, before getting to the Stoics, where the evidence is much thinner. Indeed, the textual evidence for Stoic influence is hardly compelling. Even for someone known to be parsimonious in his references to others, Spinoza mentions the Stoics very seldom – once in the *TdIE*, once in the *Ethics*, not at all in the correspondence, *TTP*, or *TP*. From a different front, we do have a record of the books in Spinoza's library on his death,[56] and it did contain some Stoic works, the details of which I shall convey below. For now, I just want to say that even though we know about those books, we do not know *all* the books he read; or, of the books he read, which ones he read carefully; or, of the ones he read carefully, which ones affected his philosophical views. For these reasons, then, we ought to be cautious about drawing inferences regarding the influence of an author or school on Spinoza just from the mere presence of their texts in his library.

We can abstract from specific texts to more general atmospherics. Stoicism was enjoying a renaissance in seventeenth-century Europe; it and the other Hellenistic schools became part of the mental framework of

---

[54] Matheron (1994), 148 (my translation).
[55] Though this is true in general, I will sometimes raise the possibility of influence. See, e.g., the end of Section 2.2 in Chapter 2, where I discuss Spinoza's reception of an edition of Simplicius' commentary on the *Enchiridion*. Other examples can be found in Chapter 3, Section 3.2.2–3, where I relate Grotius' understanding of *oikeiosis* to Spinoza's formulation of *conatus*, and Chapter 4, Section 4.2, where I note the similarity of Epictetus' talk about 'what is up to us' (*eph' hēmin*) to Spinoza's statement that 'human power is very limited and infinitely surpassed by the power of external causes. So we do not have an absolute power to adapt things outside us to our use. Nevertheless, we shall bear calmly those things that happen to us contrary to what the principle of our advantage demands, if we are conscious that we have done our duty' (IVAppXXXII).
[56] See Alter (1965).

the period.[57] In a way, though, the flourishing of Stoicism makes it harder to determine Stoicism's influence on Spinoza. Because it was so widely diffused, it is difficult to know exactly which Stoic themes Spinoza may have encountered by being attuned to the philosophical scene. Even if we could determine the answer to that question, we still would not know whether Spinoza would have recognized those ideas *as Stoic*. These and other problems[58] make me suspicious of claims of influence.[59]

At this point in my presentation of my work, I am sometimes accused of setting the bar too high. To determine influence, the charge goes, it is not necessary to provide precise historical linkages such as Stoic texts that Spinoza relied on or citations Spinoza made. There could have been Stoic conduits through Descartes or Hobbes. Moreover, I might seem to be engaged in a rearguard action, according to which my Spinoza went into his study and deduced his views entirely from his own mind, in the way that Descartes says he does in the *Meditations*. Scholarship on Descartes over the past several decades has thoroughly debunked the story Descartes tells by illustrating the many debts he owes to his philosophical predecessors. Surely it is naïve to suppose that Spinoza is any less reliant on his philosophical forebears, some of whom are undoubtedly Stoic.

To this I will make a twofold reply. First and more simply, I want to stress that while I think we ought to be careful when making claims of influence, I am not positively *denying* that Spinoza may have been influenced by the Stoics in various ways. Very likely he was. Whether he was or

---

[57] There is a large and growing body of scholarship on the reception of Hellenistic philosophy in sixteenth- and seventeenth-century Europe. Many of these works are cited in my Bibliography. See, for example, Barbour (1998), Barker and Goldstein (1984), Bridoux (1966), Brooke (2012), Buys (2010), D'Angers (1976), Kulstad (2008), Miller and Inwood (2003), ch. 9 of Schneewind (1998), some of the chapters in Strange and Zupko (2004), and Wilson (2008).

[58] Another problem: what is influence? What is it for one person or persons to influence another? Since (as seems likely) there are a number of kinds of influence, how are these kinds related to one another? Which kind (or kinds) is most applicable to the transmission and adoption of philosophical views, such as allegedly occurs when one philosopher (say, Chrysippus) influences another (Spinoza)? When a commentator casually speaks of Philosopher X being influenced by another Philosopher or Philosophy Y, I think we should treat such talk with caution unless we are told the sense in which X is supposed to have been influenced.

[59] Yitzhak Melamed identifies a quite different problem with the attempt to locate Spinoza in some 'proper historical context' (Melamed (2013a), xiv). Melamed writes, 'scholars of Jewish philosophy ... regard the medieval Jewish context as decisive; Dutch scholars choose the political and intellectual climate of seventeenth-century Netherlands as the appropriate context; and most other scholars ... stress the influence of Descartes. Obviously, this is just another example of the old story about the three blind zoologists who were examining different limbs of an elephant and concluded decisively that the animal in question was 'just a snake', 'clearly a hippopotamus', and 'undoubtedly a rhino' (xiv–xv).

was not, however, is beside the point in this volume. With just a few exceptions, my study is geared towards conceptual analysis. For that reason, the historical question of how and when the Stoics influenced Spinoza is just out of place here.

Second and more interestingly, the relationship between Spinoza and the Stoics is almost the exact inverse of some other early modern philosophers and their ancient counterparts. Take Locke and Cicero. As Phillip Mitsis has demonstrated,[60] Locke knew Cicero extremely well. There are abundant references to Cicero's works on Stoicism in Locke's writings – his published works, his letters, annotations in books from his personal library. Locke also held Cicero in high esteem, praising *De officiis* as one of only two 'discourses of morality' that a young person needs to read in order to develop a knowledge of virtue.[61] All of this leads Mitsis to argue that 'we should take seriously Locke's claim that Cicero's *De officiis* provides systematic guidance for understanding and developing the kinds of moral qualities Locke thinks necessary for a virtuous and happy life'.[62] Even if Mitsis is right,[63] however, he does not come close to calling Locke 'a Ciceronian'. The near opposite is true of Spinoza and the Stoics. We do not know whether he studied Stoicism closely but it is totally clear that he crafted a philosophical system very similar to that of the Stoics. Whereas Locke's many departures from Cicero make looking for points of influence worthwhile, it seems to me that the number of similarities makes a similar search moot in the case of Spinoza and the Stoics. Instead, I have decided to select a few prominent examples of apparent overlap between the two systems and determine whether the overlap is real or just apparent.

4   Overview of the chapters

As noted above, the apparent similarities between Spinozism and Stoicism extend across all the parts of philosophy. Insofar as I wanted to provide a comparison that explores the overall similarity between the two systems, it became incumbent upon me to look at issues in metaphysics, epistemology, philosophical psychology, and ethics. Since there are far more potential topics for comparison than I could hope to address in a single volume (and perhaps even a single lifetime), I decided to employ a two-stage filtering mechanism. First, I structured my comparison around

---

[60] See Mitsis (2003).
[61] *Some Thoughts Concerning Education*, &185 (quoted in Mitsis (2003), 45).
[62] Mitsis (2003), 59.
[63] I am persuaded by Mitsis' arguments, though others are not. See, e.g., Schneewind (2003), 2–3.

the *Ethics*: just as it has five parts which progress from metaphysics to epistemology and thence philosophical psychology, meta-ethics, and normative ethics, so I decided to incorporate five chapters in the main body of my work – one on each of these subjects. Second, I chose a major subject from each part of the *Ethics* and paired it to the Stoic equivalent. This pair of subjects appears at the beginning of each chapter in the form of epigraphs. My goal in the chapter is to probe the similarities and differences in the doctrines behind the epigraphs.

That is how the book proceeds, broadly speaking. Now let me give a more detailed overview of each chapter, to help prepare the reader for what follows. I start in Chapter 1 with the most basic thesis of Spinoza's metaphysics, that there is only one thing in the world. While it figures so prominently in Spinozism, monism does not enjoy as overt a position in Stoicism. Nonetheless, the texts show that the Stoics were monists and so the main challenge of this chapter is to assess the similarities and differences of Spinozistic versus Stoic monism. An issue that proves to be central here is just how the essential corporeality of Stoic monism relates to the infinite complexity of Spinoza's monism. Another issue concerns the conceptual foundations for monism. Unfortunately, Stoic arguments for monism are not well-preserved. Still, I speculate that their monism is ultimately based on the notion that the world 'does not lack any parts'.[64] If so, then the grounds of Stoic monism are fundamentally different from those of Spinozistic monism. For even if scholars continue to disagree about Spinoza's main argument for monism, none of the major interpretations bear any resemblance to the Stoic argument. After going through the arguments for monism, I conclude the chapter by looking into the strongly teleological nature of Stoic monism versus the equally strongly anti-teleological nature of Spinoza's substance.

Chapter 2 examines the Stoic theory of *phantasia* and its counterpart in Spinoza, his theory of ideas. Here, too, we find some significant differences between the two systems. One matter of dispute centres on how mental states which are intentional come to obtain their content. The Stoics defend a version of the externalist thesis that agents must be related to their environment in the right way for their mental states to be intentional. In opposition to this, Spinoza stands out as one of history's greatest internalists, for he thinks that all intentional mental states are attributable to agents' internal or intrinsic properties. After examining this issue, I move on to the typology of *phantasia* and ideas, another place where Stoic epistemology differs substantially from Spinozistic. Because my analysis

---

[64] Calcidius 293 (L-S 44E2).

isolated *phantasia* and ideas from the rest of the epistemological systems to which they belong, I conclude the chapter by considering the roles that the two notions play in Stoic and Spinozistic epistemology, especially in the theories of action and assent.

The next chapter takes up the most important concepts that Stoicism and Spinozism used to account for human nature. *Oikeiosis* and *conatus* were enormously complicated theories used to explain the behaviour, persistence, and essence of animals and maybe plants (in the case of *oikeiosis*) and all beings (in the case of *conatus*). In Chapter 3, I delve into two parts of the theories: the impulse to self-preservation and the nature of moral progress. When exploring self-preservation, I look into issues such as constancy of the impulse (whether it is always operational or just in force when the agent's existence is under threat) and the origins of the impulse in Nature. The latter issue once again raises the question of teleology, for the Stoics thought that Nature acted providentially when it made animals be self-preserving beings, a thought unlikely to be endorsed by Spinoza. So I spend some time going through the question of how God or Nature acts in the two systems. Once I have clarified the nature of the self-preservation, I move on to consider whether humans and other creatures are said by either system to graduate from self-preservation to another impulse that is more morally sophisticated. I attempt to show that the Stoics thought humans did while Spinoza thought we did not.

As systems, Stoicism and Spinozism are practically oriented: the ulti-mate aim of each is to articulate and defend a conception of happiness and how it can be attained. In Chapter 4, I begin to directly engage the practical aspects of their systems by discussing their views on the nature of value as such. We know that both Spinoza and the Stoics took this meta-ethical issue very seriously, for extensive portions of their *oeuvres* are dedicated to it. It has been suggested that nowhere is the gulf between Spinoza and the Stoics wider than on value theory, for Spinoza's relati-vism is diametrically opposed to the Stoics' 'absolutism'.[65] However, I argue that a close reading of the *Ethics* reveals a category of value which is non-circumstantially variable – according to Spinoza, there are no cir-cumstances in which the knowledge of God is not good for humans. For their part, most of the goods that Stoics acknowledge as valuable have their value in virtue of the circumstances in which agents find themselves. So there is more relativism to Stoic axiology than is sometimes thought. At the same time, a difference does remain. The Stoics posited the existence of a monadic set whose member alone has absolute value; the

---

[65] See Bidney (1962), 317.

member of that set is God. Not so for Spinoza, whose value theory is dyadic.

Chapter 5 descends from the heights of meta-ethics to the more concrete realm of normative ethics. Here I align the views of Spinoza and the Stoics on the nature of happiness. I begin by distinguishing between the form or syntax of a theory of happiness and the content or semantics of that theory. The form of a theory of happiness consists of all the structural conditions that a theory of happiness must satisfy before it will be recognized as a legitimate contender. In the Stoic tradition, I argue that all major Stoics agreed in taking happiness to be: (1) the highest good; (2) the ultimate end; (3) the goal of ethical inquiry; (4) not simply a feeling; and (5) achievable by a set of necessary and sufficient conditions that held for everyone. At the same time, Stoics argued vigorously about the content of happiness. The issues that they debated were: (1) whether a single virtue was necessary and sufficient for happiness; (2) whether the virtues, plural, were necessary and sufficient for happiness; (3) whether longevity was important for happiness; (4) whether pleasure had a part in happiness; and (5) whether external goods were needed for happiness. After establishing the foregoing conclusions about the form and content of eudaimonist conceptions of happiness, I proceed to Spinoza, where I attempt to show that we can find the same essential postulates constituting the form of his conception of happiness. It does not, however, follow that Spinoza's overall conception of happiness is the same as the Stoics, for they could disagree on the matter of content. I probe the issues here before concluding with the notion of living life in accordance with nature, the main ethical injunction in both Spinozism and Stoicism.

Where Chapters 1–5 follow the *Ethics* itself, the Conclusion departs from that work. Here I consider a question that I have deliberately avoided hitherto. Why does Spinoza seem so Stoical? After all, the contents of the preceding five chapters will have shown him to disagree with the Stoics on many issues, including some of great importance. Nevertheless, the picture he paints of the world and our place in it would have been recognized and basically lauded by Chrysippus and his colleagues in the ancient Stoa. So what explains the great affinity between Spinoza and the Stoics? This question is especially puzzling if, as I am supposing in this volume, Spinoza formulated his worldview without much Stoic influence. How is it that the two parties, working independently of each other, were able to arrive at conclusions which were so mutually compatible?

There is no single answer to this question. I feel the temptation to theorize with Dilthey that there is a small set of possible worldviews, defined by their positions on central metaphysical, epistemological, and ethical subjects, which all major philosophical systems such as Stoicism or

Spinozism instantiate, and that Stoicism and Spinozism are variations on the same basic worldview. However, I do not argue for the Diltheyian hypothesis here. Instead, I offer a (slightly) more modest proposal. Spinoza and the Stoics are united by their belief that: (1) the world constitutes one intrinsically active system operating by its own laws; (2) human nature is essentially the same as that of the world; and (3) both the world and ourselves are fully rationally comprehensible.

5   What is not covered in this book

If those are the subjects that will be treated in this book, a few omissions may seem glaring. Most obviously, I do not include a chapter on Spinoza's departure from Stoicism over cosmic teleology and divine providence. Some of Spinoza's best lines occur in IApp, where he excoriates the common suppositions that 'all natural things act, as men do, on account of an end' and that 'God himself directs all things to some certain end'.[66] These beliefs, Spinoza said derisively, are the product of ignorance, accepted by 'those who do not understand the nature of things, but only imagine them ...'[67] The anti-teleological and anti-providential fervour of IApp and other Spinozistic texts is, if anything, exceeded by the fervour with which the Stoics advocated for teleology and providence. Reporting the orthodox Stoic view, Cicero prosaically wrote, '[I]t was for the sake of gods and men that the world and everything in it was made.'[68] Declaiming even more grandiloquently, as one perhaps should when addressing the divine ruler, Cleanthes said that 'No deed is done on earth, god, without your offices, nor in the divine ethereal vault of heaven, nor at sea, save what bad men do in their folly.'[69]

It is not just certain points of disagreement that will not be the subject of whole chapters; the same is true for some vital areas of agreement. Of these, the most evocative is the centrality of God to each party's thought. Of course, God is central for the ontological reason that he constitutes all being, guaranteeing that any attempt to understand the nature of things would perforce dwell on his properties and productive capacities. When I write that God is central to the thinking of both Spinoza and the Stoics, however, I do not have just ontology in mind. I am also thinking of two other matters. First, they took God seriously. They thought that he played crucial roles in an enormous array of phenomena and they tried hard to develop credible interpretations of the precise contributions that he made. This is plainly shown in Spinoza's case by the only book (apart

[66] G II, 78: 2–4.   [67] G II, 81: 36–7.   [68] *ND* II.133 (L-S 54N).
[69] *Hymn to Zeus* (L-S 54I3).

from a commentary on Descartes' *Principles of Philosophy*) that he allowed to be published during his lifetime, the *Theological–Political Treatise*. In this work, God appears in discussions of issues as diverse as whether the Jews were a chosen people, how laws of nature should be conceived, and the defence of toleration.[70] Like Spinoza, most of the principal Stoics also wrote about God.[71] And like Spinoza, they thought that God was highly relevant to the adequate explanation of things ranging from the moral economy of the universe to meteorological occurrences.

The second matter is that Spinoza and the Stoics were devout, in their own way. By this, I do not mean they were conventional theists of the sort who can be found in so many modern-day churches or temples. After all, both parties identified God with Nature. They also overtly denied the anthropocentric conception of God.[72] However, once properly understood – once understood in the terms that they themselves provided – Spinoza and the Stoics did take God to be a worthy object of veneration, even love. The clearest proof of this in Spinoza lies in *Ethics* V, where he almost has trouble containing his excitement over intellectual love of God.[73] This enthusiasm is perhaps best matched in the Stoa by Cleanthes' *Hymn to Zeus* and many passages from Epictetus.[74]

Now, the preceding issues surface in the course of my discussion of other matters. I already mentioned how teleology comes up in Chapters 1 and 3; it and/or providence also arise in Chapter 5, while the high value attached to God factors into Chapter 4 and elsewhere. Nevertheless, I do not devote chapter-length discussions to them. To readers who were expecting me to say more about them, I could offer various rationales for my decision but I will not try their patience. Instead, I will try assuaging their disappointment by reiterating the limitations of this project. As I have said, much work will remain even after my book is finished. I hope that what I have accomplished here will better position us to understand how to relate Spinoza and the Stoics on things like teleology or God.

6   Historical background: Stoicism in Spinoza's day and what he knew of it

While my focus is (as it should be) generally on Stoicism *apud* Spinoza, I will make frequent allusions to the broader place of Stoicism in early

---

[70] Respectively, chs 3, 4, and 13.
[71] For an overview of these works, see Algra (2003), 153–5.
[72] For Stoics, see DL VII.147 (L-S 54A). For Spinoza, IP15Sch (at G II, 57: 3–8).
[73] See, e.g., VP32Cor, VP33Sch, and IVP36CorSch. For a clear account of Spinoza's commitment to God, see Huenemann (2014), xv–xvi.
[74] See, e.g., *Discourses* I.14 and II.8. For discussion, see Long (2002), ch. 6, section 1.

modern thought. To close this Introduction, I want to discuss some textual matters concerning Stoicism in the early modern period. Specifically, I want to discuss these three topics: first, which Stoic texts were available around 1600; second, which texts were thought to be Stoic at that time; third, which texts we have reason to believe Spinoza may have encountered.

The Latinist L. D. Reynolds uses the image of an hourglass to illuminate changes in the number and availability of classical texts from ancient times to late Renaissance. The top is the ancient world, where all the texts were extant and in varying degrees of circulation. The slender middle, according to Reynolds, is the Dark Ages, which 'so constricted the flow of classical learning that for a time it was universally reduced to a trickle'.[75] The bottom is the period post-dating the Dark Ages, when more and more texts were copied and distributed. The Renaissance is the very base, where the hourglass is at its widest. By this point in history, virtually all the classical texts that could be recovered had been recovered and, with the advent of the printing press, their place in the corpus of western literature had become secure.

This is certainly true of the texts which are of greatest relevance to my project. Though I will refer to a range of Stoic texts such as can be found in S.V.F. and more recent collections, I will draw especially on a relative handful of works from two[76] of the three traditional parts of philosophy: logic, physics/metaphysics, and ethics. Let me go through the three parts in sequence, first naming some key texts and then addressing the dates of their first post-ancient editions.

In logic, the main Stoic texts are Diogenes Laertius (DL) VII.41–83 and Sextus Empiricus – *Against the Mathematicians* (*AM*) VIII and *Outlines of Pyrrhonism* (*PH*) II. Others that are important include the following: *AM* VII; Galen – *On the Opinions of Hippocrates and Plato* (*PHP*) II and *Institutio Logica* III–V, XIV; Cicero – *Academica* II and *On Fate* (*De fato*) 11–20; Alexander of Aphrodisias – *On Aristotle's Prior Analytics* (*In Ar. An. Pr.*), various pages, and *On Aristotle's Topics* (*In Ar. Top.*), various pages; Plutarch – *On Stoic Self-Contradictions* (*Stoic. Rep.*), various pages; Aulus Gellius – *Attic Nights* (*Noct. Att.*), various pages.

Turning to physics, there are no texts that stand out as much as Diogenes Laertius and Sextus do in logic. The following, however, clearly matter: DL VII.132–160; Cicero – *On the Nature of the Gods* (*ND*) II and *De fato* 7–8, 28–30; Alexander of Aphrodisias – *On Mixture* (*De mix.*) and

---

[75] Reynolds (1983), xiii.
[76] Because Spinoza had so little to say about logic, it will not come up very much in my study. However, for the sake of completeness, I include an overview of Stoic logic texts here.

De fato, various pages; Cleomedes – *On the Circular Motions of the Celestial Bodies* (*De motu circulari corporum caelestium*), various pages; Calcidius – commentary on the *Timaeus*; Stobaeus – *Eclogues* (*Ecl.*), various pages from Books I and II; Plutarch – *Stoic. Rep.*, various pages, and *On Ccommon Opinions Against the Stoics* (*De comm. not.*), various pages; Philo – *On the Eternity of the World* (*Aet. mundi*), various pages; Sextus Empiricus – *AM* VIII–X, various pages; Galen – *PHP* II and V, various pages; Aulus Gellius – *Noct. Att.*, various pages.

Coming finally to ethics, the textual situation is more like that of logic in that there are a few specific works which are widely recognized by scholars nowadays as primary, especially DL VII.84-131, Stobaeus *Ecl.* II.57-116, and Cicero *On Ends* (*De fin.*) III.16-76. Other vitally important works include: Cicero – excerpts from *De fin.* II and remaining parts of III, *ND* II–III, *Tusculan Disputations* (*TD*) IV, *De fato*, excerpts from *On Duties* (*De off.*) III; Epictetus – *Enchiridion* and various excerpts from the *Discourses*; Seneca – excerpts from his *Epistolae* (*Ep.*), *On Anger* (*De ira*), *On Leisure* (*De otio*), *On Benefits* (*De ben.*) I–IV, *On Providence* (*De providentia*), *On the Happy Life* (*De vita beata*), and *On the Shortness of Life* (*De brevitatae vitae*).

Now, that is not an exhaustive list of key Stoical texts but these are at least central. Taking them as such, let me pose the next question: namely, were they available to the early moderns? Suppose the criterion for availability is the publication of a first edition in the post-ancient world. If that is what we mean by availability, then the texts that I have elevated above the rest as of special importance – Diogenes Laertius, Sextus' two books, Cicero's *De fin.* and other works, Seneca's various writings, Stobaeus – the *editiones principes* of all these texts predated the early modern period, often by several centuries.[77] Of the other texts that I have just named, the great majority had all been re-published by the dawn of the early modern era.

It must be granted that the criterion that I have been using for availability – mere publication in the post-ancient world – is problematic, for there is no guarantee that a published text would have circulated widely. Moreover, interest varied enormously from nearly universally read treatises such as *On the Nature of the Gods* or Seneca's *Epistolae* to the more recondite Cleomedes or Calcidius. Nonetheless, all of the truly essential texts and most of the others were known and used by important figures

---

[77] The *editio princeps* of Stobaeus was published by Christopher Plantin in Antwerp in 1575 (see Reynolds and Wilson (1991), 179). All other *editiones principes* of the mentioned works were published earlier. For a list of Stoic and neo-Stoic works published after 1424, see Moreau (1994), 9–10.

during or shortly before Spinoza's time.[78] With very few exceptions, the texts which we consider to be important for understanding Stoicism were available to early moderns.

To say that, however, is not to say anything about whether early moderns fully appreciated the resources which were at their disposal. Here, we move on to the second of the three matters to address: namely, determining early modern interpretations of Stoic texts.

This is obviously a vast subject, one which cannot be adequately examined in this Introduction.[79] I will make just one point of general significance. If the aim of contemporary history of philosophy is to provide accurate and compelling interpretations of historical figures and ideas through the close reading of texts – where possible in the original languages – without attempting to use or exploit those persons or ideas for other purposes,[80] then early moderns – and especially major early modern philosophers like Spinoza – were not historians of philosophy in our sense of the term. Granted, they were usually extremely well-read in the history of philosophy: Spinoza knew vast amounts of medieval Jewish philosophy, just as Descartes (his protests to the contrary notwithstanding) was on intimate terms with Aristotle, Augustine, and Aquinas, among others. Yet they did not normally read historical texts for their own sake; instead, they usually wanted to appropriate those contents for their own ends. This is certainly true of Descartes and Spinoza, who would probably have little interest in what is nowadays called the history of philosophy. It is also arguably true of philosophical synthesizers like Gassendi and Leibniz. They might be more sympathetic to the modern enterprise of the history of philosophy but they could not be called practitioners of it.[81] Even

---

[78] For example, even the most *recherché* of the key texts, Stobaeus, was cited widely by Lipsius in his *Manuductio ad Stoicam Philosophiam* and by Grotius in *De iure belli ac pacis* (the latter even edited a collection of his works). For more on Lipsius, see Papy (2011); for Grotius, see Miller (2009).

[79] At the beginning of her book on Epicureanism and early modern philosophy, Catherine Wilson says, 'A systematic survey of Epicurean philosophy in the seventeenth century would be an accomplishment requiring many volumes, many more years, and the efforts of many investigators' (Wilson (2008), v). The same is certainly true of Stoicism and the early moderns. Useful if piecemeal attempts, concentrating on specific points of contact between Stoicism and individual early modern thinkers, are mentioned above in note 57. More are listed in my Bibliography.

[80] This conception of the history of philosophy is called 'scientific' by Collingwood (1993). According to him, 'all modern treatment of the history of philosophy goes back to Hegel as the great modern master of the subject' (126).

[81] To quote Collingwood (1993) again, 'we owe to [Leibniz] the conception of philosophy as a continuous historical tradition in which new progress comes about not by propounding completely new and revolutionary ideas but by preserving and developing what he calls the *philosophia perennis*, the permanent and unchanging truths which have always been known' (63).

thinkers such as Lipsius and Grotius did not do history of philosophy. Though they were immensely learned and regularly employed their vast knowledge of the history of philosophy in their work, their intention in so doing was to show how historical figures and ideas supported their own projects.[82]

Now, because early moderns were not historians of philosophy in our sense of the term,[83] their understanding of historical texts was very different from our own, especially those of us who are historians of philosophy. One area in which the difference can be felt concerns the choice of texts they studied. For example, reflecting the overwhelming influence of Aristotelian logic, early moderns displayed little or no interest in works on Stoic logic. Technical stretches of Diogenes Laertius, Sextus Empiricus, and other important sources for logic were bypassed in favour of passages on physics and especially ethics. As a result, early moderns had a lop-sided conception of what counted as important about Stoicism, tilted towards the physical and the normative and away from the methodological or logical.[84]

A second effect might at first seem unimpressive but I think it is at least as important for understanding early modern interpretations of Stoic texts. Because early moderns did not approach Stoicism as historians of philosophy in our sense of the term, they often did not develop refined taxonomies of Stoic works. A quote from Descartes' correspondence with Elizabeth is illustrative. In response to some complaints that Elizabeth had expressed about her melancholia, Descartes suggested that they read together Seneca's *De vita beata*.[85] After their study group had started, Descartes wrote in his next letter, 'When I chose Seneca's *On the Happy Life* to suggest to Your Highness as an agreeable topic of discussion, I took account only of the reputation of the author and the importance of his

---

[82] The earliest biography of Lipsius shows how he used and regarded historical figures:

> He drew ethical insights from Epictetus and his interpreters Arrian and Simplicius, Plutarch's *Against Colotes*, Musonius as found in Stobaeus and Cicero's *Paradoxes*. His physics come from Cleomedes' *De motu circulari corporum caelestium*, Stobaeus' *Eclogae* and Cicero's *Academica*. Both he took from Seneca, Diogenes Laertius' *Zeno* and others. (Miraeus (1629), 128–9; my translation)

> Lipsius possessed an enviable knowledge of ancient philosophy; yet he used his knowledge for his own Christianizing purposes – he 'drew ethical insights' from Epictetus and others to produce a moral theory suitable for his day and age. For Lipsius and his contemporaries, the value of the ancients lay in the contributions they could make to their own thought. (Thanks to Jan Papy for the reference.)

[83] For more on early modern historiography of philosophy, see Brooke (2012), 139–48.

[84] Stoic logic around 1600 remains badly understudied. Some discussion can be found in Nuchelmans (1980).

[85] Descartes to Elizabeth, 21 July 1645.

topic, without thinking of his manner of treating it.'[86] Descartes did have a grasp of some finer points of Stoic doctrine[87] but an analytical study of Stoicism was not important to him. Consequently, he could be expected to know about the major Stoic texts and even, with some degree of accuracy, what they were about. Since practically all the texts which we now consider important for the study of Stoicism were available to Descartes, we can assume that he had a general impression of the Stoic system. Yet for Descartes, as for most of his contemporaries, it was not important to go beyond generalities.

This is certainly true of Spinoza, and here we can move on to the third of the three topics: viz., what Stoic texts Spinoza encountered. For what it is worth,[88] the catalogue of his library records Stoic works: Epictetus – *Enchiridion* (significantly, this was bound with Simplicius' commentary[89]) and Seneca – *Trageoediae, Epistolae, Alle de Brieven.* There is, however, no indication that Spinoza owned a copy of Diogenes Laertius, Stobaeus, or anything by Sextus. Moreover, the only work of Cicero's known to be in his possession was the *Epistolae ad Atticum.* Besides explicitly Stoic texts, there are these works by authors influenced by Stoicism: Grotius – *Defensio fidei catholicae de satisfactione Christi, De imperio summarum potestatum circa sacra commentarius*; Lipsius – editor of Seneca's *Epistolae* and Tacitus' *Opera*; Francisco de Quevedo – *Obras*;[90] and Guillame du Vair – *Philosophie morale*

---

[86] Descartes to Elizabeth, 4 August 1645 (A-T IV: 263). Trans. CSMK vol. III, 256–7.

[87] This is evident from the *Principia*, where Descartes writes: 'when we hear good news, it is first of all the mind which makes a judgment about it and rejoices with that intellectual joy which occurs without any bodily disturbance and which, for that reason, the Stoics allowed that the man of wisdom could experience' (Part IV, Art. 190; A-T VIII: 317; trans. CSM vol. I, 281). Descartes' claim about pre-passions can certainly be found in Stoic thought (see, e.g., Seneca *De ira* II.3.1–2.4).

[88] While valuable, we should use this catalogue with some caution. On the one hand, as Alan Gabbey has argued, the proportionate holding in a given subject tells us about the relative interest that the owner of the library had in that subject (see Gabbey (1996), 149). So, the fact that several of the books in Spinoza's relatively small library are by Stoics or those sympathetic to Stoicism is significant. On the other hand, we cannot be sure what was actually in Spinoza's library, since the list of his books was not compiled immediately on his death. In the intervening few days, an unknown numbers of volumes were removed by friends, perhaps to be sold in payment of some debts. For more, see Gullan-Whur (2000), 299 ff.

[89] I say significantly, because as I argue in Chapter 2, there is a possible instance of reception from Epictetus and Simplicius to Spinoza on the theory of *phantasia*/theory of ideas.

[90] This is item #116 in Alter (1965). Interestingly, there are three other works by Quevedo in the catalogue. For more on Quevedo, see the brief biography in Kraye (1997) and the book-length treatment of Ettinghausen (1972). There is an interesting discussion of whether he was a neo-Stoic in Méchoulan (1994). Quevedo will come up again in Chapter 5, Section 5.3.

de Stoïques.[91] These works prove that Spinoza was familiar with the more important Stoicizing thinkers of his time and though he apparently did not own any of their attempts at injecting Stoicism into the seventeenth century – for example, he apparently owned nothing where Lipsius speaks in his own voice – it is not unreasonable to assume that he was aware of these works.

If we turn from Spinoza's library to his corpus, we find two[92] direct references to Stoicism. In the *TdIE* he writes,

For example, some of the Stoics heard, perhaps, the word *soul* [*animus*], and also that the soul is immortal, which they only imagined confusedly; they also both imagined and at the same time understood that the most subtle bodies penetrate all others, and are not penetrated by any. Since they imagined all these things at once – while remaining certain of this axiom – they immediately became certain that the mind was those most subtle bodies and that those most subtle bodies were not divided, etc.[93]

Better known is VPref, quoted above: '[The mind] does not have an absolute dominion over [the passions]. Nevertheless, the Stoics thought that they depend entirely on our will, and that we can command them absolutely.' There are other texts where Spinoza does not name the Stoics but seems to have them in mind; these will be discussed in the chapters that follow.[94]

So what does the preceding imply about the kind of knowledge we ought to assume that Spinoza had of Stoicism and Stoic texts? He was aware of important Stoic doctrines such as the theory of blending and the control of the passions. Further, he considers them important enough to reference them in his works. Finally, he feels confident enough in his knowledge to criticize them. In sum, the safe assumption – safe because errors are less likely to result from it than its opposite – is that Spinoza encountered a great deal of Stoicism and he appreciated his

---

[91] I am not quite certain about another work of du Vair's. Item #388 in the catalogue appears to be a Dutch translation of a book of du Vair's but I have not been able to confirm this.

[92] There is a third by a correspondent. In *Ep.* 55, Hugo Boxel says, 'all philosophers, both of ancient and modern times, think themselves convinced of the existence of spirits. Plutarch bears witness to this ... and so do all the Stoics, Pythagoreans, Platonists, Peripatetics, Empedocles, Maximus Tyrius, Apuleius and others' (G IV, 258: 5–10). In his reply, Spinoza says that 'The authority of Plato, Aristotle, and Socrates carries little weight with me' (*Ep.* 56; G IV, 261: 30–1). He does not mention the Stoics.

[93] §74.

[94] See, e.g., the discussion of *pneuma* and *aether* in Chapter 3, towards the end of Section 3.3.2.

encounters.[95] It is, however, impossible to determine precisely how much he knew and how highly he valued this knowledge. Because we cannot know with any degree of certainty what Spinoza knew and thought of Stoicism, we have another reason for thinking that comparisons of the two are best undertaken conceptually and not causally or historically.

---

[95] So I only partially agree with Donald Rutherford's statement that 'there is little evidence of careful study of Stoic texts or attention to the principal doctrines of Stoic ethics' in seventeenth-century philosophers such as Spinoza (see Rutherford (2004), 178). In my opinion, it is correct to say that there is little evidence of careful study of Stoic *texts* but there is evidence of careful study of Stoic *doctrines*. The difference between the two statements has to do with the different evidentiary requirements for textual versus doctrinal claims.

1   Monism

Except God, no substance can be or be conceived.[1]

Zeno says that the whole world and heaven are the substance of god . . .[2]

At the beginning of his fourth lecture on pragmatism, William James famously said that after 'long brooding over it', he had come to consider 'the ancient problem of "the one and the many" . . . the most central of all philosophic problems'.[3] If we take 'the one' to be the idea that the world is a whole of which we humans are parts, then James' claim as a matter of history is quite correct, at least insofar as it was among the most illustrious and contentious in both the periods touched on in my book. In ancient times, it appeared early, with the Milesians' so-called 'material monism'[4] being quickly succeeded and superceded by the Eleatics' more heady talk of that which is 'imperishable, whole and of a single kind and unshaken and complete'.[5] Plato returned to it often, producing hugely influential accounts in a variety of his works.[6] Recognizing the gauntlet thrown down by his predecessors, Aristotle responded in character, clarifying the relevant terms while introducing new puzzles of his own.[7] During the Hellenistic era, all of the main schools took positions on it, the Epicureans and Stoics[8] being advocates against Sceptical

---

[1] IP14.   [2] DL VII.148 (L-S 43A1).   [3] James (1981), 61.
[4] See, e.g., Anaximenes, who held that 'the underlying nature is one and boundless [*apeiron*], not indeterminate . . . but definite, saying it is air' (DK 13A5; trans. McKirahan in Parmenides (1994)).
[5] Parmenides, *On Nature* VIII.3–4 (trans. McKirahan in Parmenides (1994)).
[6] See, e.g., the protracted analysis of 'the one' in the second part of the *Parmenides* as well as account of 'the coming to be of the universe' in the *Timaeus*, starting at 29B.
[7] Aristotle frequently deals with monism and related issues. If it is possible to enumerate which are the essential Aristotelian texts, the *Topics* 150a1–150b26 and *Metaphysics* VI.25–6 and VII.10–11 must be included on the list.
[8] Since I shall soon say much about the Stoics, I shall just justify my assertion about the Epicureans. As so often, texts are hard to come by. Nevertheless, as Jonathan Barnes writes, 'Reasonable, too, is the guess that the Epicureans worried about the matter; for their atomic theory leads directly to questions about the relationship between wholes and parts' (Barnes (1988), 228).

24

criticisms.[9] Even in late antiquity, it continued to be central to philosophical discourse, as Plotinus, Proclus, and others refined what they found in Plato and elsewhere.[10] In the early modern period, the idea became so important that someone finally coined a term for it: monism.[11] All the great rationalists of the era tangled with monism. In his *Principles of Philosophy*, Descartes provided a definition of substance which entailed that there could only be one such thing before retracting it in favour of a different definition compatible with pluralism.[12] Leibniz thought that his monad was the best defence against what he called 'Spinozism', with its doctrine of substance monism.[13] Intriguingly, however, the suggestion has arisen that even he entertained the hypothesis as a young man.[14] In Germany at the end of the 1700s, monism was briefly *the* defining issue, as philosophers were divided over Jacobi's ascription of Spinozistic monism to Lessing, and subsequent defence of monism against his critics.[15] Even Kant weighed in with a footnote that confirms the importance of monism by its very indifference towards it.[16]

---

[9] See especially Sextus Empiricus, *AM* IX.331–57.

[10] For Plotinus, see *Enneads* II.1.1, II.3.7, III.2.14, etc. For Proclus, see the *Elements of Theology* §67.

[11] Christian Wolff is normally credited for this development. He is said to have introduced it in either his *Philosophica rationalis, sive logica* (1728) or *Psychologia rationalis* (1734). See, e.g., the entry 'Monism' by R. Eucken in the authoritative *Encyclopaedia of Religion and Ethics* (1916). According to Eric Paul Jacobsen, however, the term 'monism' was not widely used until the 1870s, when Ernst Haeckel began to apply it broadly to his own work; see Jacobsen (2005), ch. 2, esp. 90 ff.

[12] The definition: 'By *substance* we can understand nothing other than a thing which exists in such a way as to depend on no other thing for its existence' (*Principles of Philosophy* I.51; CSM I: 210). The consequence of this definition, as Descartes said in the same article, is that 'there is only one substance … namely God'. His retreat from monism slowly commenced in the same article before hitting full speed in the next one with a weaker definition of substance. According to this definition, substances 'need only the concurrence of God in order to exist' (I.52; CSM I: 210).

[13] As he wrote, '[I]t is through these very monads that Spinozism is destroyed, for there are just as many true substances … as there are monads; according to Spinoza, on the contrary, there is only one substance' (Letter to Bourguet, December 1714; Leibniz (1969), 663).

[14] See Adams (1994), 129 ff., together with the criticisms of Adams found in Mercer (2001), ch. 10.

[15] As Paul Franks writes, the German idealists of the late 1700s 'are all committed, in various ways, to the view that genuine justification can be achieved only within a system that meets two conditions: the *holistic condition* that every particular (object, fact, or judgment) be determined through its role within the whole and not through any intrinsic properties; and the *monistic condition* that the whole be grounded in an absolute principle that is immanent and not transcendent' (Franks (2005), 9–10). For a treatment of Spinoza's possible contributions to German idealism, see Förster and Melamed (2012).

[16] 'The unity of the world-whole, in which all appearances have to be connected, is evidently a mere consequence of the tacitly assumed principle of the community of all substances which are coexistent. For if they were isolated, they would not as parts

Monism was central not only to the times in which they lived but also to the philosophical systems articulated by both Spinoza and the Stoics. In this chapter, I go through their conceptions of monism. After giving a brief overview of the idea of monism *per se*, I compare and contrast the key features of Stoic monism with the Spinozistic variety. Once that is completed, my focus narrows on to the argumentative bases for their theories. By way of conclusion, I look at whether the single world-system is teleological.

1.1   Monism in general

The aim of this short section, then, is to frame out the idea of monism in itself.[17] As I shall understand it, monism is a philosophical thesis about the world or cosmos, holding that (1) it has an essential unity and integration which allows it to be legitimately thought of as a whole and (2) discrete nameable members of the world, such as planets, desks, dogs, thoughts about dogs, and human beings, are parts of the world-system. This kind of monism, which I will call 'holistic monism' for the remainder of this section, must be distinguished from a different kind of monism, propounded by William James among others, which holds that though there is only one type of stuff (say, matter), there are multiple tokens of this type, each of which is substantially independent of the rest.[18] Holistic monism differs from the Jamesian variety in two respects. First, it denies that tokens of the one type of stuff are substantially independent of the world-system. It does not necessarily follow that those tokens – which include the discrete nameable members of the universe such as just mentioned – have no being or causal powers of their own. For this conclusion to follow, the additional premise that only the world as a

---

constitute a whole ... We have, however, in the proper context, shown that community is really the ground of the possibility of an empirical knowledge of coexistence, and that the inference, rightly regarded, is simply from this empirical knowledge to community as its condition' (*Critique of Pure Reason*, A218 = B 265, Note A, trans. Kemp-Smith in Kant (1965)). Franks (2005), ch. 1, offers a lucid analysis of Kant's stance *vis-à-vis* monism.

[17] To clarify my goal, I do not intend to break new ground here. Instead, I just want to provide a sketch of monism which will help us to understand Spinoza and the Stoics. For those who want a more robust discussion, see the recent work of Jonathan Schaffer (e.g., Schaffer (2003) and (2010)), together with some of Schaffer's critics (e.g., Horgan and Potrč (2012)). Schaffer offers a somewhat more accessible introduction to monism in Schaffer (2014; first edition published in 2007). The typology of Schaffer's (2014) and the earlier (2007) edition have been much discussed.

[18] See James (1978). As I understand it, James' so-called 'neutral monism' is actually slightly different from the theory alluded to in this sentence, in that it is neutral (hence the name) about the nature of the single kind of stuff out of which all individuals are derived.

whole has being or causal force is needed. To be sure, holistic monists may find themselves under considerable pressure to accept this premise, if only because they may have trouble explaining how things can have being and causal efficacy without having their own independent existence. Yet there is no immediately obvious reason why a holistic monist must be committed to the illusoriness of the parts of the whole and, as we shall see in the next section, neither Stoics nor Spinoza think of themselves as undertaking such a commitment.

The second respect in which holistic monism differs from Jamesian monism has to do with James' contention that there is only one kind or type of stuff. Holistic monists can conceive of the world in different ways. To the extent that there are holistic monists nowadays, most of them would presumably think of it as broadly material, perhaps captured by the space-time continuum of theoretical physics.[19] It is also possible to take the world as broadly mental, so that thought or intensionality lies at the basis of all reality.[20] I grant that either of these two kinds of holistic monism – the kind which takes the world to be broadly material or the other which takes it to be broadly mental – would be akin to James' monism, insofar as each takes the world to be a single kind or type of thing. However, I can see no reason why holistic monism must make this claim. A third variant holds the world to be *both* physical *and* mental. Such a theory would deny James' assumption that stuff of which all things are made is a single kind of thing. How this might work is complicated; since it is essential to both Stoic and Spinozistic monism, I shall say more about it in the pages that follow.

Moving on, holistic monism as a thesis is offered in defiance of the testimony of our senses, which shows a plurality of entities that enjoy independence from one another, even if they are conceptually or causally connected.[21] For example, when I see a robin splashing in the birdbath while a cardinal sings from the magnolia tree, both birds (not to mention the birdbath, the magnolia, and everything else in the panorama) appear to be acting and existing separately. Now, I do not mention this example because I expect it will be troubling to holistic monists. Instead of

---

[19] This seems to be the position that Theodore Sider calls 'substantivalism' (see Sider (2001), 110). Sider says that Quine toyed with it in the 1970s.

[20] If Plotinus' first Hypostasis or Principle, sometimes translated as 'the One', is the only true substance in his metaphysical system, then he may provide an example of this kind of substance monism. See, e.g., *Enneads* V.1 and Emilsson (1996), esp. n. 47.

[21] While I am discussing what the *senses* do or do not tell us about holistic monism, I might note that one recent monist, Jonathan Schaffer, has strong views regarding what *common sense* holds with respect to monism. Though many philosophers, such as Bertrand Russell, have held otherwise, Schaffer argues common sense actually prefers monism to pluralism (see section 1.2.1 of Schaffer (2010)). I am not going to engage in this particular debate here.

standing as a counter-example, it is intended to illustrate a different point. According to holistic monists, the ordinary phenomena of experience are not proof of ontological pluralism since holistic monism is an abstract thesis whose truth is discovered through philosophical reflection, not the senses.[22]

The next point that I shall make concerns the methodological and explanatory value of Nature.[23] Since I am currently limning the conceptual boundaries of holistic monism, I must admit that a holistic monist could regard Nature as having no methodological and explanatory significance. For example, if a holistic monist held that the only proposition which could be proven of Nature is that it exists, he might proceed to deny it any role of consequence in his metaphysics on the grounds that we know nothing meaningful about its nature. While possible, I do not know of any major philosophers who argued for such a view. Instead, history's important holistic monists attributed enormous methodological and explanatory importance to Nature, placing it at the centre of philosophical inquiry and invoking it to explain all manner of phenomena. This is certainly true of Spinoza and the Stoics. At the beginning of *Ethics* II, Spinoza wrote, 'I pass now to explaining those things which must necessarily follow from the essence of God ... not, indeed, all of them ... but only those that can leads us, by the hand, as it were, to the knowledge of the human Mind and its highest blessedness.' In his *Physical Propositions* Chrysippus said, 'there is no other or more suitable way of approaching the theory of good and evil or the virtues or happiness <than> from the universal nature and from the dispensation of the universe'.[24]

Finally and at risk of being *jejune*, I shall wrap up this propaedeutic section by noting the difference between a theory of substance versus a theory of monism. Very roughly speaking, the former strives to provide an account of the nature of the stuff that things are made out of; the latter tells us how many things there are. While it is possible that a particular theory of substance will ineluctably lead to the conclusion that there is only one substance, it is also possible for a theory of substance to have no implications regarding the number of substances. In this chapter, I shall focus on the theories of monism proffered by Spinoza and the Stoics. My goal is not to expound on the concept of substance itself but rather on the

[22] Schaffer holds that there is empirical evidence in favour of monism. However, the evidence is drawn from quantum mechanics and not the senses (see Schaffer (2010), 24 ff.). Since quantum mechanics is so highly theorized, even if Schaffer is right, it does not tell about the conclusion I am arguing.

[23] NB: I shall henceforth refer to the single unified entity which is the world as a whole as 'Nature' with a capital 'N'.

[24] Plutarch, *Stoic. Rep.* 1035c (trans. Cherniss in Plutarch (1976)).

idea that the whole world can be intelligibly and profitably conceived as a single being.[25]

1.2   Stoic and Spinozistic monisms

1.2.1 If monism includes the set of views outlined in the previous section, then some doubt might immediately arise as to whether the Stoics really were monists. *Stricto sensu*, substance was one of their four basic ontological categories or genera, so that many things were substances in this technical sense.[26] Given that many things were substances, pluralism seems to be built into Stoicism at a very basic metaphysical level. Such pluralism might seem flatly incompatible with monism.

Without challenging the premises, I do deny the validity of the inference. Substance can be used in many different ways. While it may be true that one sense of substance implied or was compatible with pluralism, Stoics had another which was monistic. This is shown by such passages as 'Zeno says that the whole world and heaven are the substance of god',[27] and by images which depict 'the whole cosmos as a living being [*zôion*], animate and rational'.[28] In Stoicism, the cosmos or nature (*phusis*)[29] could be conceived as a single substance unified extensionally and intensionally by a single 'breath' (*pneuma*) which was its 'commanding faculty' (*hegemonikon*).[30] As we read in one text,

Zeno said that this substance itself is finite and that only this substance is common to all things which exist ... [S]ince it is as birthless as it is deathless because it neither comes into being from the non-existent nor turns into nothing, it does not lack an eternal spirit [*pneuma*] and liveliness which will move it in a rational manner ... And they call this [i.e., the cosmos] a happy animal and a god.[31]

---

[25] I shall return to the relationship between substance and monism in Section 1.2.5 below. For now, I want to emphasize that I am holding in this paragraph that one's views on monism are not *necessarily* connected to one's views on substance, and vice versa. At the same time as they are not *necessarily* connected, there are plenty of cases where a philosopher's views on the one sculpted his views on the other. Spinoza is likely one such case: because substance is self-sufficient, there can be only one substance. My thanks to an anonymous referee for pressing me to clarify this point.

[26] See esp. Simplicius, *On Aristotle's Categories*, 222 (L-S 28H).

[27] DL VII.148 (L-S 43A1).   [28] DL VII.139 (L-S 47O3).

[29] The distinction between cosmos and nature, important in some contexts, does not enter here.

[30] See Galen, *On Bodily Mass* VII.525 (L-S 47F). Note that here and throughout I am taking Chrysippus' theory to be canonical, so where there are deviations between his doctrine and that of others, I am silently following him. In the present case, for example, Cleanthes conceived of 'vital heat' or 'designing fire' and not breath as the unifying and sustaining power of the cosmos. See Cicero's report of Cleanthean physics at *ND* II.23–30 (I-G 144–6).

[31] Calcidius, *Commentary on Plato's* Timaeus, c.292 (I-G 172; NB: the second two bracketed inserts are I-G's). Cf. Marcus Aurelius XII.30.

Referring to this text, one commentator says, 'In the last analysis the nature of the cosmos is one.'[32] Since, as another commentator writes, Stoics think of 'the world as a unitary system that contains all beings',[33] they should be registered as monists.

As for Spinoza, there is no room for doubt. From his earliest writings to his final works, evidence abounds of his commitment to monism. In the *Treatise on the Emendation of the Intellect*, for example, he frequently uses expressions suggestive of monism, such as when he speaks of the 'whole-ness', 'order', and 'unity' of 'Nature'.[34] In the *Short Treatise*, he explains that all 'attributes which are in Nature are only one, single being' and 'Nature is a being of which all attributes are predicated.'[35] Most impor-tant of all is the key text from the *Ethics*, IP14: 'Except God, no substance can be or be conceived.'

Spinoza being one of history's best exemplars of a monist, there is no need to belabour the point. Instead, let us consider whether any impor-tant differences between Spinoza and the Stoics are generated by the prominence of monism in Spinoza's thought versus the non-prominence of monism in Stoicism. Spinoza actually states that there is only one substance out of which all else is derived. Moreover, by devoting Part I of the *Ethics* to monism, he unambiguously signals that understanding the ultimate unity and cohesiveness of being is a prerequisite to understand-ing the epistemological, psychological, and moral issues broached in Parts II–V. By contrast, while the Stoics are monists, this is not comple-tely obvious; nor is it obvious that they place monism at the basis of all philosophical investigation. Now, these differences may only be a matter of emphasis, not logic or content, but they deserve notice in this compar-ison. Whereas Spinozism is unmistakeably centred on monism, the same is not true of Stoicism.

And yet if we're weighing emphasis here, we ought to place two more observations on the balance. From the Stoic side, they think that philo-sophical investigation must begin by studying Nature before advancing to logic and ethics.[36] So, one might think, Stoics do have a monistic entity

[32] Hahm (1977), 33.   [33] Long (2003), 10.
[34] For 'wholeness', see, e.g., G II 17: 7 and G II 28: 33. For 'order', see, e.g., G II 21: 1 and G II 25: 12. For 'unity', see, e.g., G II 36: 13. For 'Nature' (with a magisterial N), see, e.g., G II 22: 22 and G II 35: 9. It must be granted that in this work, Spinoza is not explicitly a substance monist, but the prevalence of words and concepts which are consonant with substance monism implies both a familiarity with and acceptance of that thesis.
[35] Part I, ch. 2 (at G I 23: 15 and G I 27: 7, respectively).
[36] See, e.g., DL VII.39–41 (I-G 110–11). For discussion, see Annas (1993), ch. 5, followed by Inwood (1995). Inwood has revisited the issue in a more recent paper that focuses especially on the reasons Seneca had for studying physics before proceeding to logic and ethics; see Inwood (2009).

whose conceptual and argumentative status is similar to Spinoza's substance. Moreover, from Spinoza's side, he engages in a series of equations
between God, substance, and Nature. These equations at least partially
validate the thought that Spinozistic philosophical investigation com-
mences with an entity whose parameters are just as wide as the Stoics'
Nature. So since Stoics have a concept that is equivalent in key respects to
Spinoza's substance, and vice versa, the differences identified in the
previous paragraph may appear not so great after all.

1.2.2 Because I want to return to first-order issues, I will let my reader
decide what to make of that methodological conundrum.[37] For now, I
want to expand on several properties that both parties attribute to their
conceptions of Nature. For the Stoics, the most important property of
Nature is corporeality. A simple argument led them to think that Nature
must be corporeal. Apparently accepting Plato's[38] idea that the ability to
act or be acted upon is the hallmark of existence,[39] Stoics argued (not
implausibly) that since only bodies have this ability,[40] it follows that only
bodies exist.[41] Since it is plain that Nature exists, it must be the case that it
is a body.[42]

 Spinoza's Nature is certainly not corporeal or, perhaps better, it is not
just corporeal. Spinoza took the single substance which constitutes
Nature to be composed of an 'infinite' number of 'attributes'.[43] There
are problems surrounding the notion of infinity which we can ignore[44] but
we must attend to the notion of attributes. In the official definition of
attribute Spinoza wrote, 'By attribute I understand that which the intellect perceives of substance, as constituting its essence' (ID4). A key
exegetical problem spawned by this definition concerns the relationship
between substance and its attributes. There are, in the words of a recent

---

[37] I will also return to a question of method at the end of Section 1.2.5.
[38] See the *Sophist* 246a–b. For analysis of how the Stoics might have read this dialogue, see
Brunschwig (1988).
[39] See, e.g., Sextus Empiricus, *AM* VIII.263 (L-S 45B).
[40] See, e.g., Cicero, *Acad.*, I.39 (L-S 45A).
[41] See, e.g., Alexander of Aphrodisias, *In Ar. Top.*, 301 (L-S 27B).
[42] Even though Stoics vigorously argued that only bodies exist, they did not also assert that
ontology is exhausted by bodies. It is possible that things could have being without having
the peculiar kind of being known as 'existence'. In the Stoics' case, they posited 'something' (*ti*) as the highest ontological category; immediately below 'something' are 'things
which are incorporeal' and 'things which are corporeal'. This is the level at which
existence enters into ontology, for it is here that bodies are encountered for the first
time. They exist and incorporeal things do not. For a helpful introduction to Stoic
ontology, see Long and Sedley (1987), 163 ff. For important criticism of Long and
Sedley's commentary, see Brunschwig (1988).
[43] See IP11. [44] For discussion of them, see Bennett (1984), 75–9.

commentator, 'two schools of thought' on this issue: first, 'attributes really do constitute the essence of substance, and do not merely appear to do so'; second, attributes do not really constitute substance's essence but only appear to do so from the perspective of the intellect.[45] If the former so-called 'objective' interpretation is correct, then since Spinoza tells us that two attributes of substance are thought and extension,[46] it follows that the essence of substance is *both* thought *and* extension. By contrast, if the latter 'subjective' interpretation is borne out, then substance is essentially neither thought nor extension, but something else altogether. The minutiae of the debate between the opposing sides are daunting.[47] Fortunately, we do not need to get into them to draw useful connections between Spinoza's monism and that of the Stoics.

Contrast the Stoic claim that Nature is ultimately wholly corporeal with Spinoza's view that the substance which forms the basis of Nature is ultimately characterized by (at least) the attributes of thought and extension. If the notion of attribute is taken 'objectively', then substance is both thinking and extended, since those two attributes really do capture two aspects of substance's being. On the other hand, if it is taken 'subjectively', it is neither thought nor extension, since those two attributes are only two ways in which substance's being is perceived. In either case, Spinoza's substance is not, ultimately, wholly corporeal.[48] We have here, then, a basic metaphysical difference between the Stoic theory of monism versus Spinoza's.

There is, however, more to the story. Although Nature is corporeal in Stoicism, it is also comprised of two fundamentally different kinds of 'principles' (*archai*), one passive (*to paschon*) and the other active (*to poioun*).[49] Regarding these principles, Seneca wrote, 'Matter lies inert, an entity ready for anything but destined to lie idle if no one moves it. Cause, on the other hand, being the same as reason, shapes matter and directs it wherever it wants, and from matter produces its manifold creations.'[50] Most commentators[51] think that both matter and cause – the passive and active principles, respectively – are bodies, so the distinction between matter and cause does not entail the introduction of an

---

[45] Lennon (2005), 19–20.   [46] See IIP1 and IIP2.
[47] For a helpful summary, including a persuasive assessment of the merits of both sides, see Lennon (2005), 20–7. More recently, Noa Shein has attempted to dissolve the dichotomy between the objective and subjective interpretations (see Shein (2009a)).
[48] As he writes in IP15Sch, 'everyone who has to any extent contemplated the divine nature denies that God is corporeal' (G II, 57: 7–9). See also IIP2 and his November or December 1675 Letter (*Ep.* 73) to Oldenburg (G IV, 307: 11–12).
[49] See, e.g., DL VII.134 (L–S 44B1–2). For commentary, see, e.g., Cooper (2009), 96–101, and Gourinat (2009), 50 ff.
[50] *Ep.* 65.2 (L–S 55E).   [51] But not all. I shall give the exceptions in Section 1.2.4.

immaterial entity. What it does introduce is the notion of two kinds of bodies characterized qualitatively, as either intrinsically passive or intrinsically active. Because this notion is absent from a common understanding of matter nowadays, scholars sometimes resist labelling Stoics 'materialists'. Instead, A. A. Long writes, 'The Stoics are better described as vitalists. Their Nature ... is a thing to which both thought and extension are attributable.'[52]

This does not change the undeniable fact that Nature in Stoicism is corporeal. What it may provide is an understanding of that corporeality which renders the Stoic Nature not as dissimilar to Spinoza's Nature as it might otherwise seem. Scholars of Stoicism take 'cause' and 'matter' to be equivalent to 'thought' and 'extension', respectively. So both thought and extension are embedded in the Stoic conception of Nature. Now consider Spinoza. The subjective interpretation of his theory of attributes does not read his substance in these terms, because it denies that attributes are anything more than how substance appears to the intellect. So if one favours the subjective interpretation, one will think that Spinoza's conception of Nature is doubly different from that of the Stoics: it is different in that (1), it is not wholly corporeal, and also (2), it is not really mental and physical.

However, things will look different from the perspective of the objective interpretation. Since it holds that substance's attributes really do reveal aspects of substance's being, then because substance has the attributes of thought and extension, it holds that substance is both thinking and extended. True, the objective interpretation does not find Spinoza's Nature to be essentially corporeal in the way that the Stoics' is, for it sees Spinoza's Nature as essentially extended *and thinking*. That disagreement notwithstanding, the objective interpretation gives us as good a reason to attribute intensionality and extensionality to Spinozistic Nature as we have to attribute those same properties to the Stoic Nature. So from the perspective of the objective interpretation – which is the consensus view among scholars today[53] – Nature in Stoicism and Spinozism does not appear so different after all.[54]

---

[52] Long (1986), 154.

[53] Cf. Lennon (2005), 20, though Michael Della Rocca among others is trying to reopen the issue (see Della Rocca (2008), 42–58). Also, I should note that Lennon (2005), 26–7, and Shein (2009a) are trying to displace the two traditional interpretations in favour of their own preferred readings. Obviously, if they are right, then the comparison to the Stoics would change.

[54] To be clear, I am not suggesting that Spinoza is a materialist. Indeed, the common early modern misinterpretation of Spinoza as a materialist might be said to read him in overly Stoical terms, for as I have said, the Stoics certainly are materialists. Rather than calling

1.2.3 Towards the end of this section I will address what the Stoics and Spinoza took thought and extension to be, but first I want to touch on how they are related. In Stoicism, matter and cause are constantly conjoined. Conceptually, they can and must be distinguished. By isolating them in our thought, we can identify their properties and understand the roles they play in the production of the universe and its constituents. Factually, however, they do not, and never can, appear apart from one another. There is no such thing as pure undifferentiated matter; it is always determined in some way or another by cause. Likewise, there is no such thing as pure undifferentiating cause; it is always determining matter in some way or another. As David Sedley describes their relationship, 'In any physical process a portion of matter [= passive principle], the essentially passive and formless locus of change, is altered by god [= active principle], the intelligent creative force which imbues it through and through and endows it with whatever properties it may have.'[55]

Bringing in Spinoza, two points should be made about his views on the relation of thought and extension. First, acknowledging that mental states plainly have something to do with physical states, he postulates a striking relationship between the mental and the physical, declaring that 'The order and connection of ideas is the same as the order and connection of things' (IIP7). According to Spinoza, for any given mental state x of substance, there is a state x* of substance, which exactly corresponds to x except that x* is physical. As he restates this doctrine of 'parallelism' in IIP7Sch, 'The thinking substance and the extended substance are one and the same substance, which is now comprehended under this attribute, now under that.'[56] Since thought and extension are attributes of the same substance, and since this substance necessarily possesses those attributes (just as it necessarily possesses all attributes), it is impossible for them to exist apart from one another.

At the same time, because thought and extension are fundamentally different ways of being, it is also impossible for them to exist in a causal or logical relation to one another. And here we come to my second point about Spinoza's views on the relationship of the mental to the physical. Mental states can give rise to other mental states; physical states can give

---

him a materialist, my point is rather to show a gap between Spinoza and the Stoics can be bridged. Because both parties endow Nature with thought and extension, their monisms are not as dissimilar as they might at first seem, when we only take into account that Stoics are materialists. In the next subsection, I will return to the crucial issue of how Spinoza and the Stoics conceive of thought and extension.
[55] Sedley (1999), 384–5 (my brackets).   [56] See also IIIP2Sch (at G II 141: 24–9).

rise to other physical states; but Spinoza writes in IIIP2, 'The Body cannot determine the Mind to thinking, and the Mind cannot determine the Body to motion, to rest or to anything else.' We can look at Spinoza's arguments for this barrier but I find the suggestion that such dualism is part of the 'cast'[57] of his mind to be at least as edifying.

Even without plumbing the depths here,[58] an intriguing similarity and a striking difference with Stoicism's two principles are evident. Like Spinoza's attributes, the Stoic principles are inseparable. Although for the purposes of theory Stoics and Spinoza argued that the principles or attributes of Nature must be distinguished, they also argued that it is impossible for thought ever to occur apart from extension (and vice versa). So everything which exists – both Nature as a whole and its products – will always be a combination of the mental and the physical. Both Stoics and Spinoza take this to be true.

On the other hand, they disagree on another matter. Whereas Spinoza's attributes stand in no causal or logical relation to one another, the Stoic principles are defined by their causal relationship. The passive principle is matter *informed by cause*; the active principle is cause *in matter*. Put another way, 'Matter needs [cause] in order to be a particular entity, and [cause] needs matter in order that there shall be some entity for [it] to characterize.'[59] While some of the differences discussed in this section may prove nugatory upon inspection, this one has implications that make it decidedly non-trivial. Let me explain.

Because of the independence of thought and extension, Spinoza cannot invoke words and ideas belonging to one attribute when explaining phenomena in terms of the other. Because all explanations must proceed solely in terms of one attribute, it follows that each attribute must possess sufficient conceptual resources to satisfy the explanatory demands being placed on it. So thought and extension, as formulated by Spinoza, are conceptually very rich. To cite but one instance, since all extended phenomena must ultimately be accounted for in terms of the attribute of extension, then since extended phenomena are active, it follows that extension itself is active. This is in sharp contrast with the Stoic concept of matter, which is simply defined as 'what has "threefold extension together with resistance"'.[60]

The broader point is that, although both parties agree that Nature is both thinking and extended, they disagree on the proper characterization of thought and extension. Stoics define thought and extension in terms of

---

[57] See Bennett (1984), 47–50.   [58] For more, see Della Rocca (1996), ch. 7.
[59] Long and Sedley (1987), 271.
[60] Galen, *On Incorporeal Qualities*, XIX.483 (L-S 45F).

activity and passivity: all agency and whatever it takes to be an agent (reason, knowledge, the ability to formulate intentions, causal efficacy, etc.) belongs to thought, while extension basically amounts to occupying space. Just as Spinoza did with Descartes,[61] so he would have found fault with what he would consider the Stoics' wrongheaded dualism of activity/ passivity and their impoverished conceptions of thought and extension.

To put the clash in different terms, there is nothing purely passive in Spinozism while there is in Stoicism. Granted, the Stoics' passive principle is incapable of independent existence, for it is always being qualified by the active principle. Nonetheless, it still exists in Stoicism while there is no possibility of a purely passive existent entity in Spinozism. Indeed, the notion of a purely passive existent being would be a contradiction in terms for Spinoza, as he thought that things exist only insofar as they are active and they cease to exist when they cease their activity. Spinoza wrote, 'The effort by which each thing tries to stay in existence is nothing but the actual essence of the thing.'[62] What is the essence of something? It is those steps or actions that thing takes to remain in existence. Or, to use Spinoza's words, 'the power of each thing . . . is nothing but the given, or [sive] actual, essence of the thing itself'.[63] The very definition of non-existence is pure passivity.[64]

1.2.4 In Section 1.2.2 above, I introduced the Stoic notion of the two principles (archai). Because the two principles are fundamental to Stoic monism, I want to extend my discussion of them in this section. Some readers may find this section to be too much of a digression from the main flow of my argument. If so, they can proceed to Section 1.2.5, where I will return to the main track. For those who have the patience, however, I think that I can present a fascinating counterfactual which may upend how Spinoza's monism should be compared to the Stoics.

Let me begin with a relatively straightforward point. It involves correcting an enduring misunderstanding. For nearly two centuries, many

---

[61] In his last two letters, Spinoza criticizes Descartes' non-dynamic conception of extension. As he writes in one of them, 'from Extension as conceived by Descartes, to wit, an inert mass, it is not only difficult, . . . but quite impossible to demonstrate the existence of bodies . . . For this reason I have not hesitated . . . to affirm that Descartes' principles of natural things are of no service' (Ep. 81).

[62] IIIP7.   [63] IIIP7Dem.

[64] As a minor aside, one could distinguish between the actual essence of a being and its eternal essence. The actual essence would have to be defined by the efforts that the being makes to remain in existence while the eternal essence – simply because it is eternal – would not have to be construed in terms of effort. Because I am talking about the actual essences of things, my argument in this subsection is not affected by this distinction. Thanks to an anonymous referee for this point.

scholars have argued that the Stoics' two principles map neatly on to Spinoza's distinction between naturing Nature (*Natura naturans*) and natured Nature (*Natura naturata*). This distinction is explained in the *Ethics* as follows:

> Before I proceed further, I wish to explain here – or rather to advise [the reader] – what we must understand by *Natura naturans* and *Natura naturata*. For from the preceding I think it is already established that by *Natura naturans* we must understand what is in itself and is conceived through itself, or such attributes of substance as express an eternal and infinite essence . . .
>
> But by *Natura naturata* I understand whatever follows from the necessity of God's nature, or from any of God's attributes, i.e., all the modes of God's attributes insofar as they are considered as things which are in God, and can neither be nor be conceived without God.[65]

In the early 1800s Hegel wrote, 'If we are now to give some further idea of what these Physics [i.e., the physics of the Stoics] are, we may say that the Stoics distinguish in the corporeal . . . the moment of activity and that of passivity: the former is . . . active reason, or, according to Spinoza, *Natura naturans*; the latter passive reason, or *Natura naturata*.'[66] Variations on this reading persist to the present day.[67] It is mistaken for two main reasons.

I stated the first of these at the end of Section 1.2.3. While natured nature (which is all of the modifications of substance) is not purely active – it cannot be, for only naturing Nature (e.g., the single substance) is purely active – it does have *some* activity. If they exist, then even the most modest of modes – a single rock on a beach or a bicycle buried deep in a garbage dump – have some capacity for action. There is nothing in Spinoza that exactly corresponds to the Stoics' passive principle.

The second reason that the Stoics' two principles do not correspond to Spinoza's distinction between *Natura naturans*/*Natura naturata* is the two pairs of concepts do dramatically different work. For Spinoza, *Natura naturans*/*Natura naturata* is just shorthand for the distinction between God or substance and all of the modifications of God/substance. Insofar as it is a handy rhetorical device, it hardly has any metaphysical significance – whatever Spinoza might have accomplished with *Natura naturans*/*Natura naturata*, he could and did accomplish with the apparatus of substance and modes. Because of this, Jonathan Bennett summarily dismisses *Natura naturans*/*Natura naturata*, writing that '[the terminology]

---

[65] IP31Dem. The other passages where Spinoza mentions *Natura naturans*/*Natura naturata* are the *Short Treatise* (Part I, chs. VIII and IX), his commentary on Descartes' *Principles of Philosophy* (at G I, 264: 3 and G I, 267: 9), and *Ep.* 9 (at G IV, 45: 32–3).
[66] Hegel (1896), vol. II, 245. [67] See, e.g., Graeser (1991) and Long (2003), 11.

is quite without significance in the *Ethics*, and we need not linger on it'.[68] The same cannot be said of the two principles. They are second in the list of five topics belonging to 'specific' physics.[69] As I have shown, they are the basic ingredients of reality as a whole. It is from them that the four elements (air, fire, water, earth) emerge.[70] In contrast to Spinoza's *Natura naturans/Natura naturata*, then, the two principles were vital to Stoic physics and metaphysics.

Aside from correcting a long-standing exegetical error, I have a deeper motivation for bringing up the foregoing, which I will introduce by drawing on the work of David Hahm. In his classic study of Stoic physics,[71] Hahm places the Stoics in a broader ancient context, showing what they may have borrowed from their predecessors and wherein lay the novel components of their theory. One theme that emerges is the importance of the drive towards explanatory and ontological simplicity in Stoicism. According to Hahm, both Aristotle and the Stoics saw Plato's theory of forms as having troublesome explanatory and ontological implications. Insofar as each form was 'separate' from the others and endowed with its own unique kind of causal efficacy, Nature had to be populated by a number of individuals which use a variety of powers to create the phenomena of the observed universe. One of Aristotle's responses to Plato, Hahm argues, dealt with what he regarded as an unjustified causal profligacy. Rather than the indeterminate number of types of causation found in Plato, Aristotle argued that there are just four, which are expressed in his theory of four causes. As Hahm reads the Stoics, they applauded Aristotle's move but they thought it was not reductive enough. While Aristotle addressed the explanatory excesses of Platonism, the Stoics thought that he failed to correct its ontological excesses. Using the resources made available by Aristotle, the Stoics took the step that Aristotle did not. Hahm writes that the Stoics distributed the 'four causes between two entities, assigning the material cause to one entity, and the motive, formal, and final causes to the other'.[72]

Now, there are many complexities to Hahm's history that I am omitting. Instead of getting into them, I want to bring in Spinoza. He would have sympathized with the drive for explanatory and ontological minimalism. However, just as the Stoics criticized Aristotle for not being

---

[68] Bennett (1984), 119. Bennett may be too dismissive of *Natura naturans/Natura naturata* but I think one can make a great deal of progress in reading the *Ethics* without being troubled by this distinction.

[69] See DL VII.132.   [70] See Stobaeus 1.129 (L-S 47A1).

[71] See Hahm (1977). I am drawing especially on ch. 2, which deals with the two principles.

[72] Hahm (1977), 44.

sufficiently deflationary, Spinoza would have criticized the Stoics for not taking the programme to its logical extreme. Of course, he would have said that the Stoics sanctioned too many kinds of causation, for the final cause must be banished as an illegitimate form of explanation, at least with regard to Nature as a whole.[73] More to the present point, however, he would have said that they employed too many entities in their search for explanations. According to Spinoza, all causal explanations must be sought in *one* entity, God or substance, including the material cause that the Stoics reserved for the passive principle.

I have steered the discussion in this direction because I want to note a fascinating possibility. While most students of Stoicism take the two principles to be autonomous, not mutually reducible material entities, a small number have demurred. These scholars typically begin building their heterodox interpretation by noting the function of the two principles in Stoic cosmogony. The Stoics held that the world goes through an endless series of cosmic cycles.[74] Each cycle begins and ends in a condition of universal conflagration, which they called *ekpyrosis*.[75] During *ekpyrosis*, all that remains is God.[76] To explain how the primordial mass that exists during the *ekpyrotic* state is able to generate the world, these scholars contend that Stoics had to endow it with the opposing qualities of activity and passivity. Hence the two principles appear as nothing more than qualities of one thing. As one commentator summarises the view, 'whereas the early Stoics conceived the universe as arising from one primary substance of fixed mass (SVF 1.87), they needed to posit two further principles in order to account for the process of genesis. Logically speaking, Stoic theory would require us to speak of one primal substance with two aspects, one active, one passive.'[77]

Now, because the two principles are mere 'aspects' of a single being, they are 'nominally distinct but essentially one'.[78] Although the single being of which they are aspects is corporeal, the principles themselves are not. In themselves, the principles are logical devices required for

---

[73] Spinoza's views on final causation continue to vex scholars. I take it to be uncontroversially true that final causes have no part to play in Spinoza's conception of God or Nature. Whether he allowed final causation any part at the level of human behaviour is more contestable. For a good recent discussion, see Carriero (2005) together with the criticisms of Carriero in Hoffman (2011). I shall discuss the related concept of teleology in the conclusion of this chapter.
[74] See, e.g., Nemesius, *On the Nature of Man*, ch. 38 (partially translated in L-S 52C).
[75] See, e.g., Eusebius, *Evangelical Preparations*, 15.14.2.
[76] See, e.g., Plutarch, *Stoic. Rep.* 1053B. [77] Lapidge (1978), 164.
[78] Lapidge (1973), 242. (I might explain that Lapidge's 1978 piece is a condensed version of Lapidge 1973.)

cosmogonical reasons. And one commentator says, 'an aspect, or logically distinguishable feature, of a body cannot itself be a body'.[79]

Pulling all of this together, according to the heterodox interpretation of the two principles, they are (A) aspects of another body and (B) not corporeal in themselves. I have been calling this the 'heterodox' interpretation, for it is in the minority today. Nevertheless, apart from the *a priori* arguments which I have just recounted, it also has some textual foundation. Concerning (A) the aspectuality of the principles, there are at least two sources:

Zeno of Citium says that the principle of the universe is god and matter, the former being responsible for acting, the latter for being acted upon.[80]

Again, if some cause exists, either [1] it is the complete cause of something, using nothing but its own power, or [2] it needs the matter affected as an auxiliary means to this, so that the effect is to be thought of in relation to the conjunction of both . . . [If 2, then] a worse result will emerge. For if the thing acting and the thing affected are thought of in conjunction with each other, there will be one conception, but with two names, 'the thing acting' and 'the thing affected'. Consequently, the productive power will reside no more in it than in the thing said to be affected. For just as it cannot act at all without the thing said to be affected, so too the thing said to be affected cannot be affected without its presence. It follows that the power productive of the effect no more exists objectively in it than in the thing affected.[81]

Those texts support the notion that the principles are aspects of another body. There is one text testifying to (B), the incorporeality of the principles. Preserved in the Suda (which is an enormous encyclopaedia of the ancient world compiled in tenth-century Byzantine Greece), the text is a variant of Diogenes Laertius VII.134. Whereas the generally accepted version of this text reads 'The principles are also bodies and without form', the Suda says 'The principles are incorporeal [*asomatous*] and without form'.[82]

Rather than explain how these texts lend support to the heterodox interpretation – this is probably plain enough – I want to compare this reading of the two principles to Spinoza. Just as the heterodox makes the two principles to be aspects of another being, so Spinoza thinks of the divine attributes as what the intellect perceives of a substance as constituting its essence.[83] Now, the way in which Spinoza's attributes are related to God's essence may not be exactly the same as the way in which the principles are related to the single being of which they are

[79] Todd (1978), 140.   [80] Achilles, *Introduction to Aratus* 3.1–3 (I-G 171).
[81] Sextus Empiricus, *AM* IX.237–40 (L-S 72N). The bracketed insertions are mine. I have removed Sextus' assertions about [1] since they are irrelevant. It is in [2] that he supports the aspectual interpretation of the two principles.
[82] SVF II.299.   [83] ID4.

aspects. Nevertheless, the form of the relationship is identical: both Spinozistic attributes and Stoics principles are reflections of the essence of the one being underlying and constituting all reality.

Moreover, just as the heterodox interpretation holds that the principles are incorporeal, the same is basically true for Spinoza's attributes. I say 'basically true', because as I noted in Section 1.2.2, there are complications. According to the subjective interpretation of Spinoza's theory of attributes, attributes are merely how substance appears to the intellect and not genuine indications of its true essence. If one favours the subjective reading, then one will agree without hesitation that attributes are not really corporeal. However, the objective interpretation holds that attributes are more than mere appearances – they really do capture the essence of substance. Since one of the attributes is extension, then one of the attributes will be something like corporeal. At the same time, the other attribute is decidedly incorporeal – it is the attribute of thought – as are the infinite number of other attributes that Spinoza says belong to God. So even those who regard attributes as providing objective insight into God's nature will think of them as mostly incorporeal.

In sum, then, the heterodox portray the two principles in ways remarkably congenial to Spinozistic attributes. Since I share the majority opinion that the heterodox interpretation is incorrect – I think that the two principles are more than mere aspects of substance and that they are corporeal in themselves – I can only present the almost total overlap between the heterodox version of the two principles and Spinoza's attributes as a fascinating counterfactual. *If* Stoic physics should be as the heterodox claim, *then* its theory of the two principles would be nearly identical to Spinoza's theory of attributes.

1.2.5 Moving on, my comparison has so far touched on five issues: the acceptance of monism (Section 1.2.1); whether Nature is corporeal (1.2.2); how thought and extension are related (the beginning of 1.2.3); how thought and extension are conceived (the end of 1.2.3); and how the Stoics' two principles relate to Spinoza's system (1.2.4). The next set of points I want to make concern questions that have surely occurred to some readers.

Spinoza is famous not just for being a monist but also, and perhaps especially, for being a monist of a particular sort – namely, a *substance* monist. So one might want to know, what about substance? How does the fact that Spinoza's monism is geared towards substance affect his relationship to the Stoics?

To answer these questions, let me start by distinguishing between the general versus narrow potential significance of Spinoza's orientation towards substance. On a general level, I do not think it matters that Spinoza's monism is centred on substance. One reason for this was because Stoics themselves thought of Nature as a system unified by and emerging from a single substance that was itself eternal and immutable. According to Diogenes Laertius, the Stoics regarded God as 'the peculiarly qualified individual consisting of all substance, who is indestructible and ingenerable, since he is the manufacturer of the world-order'.[84] Though the properties of the Stoic substance may differ from those of Spinoza's, its role in their theory of monism is very similar to that played by substance in Spinozism. This leads to my second reason for thinking it irrelevant that Spinoza's monism is centred on substance. While there are fairly technical ways in which talk about substance is significant (and I shall start discussing them in the next paragraph), there are other ways in which it is just a linguistic quibble whether we use the terminology of substance. As I have tried to argue, both Spinoza and the Stoics are holistic monists who take the world to be one because of the presence of a dynamic cohesive force. If Spinoza chose to speak of 'substance' while Stoics tended to use words such as *hexis, nous, pneuma*, and *theos*,[85] it is plain that they have approximately the same referent in mind.

While the orientation of Spinoza's monism towards substance may not matter on a general level, it is of significance for more narrow or technical reasons. To get into this, I want to illustrate Spinoza's ontology by working through an example – say, one involving the attribute of extension. Spinoza denies that individual extended objects such as bicycles and flowers 'follow' immediately from that attribute.[86] This is because the attribute of extension is by definition always and everywhere the same, whereas individual extended objects are by definition temporally limited and non-uniform. The only modifications that the attribute of extension can have immediately are those features of the extended world which hold true constantly and universally. In a letter, Spinoza names one such mode: motion-and-rest.[87] It is always and everywhere true that extension will undergo motion-and-rest; therefore, the attribute of extension may

---

[84] DL VII.137 (L-S 44F).   [85] See, e.g., the list at DL VII.147 (L-S 54A).

[86] As he writes in IP21, 'All the things which follow from the absolute nature of any of God's attributes have always had to exist and be infinite'.

[87] See his 29 July 1675 letter to Schuller (*Ep.* 64). In that same letter, he also names such a modification of the attribute of thought, saying it is 'absolutely infinite intellect'. For brief discussion and references, see Miller (2003a), n. 14. For a more recent and much more robust attempt to make sense of infinite modes, see Melamed (2013), ch. 4. As fruitful as Melamed's discussion is, what he can say is limited by the parsimonious evidence. He concludes, 'Instead of presenting speculations . . ., let me suggest that I am not sure Spinoza's text allows us to provide definite answers' to the many questions surrounding infinite modes (136).

be said to be modified by motion-and-rest. In Spinoza's parlance, motion-and-rest is an 'immediate infinite modification' of the attribute of extension. Like the attributes, the immediate infinite modes are also modified; in their case, they are modified by what are sometimes called 'mediate infinite modes'.[88] And so ensues a series in which one mode is modified by another more limited mode, until finally we arrive at the most finite of modes, such as bicycles and flowers.[89] In this way, a hierarchy of being can be seen to exist, all firmly rooted in God or substance, but all real in its own way.[90]

This ontology is reflected in the method that Spinoza recommends for philosophical investigation. He writes in the *Theological–Political Treatise*,

Now in examining natural phenomena we first of all try to discover those features that are most universal and common to the whole of Nature, to wit, motion-and-rest and the laws and rules governing them which Nature always observes and through which she constantly acts; and then we advance gradually from these to other less universal features.[91]

Spinoza subscribes to a top-down model of philosophical and scientific investigation: he thinks we must start with the most abstract theoretical entities, learn their properties, and then deduce the ways in which they can be modified.[92] This process is repeated for each level in the scale of Nature, until eventually we deduce the properties and activities of the most finite or particular of modes.

Two features of Spinoza's prescription for philosophical investigation must be stressed. First, it is inherently nomological: the 'laws and rules governing' natural phenomena structure all inferences we are to make about the phenomena under investigation. Second, it is deductive, not

---

[88] The best (and perhaps only) example of a mediate infinite mode is the whole of the physical universe, taken as one individual. This is what Spinoza calls the 'face of the whole universe' (*Ep.* 64). This follows directly upon the attribute of extension and the immediate infinite mode of motion-and-rest because it presupposes both of them – and nothing else.

[89] I deliberately speak in generalities, as I cannot afford precision here. As any Spinoza commentator knows, saying exactly how Spinoza moves from the infinite to the finite is extremely difficult. I hope my general sketch is enough to sustain my comparison.

[90] One way in which modes like bicycles or flowers are real is that they possess genuine causal powers. As Valterri Viljanen puts it, finite particular modes like bicycles or flowers are nothing less than 'essential causers of properties' (Viljanen (2011), 41).

[91] *TTP* ch. 7 (G III, 102).

[92] Thus his is a version of what Ian Hacking calls 'the method of hypothesis' (see Hacking (1999), 197). As opposed to the bottom-up approach of the 'method of induction', which proceeds from simple observations and modest generalizations based on those observations to grander generalizations and ultimately theories and laws of nature, the method of hypothesis enjoins us to 'make guesses, deduce testable consequences, conduct experiments, throw out the bad guesses that are refuted by experiment, and proceed to new conjectures' (ibid.).

inductive: from the correct laws of nature plus the relevant particular facts, we are always able to arrive at the right understanding of the phenomena before us. Justifying this view of philosophizing is Spinoza's belief that the world itself is as interconnected as the philosophical system he is creating. In the words of one commentator, 'Spinoza's *Ethics* is intended to exhibit the structure of nature', with the geometrical method 'mirroring the immanent necessity of nature'.[93]

Comparing these ideas to Stoicism, it must be admitted that Stoics lacked the formal apparatus – both the substance-mode ontology as well as the *mos geometricus* – so prominent in Spinoza. Yet there is no reason to think that they would object to it. Like Spinoza, Stoics were substance monists only at the level of fundamental metaphysics: it is only when considering the ultimate object of the world that they defend monism. Because the single substance – that is, the world – as constituted by matter, and reason can account for only purely general matters such as the possibility of change, it cannot explain localized phenomena. To obtain these explanations, Stoics accepted a pluralism in which the variety of phenomena are equivalent to what Spinoza calls modifications of substance. For example, as I have said, the Stoics subscribed to the traditional four-elements theory of fire, water, air, and earth. Inter alia, these elements are necessary for cosmological purposes, serving to explain how the world came to have earth at its centre and fire at the periphery.[94] Although the elements are reducible to the irreducibly basic substance described above, Stoics resisted the reduction when they were engaged in cosmology, climatology, and other matters.

More proof that lesser beings are held to be authentic causal agents can be gathered from Chrysippus' discussions of responsibility. He carefully distinguished types of causes in order to show how humans can be held accountable for their actions even in the face of universal causal determinism.[95] Chrysippus did not try to insulate humans from the causal order which incorporates all beings but instead he tried to show how humans have causal efficacy because they share in the divine rationality governing the universe.[96] From his day to ours, his readers have been puzzled by his arguments but that is beside the present point.[97] Instead,

---

[93] Garrett (2003), 100–1.
[94] Cf. Stobaeus I.129–30 (L-S 47A) and Cicero *ND* II.23–5 (L-S 47C1–3).
[95] See, above all, Cicero, *De fato* 39–43. Also interesting is Leibniz's commentary on Chrysippus' views starting at §331 in the *Theodicy* (Leibniz (1985), 324 ff.).
[96] See Aulus Gellius, *Noct. Att.* VII.2.6–13 (L-S 62D).
[97] Susanne Bobzien tries hard to resolve some of the puzzles in the monumental Bobzien (1998). She specifically addresses the Gellius passage in Section 6.3.1. I shall return to this in Chapter 2, Section 2.3.2 and 2.3.3.

Chrysippus' analyses show that in both the hierarchy of beings it posits, and its refusal to reduce finite beings to God, Stoic ontology resembles Spinoza's.

The assertion of such ontological similarity is strengthened by the similarity of their methods. Consider this passage from Cicero:

> I have been led on by the marvellous structure of the Stoic system and the miraculous sequence of its topics ... Nothing is more finished, more nicely ordered, than nature; but what has nature, what have the products of handicraft to show that is so well constructed, so firmly jointed and welded into one? Where do you find a conclusion inconsistent with its premise, or a discrepancy between an earlier and a later statement? Where is lacking such close interconnexion of the parts that, if you alter a single letter, you shake the whole structure?[98]

It seems that Stoicism aspired to craft a system every bit as rigorous as Spinoza's.[99] Moreover, the rationale for this aspiration seems the same as we find in Spinoza: philosophy ought to be systematic, because that which it seeks to understand – Nature and all it contains – are seamlessly linked by an unbroken and unbreakable series of causal links.[100]

For all these similarities, there is one possible and possibly significant difference. As noted, Spinoza's method is thoroughly nomological. The same cannot be said of the Stoics, for as Michael White writes,

> [W]hat the Stoics expected from physics, as a principal subdivision of philosophy, is not the same ideal of 'explanation of nature' attached to many classical modern and contemporary conceptions of physics: a nomic–deductive picture according to which the 'covering laws' of physics plus a complete description of an instantaneous world-state allows an omniscient observer to *predict* the subsequent history of the world to the finest detail.[101]

White is specifically addressing Stoic physics and not logic or ethics. Still, I think we can generalize his point to hold for all forms of Stoic explanation. Whatever the domain – physical, logical, or moral – the Stoics did not conceive of explanation as having to be 'nomic–deductive'.

---

[98] *De fin.* III.74 (trans. Rackham in Cicero (1931)).

[99] Speaking about the passage of *De fin.* III just quoted, Long writes, 'What is undeniable is the attempt to present a set of moral truths which are so related that the last is entirely consistent with the first ... The procedure, like some of the thought itself, reminds one of nothing so much as the *mos geometricus* of Spinoza' (Long (1986), 185). Long presents the dominant view about the internal unity of the Stoic system; I shall return to it briefly at the end of this subsection. In the meantime, I ought to note that Brad Inwood has recently published a paper inveighing against the dominant view; among other things, he tries to show how *De fin.* III.74–5 does not support it. See Inwood (2012).

[100] See Alexander of Aphrodisias, *De fato* 191–2 (L-S 55N). Also, Sextus Empiricus, *P.H.* III.242.

[101] White (2003), 141.

Whether or not one will be impressed by the nomologicalness of Spinoza's preferred method of philosophical investigation and justification versus the non-nomologicalness of Stoicism will depend on one's views about the importance of laws of nature. On an influential view, however, scientific explanation *just is* explanation by reference to laws of nature.[102] If that is correct, then non-nomologicalness of Stoicism means that any explanations of natural phenomena it offers will not be scientific, whereas the nomologicalness of Spinozistic explanations makes them possibly scientific (whether they will in fact pass the bar depends on how Spinoza has employed his laws).

To be clear, I am not saying that Stoics did not value or even see the possibilities latent in natural laws. There is ample evidence to the contrary. Take this passage, the exordium to Chrysippus' *Peri Nomou*: 'Law is kind of all things human and divine. Law must preside over what is honourable and base, as ruler and as guide, and thus be the standard [*kanon*] of justice and injustice, prescribing to animals whose nature is political what they should do, and prohibiting them from what they should not do.'[103] At least one Stoic, Chrysippus, conceived the universe to be governed by law in much the same way as Spinoza. Moreover, Chrysippus thought natural law had enormous significance. The passage just quoted emphasizes the moral import of natural law but it would be a mistake to limit the import of the laws to just the moral realm. In addition, natural laws could be applied to what might be called non-moral[104] phenomena. As one commentator has written, 'it is fundamental to Stoicism that' the world could 'be analysed entirely by reference to Natural Law'.[105]

Given the foregoing, one might wonder how I could say that Spinoza's system is scientific in a way that Stoicism is not. The reason for my statement is that while Chrysippus and other Stoics may have seen the

---

[102] This view flourished especially in the middle of the twentieth century, when it was defended by the likes of Carnap and Hempel. As Carnap bluntly put it, 'you cannot give an explanation without also giving a law' (Carnap (1998), 680).

[103] Marcian, *Institutiones* 1 (L-S 67R (trans. slightly modified)). This is not the only text testifying to the importance of laws of nature in Stoicism. See also, for example, DL VII.88 and Plutarch, *Stoic. Rep.* 1037c–1038A.

[104] There is a sense in which all phenomena are moral phenomena in Stoicism, for the Stoics (unlike Spinoza) think of Nature as a living being, providentially directing all things towards what is best. As one commentator has written, 'the universe pulses with rationality, directionality, normativity. How things ought to be is given by the natural universe itself' (Shields (2012), 186). By speaking of 'non-moral phenomena', I mean those objects and events that do not immediately involve human welfare, such as celestial motions, the behaviour of bees, and the valence of hydrogen atoms.

[105] Long (1986), 165.

potential for natural laws, they did not fully actualize that potential.[106] While his efforts may not have been successful, Spinoza came closer to bringing into fruition the full value of natural laws. Since Spinoza's actual appreciation of natural laws makes his system appreciably closer to contemporary philosophical views on the importance of said laws, he occupies a different place in the history of ideas from the ancient Stoics.

1.3   Arguments for monism

The broad comparison that I have been conducting could be continued. However, while I will return to one last issue in the final section of this chapter, I shall change my approach for the next few pages as I probe each party's argument for monism.

As an opening point, let me observe that most scholars of Stoicism take a dim view of the prospects here. Some think that Stoics simply did not have an argument for monism. So Long and Sedley write, 'Stoic physical theory starts from the presupposition that a single world-order exists.'[107] Others are of the more charitable opinion that transmission is at least partially to blame for the paucity of argument. In this vein David Furley says,

Stoic cosmology is known to us mainly through doxographers, who as a rule were not interested in the reasoning with which the philosophers defended their doctrines, and through the works of opponents of the Stoics, who were generally not as concerned as they should have been to give a fair account of Stoic arguments. As a result, although we know the doctrines at least in outline, we know too little about the context within which they were framed.[108]

The contrast with Spinozism on the known rational basis for monism could hardly be greater. Unlike the Stoics, Spinoza argues at length and with great care for his monism. Also unlike the Stoics, Spinoza's arguments for monism have been preserved. Lest one wonder about the import of these differences, I shall only say that arguments are the essence of philosophy. Insofar as Stoicism as it is known to us lacks the arguments

---

[106] Even Long (1986), who goes farthest in establishing the *rapport* between Spinoza and the Stoics on the value of natural laws, has to admit this point. He writes, 'Spinoza is of course still more formal, but his practice of setting down one continuous chain of reasoning consisting of propositions, proofs and corollaries *would* have won the firm approval of Chrysippus' (185). Though Chrysippus would (or might) have approved of Spinoza's *mos geometricus*, there is nothing in his or any other Stoic's surviving writings to indicate that he or any other Stoic actually accomplished what Spinoza did.

[107] Long and Sedley (1987), 270. As Sedley reiterated a dozen years later, 'Unlike the case of Epicurean physics, for Stoic physics we do not have any text which *argues* for the theory from first principles' (Sedley (1999), 382).

[108] Furley (1999), 433.

which we find in abundance in Spinozism, the latter's monism is going to be more philosophically satisfying. In any case, these differences must be mentioned in the comparison I am undertaking. It is significant that the known Stoic arguments for monism are so thin whereas Spinoza's are robust.

With that said, I return to the Stoics. Though I accept what the above scholars said about Stoic arguments, I still want to advance – if only for the purposes of discussion – a tentative guess as to why they were monists. Stoics held that the world 'does not lack any parts'.[109] Since it does not lack any parts, there are no possible parts which would constitute additions to the world if they were actualized. Since the world cannot be added on to in any way, it must be thought of as the whole.[110] Now, we can distinguish a range of ways in which something could be a whole, from a loose collective whose parts are unified only by physical or temporal proximity, to a fully integrated organism, all of whose individual members and actions are subordinated to a set of impulses or ends emanating from a single controlling authority. As various texts show, when Stoics describe the world as a whole, they had the latter model in mind.[111] The world has this high degree of integration thanks to the existence of a 'breath [*pneuma*] which pervades the whole' of it, so 'unifying' and 'sustaining' the world's parts that they are rendered 'inseparable and mutually coherent with themselves'.[112] Once the world has been shown to be a whole akin to a living organism, the possibility that there could be members of the world which are nonetheless independent of the world is eliminated. Since (1) there are no possible parts that would constitute additions to the world if actualized and (2) all possible parts belong to a single unified and coherent whole, the monistic thesis must be true.

Turning now to Spinoza, since this is beyond the purview of this chapter, I will not try to advance a novel interpretation of his argument for monism or even summarise all of the extant readings. Instead, I shall rely on a helpful synopsis recently given by John Carriero.[113]

There are, Carriero explains, two basic approaches to Spinoza's argument for monism.[114] One of these, which Carriero coins 'Individuation-Oriented Interpretations' (IOI), takes it to be based on the impossibility

---

[109] Calcidius 293 (L-S 44E2).   [110] Sextus Empiricus, *AM*, IX.332 (L-S 44A).
[111] See the arguments from natural philosophy in Cicero, *ND* starting at II.23. See also DL VII.139 and Sextus Empiricus, *AM* IX.104.
[112] Alexander of Aphrodisias, *De mix.*, 223 (L-S 47L1). Cf. Stobaeus *Ecl.* I.166 (L-S 50J).
[113] See Carriero (2002).
[114] Even if there are more than these two – and after criticizing both of them, Carriero tries to advance his own third reading – it is certainly true that *most* interpretations can be placed under one or the other.

of any real differences occurring in nature. In IP4, Spinoza stated what he takes the requirements for individuation to be: 'Two or more distinct things are distinguished from one another, either by a difference in the attributes of the substances or by a difference in their affections.' There are two conceivable ways in which a pair of objects, x and y, may be differentiated from one another: either by being different substances/ having different natures, or by being in different states/having different properties. In IP5Dem, Spinoza eliminated the latter possibility, arguing that since states/properties are derivative of natures, they ought to be 'put to one side' in favour of directly considering the natures of x and y in themselves. Thus it turns out that the only way in which x and y can be distinguished is if they have different natures or are different substances. This reflection on individuation, supporters of IOI contend, quickly leads to the conclusion that two things are really distinct iff they are different substances. Now, since Spinoza elsewhere proved that finite things such as cups and cars do not qualify as substances, it follows they are not really distinct. It is true that IOI must allow the actual demonstration for monism, IP14Dem, to carry some weight, since Spinoza's reflections on individuation only led him to grant real distinction to substances. This is not embarrassing to IOI, however, since they never need be seen as elevating individuation to the exclusion of all else. Rather, all they maintain is that individuation is the linchpin of Spinoza's monism.

Opposed to IOI are what Carriero calls 'Substance-Oriented Interpretations' (SOI), whose essential claim is that Spinoza 'is led to monism through reflecting on the notion of substance'.[115] For example, one common SOI has Spinoza dissatisfied with Descartes' remarks on substance in the *Principles of Philosophy*, Part I, Articles 52 and 53. There Descartes defined a substance as that 'which exists in such a way as to depend on no other thing for its existence'. Since he realized that only God would satisfy this definition, he quickly advanced a second, weaker one, which says that things are substances which 'need only the concurrence of God in order to exist'. According to the current SOI, Spinoza reacted with disgust to Descartes' relaxing of the conditions for substancehood: moving boldly where Descartes hesitated, he argued unequivocally for the monism implied by the strong conception of substance.

A different SOI would also find Spinoza disgusted with Descartes but it takes his disgust to be based on an antecedently developed conception of substance, not indebted to his study of the Frenchman. On this reading, Spinoza accepted some conception of substance, such as that 'a substance

---

[115] Carriero (2002), 38.

is something that does not exist in another thing'.[116] Where he differed
from others who embrace this same conception is that Spinoza (in the
words of one commentator) 'restricts its application by firmly insisting
upon its rigid logical meaning'.[117] If one reflects hard enough on the
meaning of substance, one will ultimately find that only one thing can
satisfy its conditions. According to this SOI, Spinoza is supposed to have
reached this insight. And so he was led to monism.

Now, if Spinoza's case for monism is to be understood in either of the
foregoing ways, how does it relate to that of the Stoics? What lies at the
basis of Stoic monism is the intuition that the world constitutes a genuine
and well-integrated whole. By contrast, Spinoza's monism is usually held
to be based on either individuation or the nature of substance.[118] Since it
would take me too far afield to demonstrate this claim, I will simply assert
that the foundations of Stoic monism, so conceived, are not equivalent to
the foundations of Spinozistic monism, so conceived. This underscores a
point which, while familiar, bears repeating. What I have sometimes
called holistic monism is a substantive philosophical thesis; substantive
philosophical theses can be proven by many different means; as a result,
even parties which agree about the theses themselves will not necessarily
agree about why they are so.

If the foundations for Stoic and Spinozistic monism are different,
however, are they incompatible? Or would each side have welcomed the
arguments of the other as further reinforcing a conclusion it was keen to
establish? In particular, what would Spinoza say of the Stoics' line of
reasoning? The rest of this section will be devoted to that question.

Consider my reconstruction of the Stoic argument. As I have presented
it, the universe can be conceived as a whole, according to Stoics, because
of a ubiquitous physical force rendering all its parts inseparable and
mutually coherent. Now, I previously left indeterminate the character of
this force. To specify it only very partially, *pneuma* is both 'endowed with
sense-perception and reason' and 'divine'.[119] Even without expanding on
them, these properties are important clues to the way in which *pneuma*
organizes the universe's parts into a coherent whole. There are two basic
(and not necessarily mutually exclusive) explanations for how it is that
complex entities qualify as true individuals and not mere collections of
parts: teleological and non-teleological. The teleological explanation

---

[116] Carriero (2002), 43.   [117] H. A. Wolfson, as quoted by Carriero (2002), 43.

[118] Even though he offers an interpretation which is neither individuation- nor substance-
based, Carriero's take on Spinoza's monism also grants no part to the wholeness of the
world, for he makes his monism be 'a response to revisions in the concept of matter
wrought by Descartes' science' (Carriero (2002), 38).

[119] Cicero, *ND* II.29 (I-G 146).

holds that a complex entity is an individual when and only when all of its parts are acting in concert for the attainment of some end(s). By contrast the non-teleological account says that complex wholes are real individuals only in the case that their constituents attain and preserve a certain relation to one another. Given the anthropomorphic and theological properties that Stoics attributed to the universal breath responsible for turning the universe into a whole and therefore a substance, it is plain that they opt for the former. That is, Stoics regarded the most complex of all possible entities – the universe and all it contains – as a genuine individual partially[120] because they believed there to be a divine being which both establishes a set of ends and compels all members of the universe to serve those ends.

Turning to Spinoza, though there is scholarly dispute about his views on teleology,[121] there is no doubting his opposition to universal teleology of the sort ascribed by Stoics to Nature. As he declared in one of the more famous passages of the *Ethics*, 'All the prejudices I here undertake to expose depend on this one: that men commonly suppose that all natural things act, as men do, on account of an end; indeed, they maintain as certain that God himself directs all things to some certain end.'[122] Because the Stoic case for monism presupposes precisely this kind of teleology, Spinoza would have no truck with it.

And yet Spinoza did have a sophisticated and powerful theory regarding the nature of wholes or complex individuals[123] which he deployed to areas as diverse as physics and the philosophy of mind.[124] Moreover, it is arguable that his views on wholeness influenced his views on other matters.[125] Given that he took wholeness so seriously, it is certainly possible that his monism was partially motivated by thinking of the world as a whole. If that were so, then whatever their differences over teleology, Stoics and Spinoza would both concede roughly the same pivotal role to wholeness in their acceptance of monism.

---

[120] Let me stress that Stoics' account of the universe's wholeness could also draw upon non-teleological factors. It only matters to my argument that teleology be a necessary and not a sufficient part of their case for wholeness.

[121] For opinionated guides through the terrain, see Curley (1990) and, more recently, Carriero (2005). Curley focuses specifically on teleology while Carriero treats final causation. Lin (2006) is also helpful, especially with his distinctions among types of teleology.

[122] IApp (G II, 78: 1–4).

[123] The theory is most fully developed in the digression into physics after IIP13Sch.

[124] See the material following IIP13Sch and IIP15, respectively.

[125] For example, it is plausible to think that he was able to conceive of the 'whole of Nature' as one complex individual (IIILe7Sch), precisely because of his theory of wholeness.

Now, to do full justice to this proposal, various refinements would need to be introduced.[126] However, since I believe there is one problem which would eventually torpedo it, regardless of all the qualifications and complications, I will cut to the chase. The problem is this: Spinoza's account of the wholeness of complex entities pertains to objects *within* Nature. It is not at all obvious that he could or would apply it to Nature taken as a whole. The reason is that Nature does not have parts.[127] Because Nature does not have parts, it does not have parts which need to retain their relationship to one another in order for it to be and remain in existence. So there must be some entirely different explanation for the being and continued existence of nature as a whole.

What we learn from comparing Stoic versus Spinozistic arguments for monism, then, is that they are *both* different *and* incommensurable. Stoic arguments rely on views about the nature of wholeness; they are also deeply teleological.[128] Spinozistic arguments draw on a theory of either individuation or the nature of substance *per se*; they are utterly devoid of teleology.[129]

---

[126] For example, since the discussion after IIP13Sch is of bodies, not ideas, changes will have to be made before we can apply that account of wholeness to intensional entities. But given his parallelism, we should suppose that such changes are possible: complex mental entities come to be and perdure when their parts (which would be individual ideas) attain a stable intensional relationship with one another.

[127] IP12. See also the close discussion of the mereology of Spinoza's monism in Guigon (2012). A counter-example to my claim that Nature does not have parts might be thought to reside in *Ep*. 32, where Spinoza offers his celebrated worm-in-the-blood analogy to illustrate how beings within a complex system such as a living body exist and act in ignorance of the nature of the whole of which they are parts. When read carefully, however, the language of the letter shows that Spinoza is talking about beings *within* the whole, not the whole itself. *Qua* complete system, the whole does not have parts.

[128] An early modern who may come closer to the Stoics than Spinoza on these issues is Francis Hutcheson. A strong proponent of providentialism throughout his career, Hutcheson apparently began to connect his providentialism to a kind of monistic worldview in his later works (especially the *Philosophiae Moralis Institutio Compendiaria* (1642)). Moreover, he allegedly did so specifically under the influence of Stoicism. For more on this, see Scott (1900), ch. 12 (esp. 247–56). Irwin (2007–9), vol. II, states without further explanation that Scott 'emphasizes (indeed exaggerates) Hutcheson's closeness to Stoicism' (400 n. 7).

[129] As we leave monism behind, it is worth pointing out there is a cost to Spinoza's version of the theory. He may be able to avoid the problems that Stoicism encounters when it posits that the world is whole because it is alive and driven for an end. At the same time, he faces a set of challenges that are no less daunting, for his monism must try to explain how an infinity of attributes can be unified in one substance. IP9 tries to address this problem but it is far from clear whether it does so successfully. Besides the sources mentioned in note 47 above, see also the excellent encapsulation of this so-called problem of the attributes in Shein (2009b).

1.4   Conclusion: teleology

The issue of natural teleology – which is to say whether Nature is teleological – has arisen several times in the course of discussing other
matters. To conclude this chapter, I shall confront it directly. I start
with the Stoics.

1.4.1 In Section 1.2.4, I noted that Stoic cosmology takes the world to
have a history which is cyclical in character. As it will provide a useful
conduit into Stoic teleology, I shall begin by amplifying on this idea.[130]

At the beginning of each cycle, in the phase that the Stoics called
'universal conflagration' (ekpyrosis), Stoics believed that God alone exists.
He has the form of either pure flame or pure light.[131] During this phase,
all matter has been consumed by God.[132] Residing alone, he contains
within himself 'the principles [logoi] of all things and the causes of past,
present, and future events'.[133] As fire, God is not destructive but rather he
is 'designing, causing growth and preservation'.[134] Being inherently creative, God produces the world out of himself. He is not separated from his
creation, in the way that the Christian God is typically construed, but
rather he is identical with it.[135] As God creates the world out of himself,
he follows a plan that he has formulated or, better, he acts out the plan
which is embedded in his essence.[136] The details of how the world is
created are irrelevant for our purposes. Eventually and solely as a result of
God's actions, the world-system (cosmos) comes into being and it will
remain in being until the end of the present cycle. When the pre-ordained
time arrives, God will absorb the entire world back into himself, so that
things are as they began, with universal conflagration again consuming all
lesser beings and matter, and God existing alone by himself.

It is easy to dismiss Stoic cosmogony and cosmology as fanciful. Other
than observing that it was based on the best scientific knowledge of the

[130] The account of the world cycle that I am about to present was perhaps held by no
individual Stoic, for there are elements in it that each Stoic might object to. For
example, many important Stoics (Zeno of Tarsus, Panaetius and Boethus) questioned
or even flatly denied that a conflagration ever occurs. To cite another example,
Cleanthes and Chrysippus took opposing sides on the question of whether the cosmos
was destroyed in each conflagration (Cleanthes thought it was but Chrysippus thought
it was not). Even if my account is not attributable to any specific Stoic, it is still broadly
Stoic in outline. For a recent discussion, see Salles (2009b).
[131] Philo, Aet. mundi 90 (L-S 46M).
[132] See, e.g., Plutarch, Stoic. Rep. 1052c (L-S 46E).
[133] Eusebius, Evangelical Preparation 15.14.2 (L-S 46G2).
[134] Stobaeus Ecl. I.213 (L-S 46D2 (translation slightly modified)).
[135] See, e.g., Cicero, ND I.39 (L-S 54B).
[136] See, e.g., Eusebius, Evangelical Preparation 15.19.1–2 (L-S 52D3).

day, I will not mount a defence, referring interested readers to those who are better equipped for the job.[137] Instead, I want to expound on a central tenet of the theory: the thoroughly teleological nature of God. Before commencing my exposition, however, permit me to say that 'God' in the present context is extensionally equivalent to 'Nature'. So when the Stoics speak of 'God', they could also employ the term 'Nature'.[138] Because I want to emphasize that Stoics are speaking of the world taken as a whole and not a person-like deity, I will use 'Nature'.[139]

Now, according to the Stoics, the plan that Nature enacts as it creates the world places nearly everything in the position of serving something else. Cicero wrote,

[W]ith the exception of the world everything was made for the sake of other things: for example, the crops and fruits which the earth brings forth were made for the sake of animals, and the animals which it brings forth were made for the sake of men ... Man himself has come to be in order to contemplate and imitate the world, being by no means perfect, but a tiny constituent of that which is perfect. But the world, since it embraces everything and there is nothing which is not included in it, is perfect from every point of view.[140]

Apart from Nature itself, everything else is 'made for the sake of other things'. One noteworthy feature of what is sometimes called, slightly mis-leadingly, Stoic cosmic teleology[141] is the extraordinary detail of the vision. Above we read generically about crops, fruits, and animals. Elsewhere there are specific assertions – for example, that 'bed bugs are useful for waking us, that mice encourage us not to be untidy' or that 'the pig, that most appetizing of delicacies, was created for no other purpose than slaughter'.[142] Such details show the extent to which Stoics deliberated over Nature's teleology. It also demonstrates a second feature of Stoic teleology worth emphasizing – viz., the concomitant degree of control which Nature must wield over its members. If all things exist and act because of a plan executed by Nature, then Nature must be the ultimate agent. Cleanthes said, 'All this cosmos ... obeys you, whichever way you lead, and willingly submits to your sway ... [Y]ou direct the universal reason which runs through all things and

---

[137] See, e.g., Hahm (1977), chs. 3 and 4. A briefer but still compelling account can be found in L-S vol. 1, 277–9.
[138] Indeed, they sometimes do precisely that. See, e.g., Cicero, *ND* II.38, Eusebius, *Evangelical Preparation* 15.19.1, Sextus Empiricus, *AM* IX.104.
[139] The non-anthropomorphic nature of God is explicitly stated in various texts, including DL VII.147.
[140] *ND* II.37–8 (L-S 54H1–2).
[141] It is misleading because there are three senses of cosmos (cf. DL VII.137–8), only one of which includes Nature in my sense – viz., both the world existing between conflagrations and God existing alone during conflagration.
[142] Plutarch, *Stoic. Rep.* 1044d (L-S 54O), and Porphyry, *On Abstinence* 3.20.1 (L-S 54P1).

intermingles with the lights of heaven both great and small ... No deed is done on earth, god, without your offices.'[143] A third feature is the progressive character of Nature's teleology. There are two ways in which it is progressive. First, there is a sequence of events through which the cosmos progresses. This kind of progression is value-neutral, in that it merely references the necessary order in which things must happen. In addition, there is a second, value-laden sense of progress according to which Nature realizes the *good* by its actions. Thus, we read in the passage from Cicero quoted above that 'the world ... is perfect from every point of view'. Elsewhere we read that through Nature's actions 'the world is excellently organized as in a perfectly ordered society'.[144]

In sum, then, the Stoic theory of cosmic teleology is a carefully worked-out vision of the natural order of things. It takes God or Nature to be the immanent agent directing the cosmos towards the achievement of an end. That end is the flourishing of God/Nature and human beings.[145] Because the essential trait connecting God/Nature with human beings is their common rationality, we can say that the world is made for the sake of reason itself. By the providence of God/Nature, all things can be said to be for the best and because of the best. The resulting world-system merits all positive appellations, for it truly is beautiful, just, good, etc.

Bringing in Spinoza, I said towards the end of Section 1.3 that he rejected universal or cosmic teleology. Though I do not think this is actually the case,[146] much of the Appendix to Part 1 seems like it could be specifically targeted at the Stoics. For example, this passage could almost be a paraphrase of Stoic arguments for the existence of a providential God such as are found in Cicero's *De natura deorum*:

[People] find ... many means that are very helpful in seeking their own advantage, e.g., eyes for seeing, teeth for chewing, plants and animals for food, the sun for light, the sea for supporting fish. Hence, they consider all natural things as means to their own advantage. And knowing that they had found these means, not provided them for themselves, they had reason to believe that there was somebody else who had prepared those means for their use ... [This led them] to infer that there was a ruler ... who had taken care of all things for them, and made all things for their use.[147]

---

[143] *Hymn to Zeus* (L-S 54I2–3). Cf. Chrysippus as quoted by Plutarch: 'For since universal nature reaches everywhere, it must be the case that however anything happens in the whole and in any of its parts it happens in accordance with universal nature and its reasons in unhindered sequence' (*Stoic. Rep.* 1050c–d (L-S 54T)).

[144] Aristocles in Eusebius, *Evangelical Preparations* 15.14.2 (L-S 46G3).

[145] See, e.g., Cicero, *De fin.* III.67 and *ND* II.133, and Gellius, *Noct. Att.* VII.1.1–2.

[146] The larger context of IApp shows that he has not the Stoics but the Judeo-Christian tradition of a transcendent creator God in mind.

[147] G II, 78: 29 ff.

After giving this account of how people came to believe in a providential creator-God, Spinoza immediately parodies it:

But while they sought to show that nature does nothing in vain (i.e., nothing which is not of use to men), they seem to have shown only that nature and the Gods are as mad as men. See, I ask you, how the matter has turned out in the end! Among so many conveniences in nature they had to find many inconveniences: storms, earthquakes, diseases, etc. These, they maintain, happen because the Gods are angry on account of wrongs done to men, or on account of sins committed in their worship.[148]

While he thinks of cosmic teleology and its partner, divine providence, as farce, Spinoza does not dismiss them without argument. The most thoughtful refutation appears in IP33Sch2. Because Nature is the whole of being, there is nothing outside of Nature to which it could refer when it acts. Because there is nothing outside of Nature to which it could refer when it acts, all of Nature's 'goals' must be internal to itself. If they are internal to itself, Spinoza contends, then they are not proper objectives which Nature can seek to achieve. For they are states of Nature itself and so they are already achievements of Nature. Moreover, because Nature necessarily exists in exactly its actual condition, there is no alternative state of affairs different from the actual one that could be instantiated. Since there are no alternative states of affairs that could possibly be instantiated, it makes no sense to say that Nature 'chose' to render the world as we find it. Instead, Nature caused the world out of sheer necessity. Nature and its product can be called 'perfect' but only in the old sense of the word, meaning something completed or finished. It makes no sense to say, as the Stoics did, that the world is a genuine bearer of moral or other normative predicates. These two arguments alone, Spinoza thinks, suffice to demolish the twin theses of cosmic teleology and providence.

And yet once I introduce his arguments against teleology and providence, a puzzle appears. The Stoics would *agree* with Spinoza that there is nothing outside Nature which Nature could take as a goal for its actions.[149] So both Spinoza and the Stoics think that Nature does not act for the sake of ends which it does not possess. If both parties agree on this issue, then how can they differ on teleology?

The answer has to do with the opposing answers they give to the question of whether Nature has purposes favouring certain kinds of individuals. The Stoics think that Nature does have such purposes, since it structures the cosmos for the benefit of rational beings. By contrast, Spinoza does *not* think Nature has such purposes, since Nature is

[148] G II, 79: 16–23.   [149] See, e.g., Cicero, *ND* II.38.

equally beneficial or harmful to all beings. Put another way, the Stoics conceive of a special bond between Nature and humans, for the essence of both beings is reason, and they argue that this bond gives Nature a special purpose for action.[150] Not so for Spinoza. There are no unique kinds of individuals in Spinoza's metaphysics, where differences among kinds are a matter of more-or-less.[151] Because Nature has no special connections to any particular beings within Nature, it has no reason to act preferentially towards them.[152] And because it has no reason in act preferentially towards them, it will not act in such a way, for Nature never acts when it does not have a reason.

1.4.2 Thus far, I have been supposing that the Stoic Nature is teleological. For the remainder of my Conclusion, I will drop that supposition.[153]

At this juncture, some of my readers are surely questioning my purpose. The Stoic conception of Nature involves cosmic teleology, full stop.[154] So why think otherwise? I will get to that question but first let me try to motivate the very idea of a non-teleological Stoic cosmology.

It begins with a point rather offhandedly made earlier, towards the beginning of Section 1.4.1. The Stoics believed in cosmic teleology partly because it was supported by the best scientific evidence available to them. In our day, science no longer lends credence to the idea that the universe has a purpose or that human beings occupy a special place in the hierarchy

[150] Besides the texts already cited, see Epictetus, *Discourses* I.16 (called 'On Providence').
[151] This is what Don Garrett calls Spinoza's 'incrementalism'. According to Garrett, Spinoza treats 'important explanatory properties and relations not as simply present-or-absent but rather as properties and relations that are pervasively present to greater or lesser degrees' (Garrett (2008), 18–19). Examples of properties that are present in rudimentary 'forms throughout all of nature' include desire, belief, understanding, and consciousness (ibid.).
[152] Cf. *TTP* ch. 3, where Spinoza denies that the Jews are a special or chosen people (G III: 57), and Letter 19, where he denies that God 'felt sympathy with some things and antipathy to others' (G IV: 90a).
[153] To be clear, I am dropping this supposition only for this part of the chapter. I am doing so as it raises interesting interpretive possibilities which otherwise could not arise. Like Long (see next note), I think that Stoicism is intrinsically teleological and so the case made by Becker (1998) cannot succeed.
[154] When I say that Stoic Nature must be teleological, this is not just for strictly textual reasons. Yes, the textual evidence is overwhelming. In addition, however, Stoic Nature must be teleological for conceptual reasons. If it is not, then the whole Stoic system – physics, logic, and ethics – becomes incoherent. As A. A. Long writes, 'Stoic eudaimonism makes good sense if and only if one adopts a Stoic view of the way things are. If, as I have claimed, determinism and divine providence are crucial features of that view, any attempt to elucidate Stoic ethics which ignores these features will be broken-backed' (Long (1989), 201). If Long is correct, then Becker's version of Stoic ethics (which I am about to outline) must indeed be 'stoic' with a small 's'.

of being (if, indeed, there is a hierarchy). So if there should be any present-day Stoics, then since they would want their cosmology to be consistent with the teachings of science, they would drop their teleological vision of Nature in favour of a non-teleological one.

This very idea has recently been argued by Lawrence Becker in his attempt to revitalize Stoic ethics for the twenty-first century. While adamant that the ethical system which he advocates is Stoical, Becker does allow that it will be different from the ethics of the ancient Stoics. He writes, 'Many ancient stoic ideas would be missing, of course, and a major one would be cosmic *telos* – the notion that the natural world is a purposive system with a end or goal that practical reason directs us to follow.'[155] To those who hold that Stoic ethics shorn of cosmic teleology would not be Stoic ethics, Becker says the following,

[I]t is interesting to try to imagine what might have happened if stoicism had had a continuous twenty-three-hundred-year history; if stoics had had to confront Bacon and Descartes, Newton and Locke, Hobbes and Bentham, Hume and Kant . . . It is reasonable to suppose that stoics would have found a way to reject teleological physics and biology when the scientific consensus did[.][156]

To be sure, Becker's interest in ethics somewhat alters the point, for I am proposing that we de-teleologize Stoic cosmology, which belongs to the domain of physics. Nevertheless, he gestures my way, for he directs attention to the possibility of a reformed Stoicism which has dropped outmoded ideas in favour of current best practice. Inter alia, we may suppose that this school of reformed Stoics – if we want to follow Becker, we could call them 'stoics' with a small 's' to differentiate them from their ancient predecessors – would abandon the very teleological ideas abhorrent to Spinoza.

So let us suppose a reformed stoical conception of Nature that has been shorn of teleology but is otherwise unchanged from the original Stoics' Nature. When we ask what Spinoza would make of such a non-teleological Stoicism, the answer has already been given by the preceding sections of this chapter. He would reject the essential corporeality of Nature. He would embrace the vision of Nature as animate. He would deny that two principles, defined as pure activity and pure passivity, constitute Nature. In place of the principles, he would substitute attributes. He would applaud the stoics' attempts to derive the phenomena that we directly experience – things that he called 'modes' – from Nature. Most generally, he would say with the stoics that we can and must conceive of the universe as a single, unified, coherent being. In sum,

---

[155] Becker (1998), 6.   [156] Ibid.

then, if we take as our *comparatum* not the actual historical Stoics but a reformed and possibly non-existent school of non-teleological stoics, the relationship between Spinozistic monism and that of these stoics would be nearly as complicated, fraught with tension but filled with possibility as his relationship to Zeno, Cleanthes, Chrysippus et al.

Now I can return to the question posed at the beginning of this sub-section – viz., why think of Stoic Nature as non-teleological when it so obviously is? There are four different answers. The first harkens back to a point made in Section 2 of my Introduction. Inter alia, we ought to study Spinoza's relationship to Stoicism because doing so will let us see what was happening to Stoicism in the seventeenth century more broadly. Many philosophers (Hobbes, Descartes, Spinoza) were sympathetic to certain aspects of Stoicism but hostile to others. For many philosophers, Spinoza among them, the most rebarbative feature of Stoicism would have been its natural teleology. So it is worthwhile to speculate what philosophers such as Spinoza might have thought about Stoicism stripped of natural teleology.

The second answer is connected. Insofar as I want to map Spinoza's relationship to all variants of Stoicism, it is necessary for me to consider how his conception of Nature relates to those variants. As I have just argued, even if we could conceive of a non-teleological Stoicism, Spinoza's relationship to such a system would be almost as difficult and filled with potential as his relationship to teleological Stoicism.

The third answer concerns the value of the thought-experiment. If we consider something that is not the case – namely, a non-teleological Stoicism – then we can see the issue of teleology for what it is: an important division between Spinoza and the Stoics but not so important as to obviate all affinities between them. For as I have just argued, even after subtracting teleology, there is much to be said about how their conceptions of Nature compare.

Fourth and finally, it allows me to raise an important question: to wit, just who or what are the Stoics? The actual historical Stoa whose founding Scholarchs were Zeno, Cleanthes, and Chrysippus? The idealized school envisaged by Becker? Or someone/something else entirely? With whom or what am I comparing Spinoza, when I say that I am investigating the relationship of his philosophical system to 'the Stoics'? There is no definitive answer to this question. At times, such as I just did in the case of a non-teleological Nature, I will speculate about how Spinoza's views compare to an idealized stoa (small 's'). For the most part, however, I seek to place Spinoza against the actual historical school as reconstructed by contemporary scholarship. I do not seek to place Spinoza against *his* understanding of Stoicism, since (as I argued in my

Introduction (see Section 3)) I think we have very little chance of knowing what he took Stoicism to be. Nor am I interested in how Spinoza's views compare to those of the Stoics, as interpreted by any of the many people who have remarked on his Stoicalness – Leibniz, Bayle, Hegel, etc. Instead, I want to know the relationship in which Spinoza stands to our own best guess as to Stoicism.

2   *Phantasia* and ideas

> By idea I understand a concept of the Mind that the Mind forms because it is a thinking thing.[1]

> [A]n impression is a printing in the soul ...[2]

A seminal development in seventeenth-century philosophy involved the appropriation of the old philosophical word 'idea' for new purposes.[3] This change occurred both as a result of, and in the service to, the articulation of a new way of thinking about the connection between the individual and the world. It has been argued that the representationalist schemas which emerged out of early modern philosophy constitute one of the early moderns' most significant legacies.[4] Given the centrality of ideas to early modern representationalism, and the importance of those representationalist theories themselves, it is no surprise that an enduring exegetical and argumentative problem confronting scholarship of early modern philosophy is understanding the nature and role of ideas in the philosophy of that time.

Substitute '*phantasia*' for 'idea' and much the same can be said of Hellenistic philosophy. Hellenistic philosophers crafted theories of *phantasia* which were unprecedented in both the distinctions they drew among types of *phantasia* and the specific tasks they assigned to each of these types.[5] Moreover, the opposition between those Stoics who argued that *phantasia* can be and are trustworthy warrants to knowledge claims about the external world, and the Sceptics who denied the same, formed the core of the 'epistemological turn' that philosophy is sometimes said to have taken in the Hellenistic era.[6] These and other factors help to explain

---

[1] IID3.   [2] DL VII.50 (L-S 39A3).   [3] A classic piece on the subject is McRae (1965).

[4] See especially the polemical 'Introduction' to Rorty (1979).

[5] So A. A. Long writes, 'As one studies Stoicism from its fragmentary Zenonian origins down to the continuous *Discourses* of Epictetus and the *Meditations* of Marcus Aurelius, it becomes evident that *phantasia* has a centrality that it lacks in Plato and Aristotle' (Long (1991), 265). Though Long speaks only of the Stoics, I would argue that the same is true of the Sceptics, who vigorously opposed Stoic claims to knowledge based on *phantasia*.

[6] The phrase 'epistemological turn' is borrowed from Brunschwig (1999), 229 ff.

the considerable energy expended by scholars on trying to clarify the status of *phantasia* in Hellenistic thought.[7]

In this chapter, I compare aspects of the Stoic theory of *phantasia* to Spinoza's theory of ideas. In the first section, I discuss the origins and nature of *phantasia* (or, as I shall call them, impressions) and ideas. Then, I explore the range of types of impressions posited by Stoicism, and consider whether there is an equivalent in Spinozism. Finally, I situate impressions/ideas in the larger context of the two systems, looking at two issues: their place in action theory, and whether and how we are able to control our response to them.

2.1   Externalism versus internalism

There are two broad and interrelated questions I address in this section. The primary one concerns the extent to which the contents of impressions/ideas are determined by the world versus the cognitive states of the agents forming those impressions/ideas. The process of addressing this question will give me occasion to ask another: namely, just how dependent are *all* of our mental states on our beliefs, dispositions and other commitments? I shall start with the Stoics and then move to Spinoza.

2.1.1   The Stoics

Described in the most general of terms, impressions are affections (*pathe*) that occur in the soul.[8] While it is true that not all impressions are sense-impressions – we have purely intellectual impressions,[9] such as our idea of God, as well as purely internal impressions, such as the impression of

---

[7] A further interesting parallel between *phantasia* and ideas is the trajectory they followed: both became terms of art rather quickly, flourishing during the heyday of their respective periods, only to see their technical meaning disappear just as quickly as philosophical discourse progressed. Gerard Watson writes of the ancients, 'It is obvious, then, that by the late Hellenistic period φαντασια is a well-known term in technical philosophical debate. It is apparently at this period that the range of meaning is clearly extended, although earlier uses are not abandoned' (Watson (1994), 4766). Robert McRae says that a generation after Berkeley wrote in his *Third Dialogue* that 'idea' is a word 'commonly used by philosophers to denote the immediate objects of the understanding', 'the significance of idea in any technical sense derived from Descartes begins to dissolve' (McRae (1965), 175).

[8] See, e.g., Aetius 4.12.2 (L-S 39B2).

[9] '[Stoics] divide impressions into those which are sensory and those which are not. Sensory impressions are ones obtained through one or more sense-organs, non-sensory are ones obtained through thought such as those of the incorporeals and of the other things acquired by reason' (DL VII.51 (L-S 39A4)).

ourselves at birth[10] – the most important source of impressions are external to the soul: they arise as a result of stimuli – impressers – impacting the soul. Perhaps this is why Philo omits both non-sensory and internal impressions from his general definition of an impression: 'An impression is formed by the approach of an external object which strikes the mind through sensation.'[11]

One might well wonder what it could mean for an impresser to strike the mind or soul. The flavour of the theory is conveyed by Diogenes Laertius' description of visual impressions:

Seeing takes place when the light between the visual faculty and the object is stretched into the shape of a cone ... The air adjacent to the pupil forms the tip of the cone with its base next to the visual object. What is seen is reported by means of the stretched air, as by a walking stick.[12]

Given the state of science at the time, the account of the actual mechanics of sensation is unavoidably simplified. Such simplicity is also evident in the analogies supplied to clarify how the soul is capable of receiving impressions: for example, Chrysippus is reported to have conceived of an impression as an 'alteration of the soul', not an imprint 'like that of a signet-ring, since it is impossible for there to be many such prints at the same time affecting the same subject'.[13] While Stoics may be vague on details, the basic picture is clear enough. As we learned in Section 1.2, Stoic ontology holds that all existing things are corporeal. As an existing thing, then, the soul or mind must also be corporeal or physical. For the same reason, the same will also be true of impressions. So when Stoics hold that the impresser strikes the mind to give rise to an impression, they are saying that one physical entity (the object being experienced) is impressing itself upon another (the mind).

Although most impressions are passive affections of the mind – they happen when external objects act on the soul – it would be a mistake to infer that those forming the impressions contribute nothing to them. Far from it: an interesting and important interplay occurs between impressers and agents which directly affects the nature of impressions. This interplay can be seen as occurring on two levels: first, on the level of groups (such as non-rational or rational animals); second, on the level of individuals (such as Socrates or Descartes). To give a simple example of the former,[14] when

---

[10] See, e.g., Hierocles 1.38–9 (L-S 57C2).   [11] *Allegories of the Laws* 1.30 (L-S 53P2).
[12] DL VII.157 (L-S 53N).   [13] DL VII.50 (L-S 39A3).
[14] To be clear, I am not suggesting the only two groups are rational versus non-rational agents. There are others as well. For example, there is the group of actually rational versus potentially rational agents; the former would be the sages while the latter are fools. Sages would share some impressions simply in virtue of their sagacity. For example, all

my dog and I form impressions of a substance that I would describe as potable water, we are each forming our own impression of the same substance. Moreover, if we are thirsty, we may suppose that our impressions are capable of stimulating action for both of us. Yet because I am rational, my impression differs crucially from my dog's: mine is also attended by a number of propositions, one of which will be something like 'It is appropriate for me to drink this water'. It is not just that my nature differs from my dog's and so my understanding of my impressions differs from my dog's. That is quite true but the Stoics argue that in addition, my *impressions* – the very input I receive about the world – differ from my dog's.[15] To put the matter in Stoic terms, the impressions of rational versus non-rational animals must be sharply distinguished because rational animals' impressions are, and non-rational animals' are not, necessarily attended by *lekta*.[16]

As many scholars have noted, the Greek word *lekton* (plural: *lekta*) is difficult to translate into modern European languages.[17] It is loosely construable as 'sayable' or 'proposition'.[18] An utterance's *lekton* is the meaning or sense that the utterance possesses; it is not what *is* said but what *could be* said of an impression.[19] So when I receive a particular impression, a particular part of my soul, the *hegemonikon* or commanding part, is altered in such a way that the alteration is displayable in language. This does not and cannot happen with non-rational animals.

The dependence of impressions on the natures of those receiving them occurs not just on the macro-level of groups but also on the micro-level of individuals. To borrow an example from Diogenes Laertius,[20] the impression of a human who is knowledgeable about art will differ from the neophyte's. To the latter, a work by Jackson Pollock might seem to be

---

similarly situated sages would experience the same cataleptic *phantasia*. I shall return to the notion of cataleptic *phantasia* below.

[15] See, e.g., DL VII.51.

[16] See, e.g., Sextus Empiricus, *AM* VIII.70 (L-S 33C). The interpretation that I have just given is widely accepted by scholars; one of its principal advocates is Michael Frede in Frede (1983). Not surprisingly, there are critics of the standard view; see above all Richard Sorabji in Sorabji (1990). A reading that tries to mediate the dispute is Lesses (1998). Needless to say, if Sorabji or Lesses proves to be correct, then the comparison that I am making between Spinoza and the Stoics on this set of issues would have to change.

[17] Some of the difficulties are discussed in Shields (1994), 205–6.

[18] I say 'loosely construable', because propositions are strictly speaking only one of a number of types of *lekta*. L-S's translation of *lekton* as 'sayable' (see L-S 33) indicates the full range of entities that are *lekta*: namely, all those things which are expressible in language and thought. Long (1971b) argues persuasively that these things include both propositions and the material of the mental language or 'internal speech' (as Sextus Empiricus puts it in *AM* VIII.275) which Stoics took to be constitutive of thought.

[19] See Brunschwig (2003), 218.   [20] See DL VII.51 (L-S 39A7).

so many dribbles of paint on canvas but to the former, it will be redolent with meaning. The difference in impressions here is not explicable in terms of group differences, since both individuals belong to the same group: they are both rational animals. Instead, Stoics would say that the difference is due to variations in the cognitive abilities or, more generally, the characters of the two.[21] Because the neophyte has an unrefined understanding of art, his impressions of the artwork are unrefined; not so the aficionado. Since no two people will ever have exactly the same cognitive abilities, much less the same character, the dependency of impressions on those things means that no pair of individuals will ever receive all the same impressions. That is, just as my dog and I will receive different impressions when we both perceive what I as a human would describe as fresh, clean water, so any two humans will receive different impressions when they receive sensory input of the same phenomenon.[22]

At the same time as impressions depend on the natures of those forming them, agents do not have total control over them. Such is a key point of this passage from Gellius:

When some terrifying sound occurs, either from the sky or from a building's collapse or as the sudden herald of a danger, even a wise man's mind must be slightly moved and contracted and frightened – not by a preconceived opinion of anything bad but by certain rapid and involuntary movements which forestall the proper function of mind and reason. Soon, however, the wise man in that situation withholds assent to such impressions . . . but he rejects and belittles them and finds nothing in them that should be feared.[23]

Stoics do not hold that all our impressions depend wholly on us. While they do insist that our impressions of the world depend to a certain extent on us, they reserve the leading role for the phenomena outside us which trigger them. Bobzien concisely expresses the view: the impression is 'a function of the external object and the state of our soul'.[24]

As a final point, I want to draw attention to an important distinction. The distinction is between what might be called a mere physiological response to input from one's environment and a full-fledged mental state. A mere physiological response is the initial reaction one has to what is

---

[21] As Michael Frede puts it, '[I]t is perfectly true that an impression is something which we find ourselves with. But it is by no means true that we are completely innocent of the particular details of the impressions we individually form. They very much reflect the beliefs, habits, and attitudes of the particular mind in which and by which they are formed' (Frede (2011), 38).

[22] To be clear, I am saying that no two people will ever experience all the same impressions. This is consistent with allowing that similarly situated sages will experience the same cataleptic *phantasia*.

[23] *Noct. Att.* 19.1.17–18 (L-S 65Y (trans. slightly modified)).   [24] Bobzien (1998), 240.

happening around oneself. In the passage from Gellius, it is the 'moving' and 'contracting' of the sage's soul when he hears a terrifying sound. In this passage from Seneca, it is given a different description:

Involuntary movements can neither be overcome nor avoided. Take the way we shiver when cold water is sprinkled on us . . . Take the way that bad news makes our hair stand on end and indecent language brings on a blush. Take the vertigo that follows the sight of a precipice. None of these is in our power; no amount of reasoning can induce them not to happen. But anger *is* put to flight by precept.[25]

One's body will automatically respond to certain stimuli from the environment without any intervention or action by oneself. This is a matter of physiology; it has nothing to do with what counts as a mental state. A mental state, strictly speaking, happens after one has decided how to respond to the events unfolding around oneself. In Seneca's example, the mental state is anger; it happens because one judges that the events unfolding around oneself are deleterious.[26]

Setting aside the physiological response, Stoics held that there is no such thing as a pure, unprocessed mental state; instead, all mental states include an evaluative component. This thesis is most familiar in the Stoic theory of the emotions, where they famously argued that emotions include or are conditioned by judgments.[27] Their analysis of the emotions, however, is symptomatic of their broader analysis of mental states. Just as Stoics denied that there is or could be an entirely reactive emotion – one which was not at all conditioned by the agent's judgment of the state of affairs which the emotion depicts – so they denied that there is or could be any entirely reactive mental state. As Long puts it, 'we do not experience the world without the mediation of our own assessments'.[28] Because impressions are the primary way in which we experience the world, it follows that they are mediated by our own assessments.[29]

---

[25] *De ira* II.2.1–2 (trans. Cooper and Procopé in Seneca (1995)).

[26] For more on the distinction in Gellius, see Graver (2007), 85–7. For more on Seneca and a critique of the Gellius material, see Sorabji (2000), 375–8.

[27] In saying that emotions 'include or are conditioned by judgments', I am alluding to the scholarly debate over how to take the place of judgments in emotions. Some think that emotions *just are* (false) judgments, while others hold that they follow from such judgments. Evidence for both views can be found in the ancient texts (see, e.g., the dispute recorded by Galen in *PHP* 4.3.2 (L–S 65K1)). For my part, I agree with Margaret Graver that it is an exegetical problem of small importance, for both ways of reading the Stoics grant that emotions are deeply problematic (see Graver (2007), 33–4). In any case, because I am talking about the possibility of unmediated mental states, the debate is beside my main point here.

[28] Long (2002), 28. Cf. Frede (1986), 103–4.

[29] Cf. Annas (1992): 'Perceiving is thinking, not the reception of raw data' (75).

2.1.2   *Spinoza*

Leaving the Stoics for the time being, one place to start with Spinoza is his official definition of idea, IID3: 'By idea I understand a concept of the Mind that the Mind forms because it is a thinking thing.' According to Spinoza, ideas are actions. Two considerations led him to this conclusion, the first of which involves the causal or psychological origins of ideas. They do not exist independently of any thinking entity; he denies that there are ideas independent of the mind which it perceives when it has experiences of external objects. Instead, they are the product of the mind: whenever an idea occurs, it is because some mind is thinking. Moreover, ideas are caused *only* by the mind. In the Explanation to IID3, Spinoza explicitly contrasts his theory of the origins of ideas with the view that an idea arises when 'the Mind is acted on by the subject'. While this view allows that the mind is partially responsible for ideas, it also grants an essential role to an agent outside of or apart from the mind. Spinoza denies the second element; he thinks that ideas happen when and only because the mind has acted. As he explains in IID3Exp, it is because he wants to stress the origins of ideas in the mind that he calls them 'concepts' rather than 'perceptions'.

The second reason for thinking of ideas as actions stems from the supposition that they are inherently propositional. Since they are inherently propositional, it is necessary for them to have content. Because they must have content, they will always hold that something is (or is not) the case. To say that something is (or is not) the case is to offer an affirmation (or negation). Affirmations (or negations) are judgments. And judgments are actions. So from the supposition that ideas are propositional, it follows that they must be or involve actions.

It may help to work through an example.[30] Suppose we form the idea of a triangle. Whenever we form an idea of a triangle, we will have thoughts about enclosed three-sided objects and the like. By having those thoughts, we will necessarily be making certain affirmations, such as that a triangle is an enclosed three-sided object. We cannot have the idea without simultaneously making the judgment. Casting Spinoza's point in contemporary terms, it is customary nowadays to analyse beliefs as complexes of two distinct elements, propositional content and propositional attitudes. As Lilli Alanen has written, to believe something is 'to entertain a proposition plus have an epistemic attitude to it: taking it to be true or false, or doubtful, or likely, or whatever'.[31] Spinoza denies that content and attitude can be separated. For him, agents are able to have ideas with

---

[30] This is adapted from IIP49Dem.   [31] Alanen (2003), 152.

propositional content if and only if those agents have certain propositional attitudes about the matters at hand.[32]

Now, because ideas are 'acts of apprehension, not [sic] objects of awareness',[33] the possibility of their being totally determined by the external environment is eliminated. To see why this should be so, suppose the opposite: assume they were totally determined by the external environment. In that case, both the occasion on which they arose and the contents they possess would be fully established by factors outside those whose ideas they are. If that happened, then it is hard to see how those whose ideas they are would be the progenitors of the ideas. Because of his views on the activity of ideas, however, Spinoza resists any account of ideas which does not make the possessors of ideas their authors. Since we arrive at this unacceptable conclusion by supposing that ideas are totally determined by externalities, it follows that we must reject it and instead take Spinoza as saying the opposite: viz., that it is not the case that ideas are totally determined by factors outside the agent. Since this is Spinoza's view, he should be seen as subscribing to a form of internalism with respect to the formation of beliefs. In common with internalists nowadays, he does not think that the appearance in one's idea of an object outside oneself can be wholly explained by the relations that idea has to states of affairs in the world outside oneself.[34]

Of course, to say that ideas are not *totally* determined by external factors is to allow that they could be *partially* determined by them. I think Spinoza wants to deny even this much, only in such a way as to allow an indirect role for externalities in the formation of ideas. To understand all of this, we need to turn to the all-important doctrine of parallelism, first vetted in Section 1.2.3 of the last chapter.

As I explained there, parallelism is the thesis that there is a one-to-one correspondence between modes of extension and modes of thought, such that for every physical state x, there is a mental state x* which is about the physical state x. This is a universal claim regarding all of being; as such, it applies to human beings. With regard to humans, Spinoza says that 'The

---

[32] Alanen goes on to say that while Descartes incorporates the distinction between content and attitude into his own theory of belief Spinoza does not. As she reads Spinoza, 'he does not allow for any distinction between propositions and propositional attitudes. Ideas or propositions come to the mind as judgments, that is, as affirmations or denials' (153). I disagree only slightly with the way she puts it: insofar as the expression 'ideas or propositions *come to the mind*' implies that they exist prior to the mind's action, this is contrary to Spinoza's thought. For more discussion, see Della Rocca (2003), 201–2.

[33] Mark (1978), 13.

[34] Cf. Della Rocca (1996b), 16–17. In this passage, Della Rocca attributes to Spinoza the radical internalist view that 'accords extreme explanatory independence to the mental, that is, according to which the mental is more autonomous than the current proponents of both internalism and non-reductionism would allow'.

object of the idea constituting the human Mind is the body ... and nothing else.'[35] Take any person. His mind is made up of many ideas.[36] Apart from second-order ideas,[37] all of his ideas are ideas of his body. And they will be *only* about his body: that is the point of the qualifying clause 'and nothing else'. Since ideas are only about one's own body, then because one's own body is internal to oneself, ideas are not determined by factors external to oneself. That is to say, one's ideas are not even partially determined by what is transpiring outside oneself.

Nevertheless, one's bodily states are affected by things outside oneself. Since these things are affecting one's body, then insofar as one's bodily states bear the imprint of such externalities, one's ideas can be said to be indirectly caused by externals. Spinoza acknowledges this in a pair of texts. In IIP16 he writes, 'The idea of any mode in which the human Body is affected by external bodies must involve the nature of the human Body and at the same time the nature of the external body.' When a part of one's body has been affected by an external body, the idea one will have of the affected part includes information about both the bodily part and the external agent which impacted it. For example, if a pin pricks my finger, my idea of my pin-pricked finger will include both the finger itself and the pin which has caused the damage: I will think about the hard, sharp object which caused me pain as I think about the hurt finger itself. At the same time, because that part of my idea which is about the external agent is always mediated through my internal bodily states, Spinoza ascribes a secondary place to it. He writes in the second Corollary to IIP16 that 'the ideas which we have of external bodies indicate the condition of our own body more than the nature of the external bodies'. We know external bodies only because, and only to the extent that, they impact our bodies; hence, our understanding of them is always in terms of their influence on our bodies.

In sum, then, Spinozistic ideas are ideas of the body. As such, they will not be directly caused by external agents: their direct causes[38] are the

---

[35] IIP13. A word on the translation. Curley supplies 'the' before 'body' where of course the Latin leaves open the possibility of either a definite or an indefinite article. Della Rocca (1996b), 25–9, assesses the merits of both translations. I obviously agree with him that on balance the evidence favours the use of the definite article.

[36] IIP15.

[37] Second-order ideas, or what Spinoza calls 'ideas of ideas' (see, e.g., IIP21Dem), take as their object first-order ideas. So they will not have the body as their immediate object. Nonetheless, since they are ideas of ideas which do take the body as their object, even their contents will be importantly determined by the body.

[38] Of course, given the causal barrier between body and mind stipulated by IIID2, it is strictly speaking inaccurate to say that any body *causes* the mind to form ideas. A more cumbersome but more accurate way of expressing the claim I am making would be to say that changes in one's ideas occur in parallel to changes in one's body. The essential point, however, remains the same: namely, that new ideas are formed only in tandem with new

body to which they stand in a parallel relation, since they come into being only when the body assumes new forms. Moreover, they will not be about states of affairs which are external to the body, since they are always and only about one's body and its states. At the same time, because one's body is a mode occupying space in a plenum filled with other extended and active modes, one's body is constantly being acted upon by other bodies. The actions of these other bodies affect one's body. To the extent that they have these effects, the contents of one's ideas of one's body can be said to include information about bodies external to oneself.

2.1.3   Comparisons (1): on the origins of mental content

The terms 'externalism' and 'internalism' can be used in relation to a wide range of phenomena. In this chapter, I apply them to two basic issues: first, the origins of impressions/ideas; second, the contents of impressions/ideas. As I use the terms, a purely externalist theory of impressions/ideas would regard the occurrence of all of one's impressions/ideas, and all of the contents of one's impressions/ideas, as ultimately derived from or caused by relations which those impressions/ideas have to states of affairs outside oneself.[39] Pure internalism would hold the opposite: all of one's impressions/ideas and their contents are attributable only to states of affairs internal to oneself.[40] A plethora of positions lie between the two pure extremes, varying according to whether and how they admit or deny the relevance of externalities to the origins and contents of impressions/ideas.[41]

states of one's body; new states of other bodies, external to one's own body, are irrelevant. Thanks to an anonymous referee for pressing me to clarify this point.

[39] While I am speaking about mental content and not knowledge, there are relations between the two. So, to understand better externalism about mental content, it might be helpful to cite Hilary Kornblith's loose characterization of externalism as applied to knowledge: '"externalism" is a view about knowledge, and it is the view that when a person knows that a particular claim p is true, there is some sort of "natural relation" which holds between that person's belief that p and the world' (Kornblith (2001b), 2).

[40] As William P. Alston has said about internalist views of knowledge, they hold that 'only what is within the subject's "perspective" can determine the justification of a belief' (Alston (1980), 70). Or, as Alvin Goldman puts it, internalism about knowledge is the view that knowledge occurs only when there is a suitable 'doxastic principle or procedure *from the inside*, from our own individual vantage point. To adopt a Kantian idiom, a [doxastic decision principle] must not be "heteronomous," or "dictated from without." It must be "autonomous," a law we can give to ourselves' (Goldman (1980), 42–3).

[41] My statements of externalism and internalism *vis-à-vis* mental content are admittedly and intentionally vague, for the same reasons that Kornblith kept his accounts of externalism and internalism about knowledge vague. Kornblith writes, 'While the broad outlines of these two views are clear enough, precisely what each position comes to is itself a subject of current controversy. It would thus be a mistake to provide precise accounts of these two views ... the state of the art will not allow it' (Kornblith (2001b), 7).

If we think in terms of such a spectrum, it is plain that the Stoics are moderate externalists.[42] Regarding the occurrence of impressions/ideas, Stoics believe most[43] impressions happen when external objects impress themselves upon the soul and force alterations thereto. Though they also think that the character of the soul affects the nature and extent of the impression (this is part of what prevents them from being pure externalists), if no external object ever acted on the soul, there would never be any impressions. Concerning the contents of impressions, Stoics hold that impressions evince traces of their causal origins. This is clearest in the case of cataleptic impressions[44], where impressions are supposed to be reliable indicators of the states of the world because their contents are fixed by their causal history. But it is also true of other impressions.

Spinoza would disagree with all of this. He denies that ideas are caused by externalities: instead, they are intentional counterparts to extensional states which are internal to oneself. That is to say, because ideas are ideas of one's body, and because one's body is internal to oneself, the origins of one's ideas are also fully internal. Concomitantly, because the origins of ideas are other internal states, Spinoza also thinks that the contents of ideas are fully determined by internalities. Ideas have content solely because the bodies they represent (or – if you do not like to think of Spinozistic ideas as representational[45] – the bodies are that the ideas are ideas of) are in the states that they are. There is no need, and indeed it would be incorrect, to cite external states as explanations for their contents. Because of his views on the origins and contents of ideas, Spinoza qualifies as a strict internalist.[46]

---

[42] I deliberately call Stoics '*moderate* externalists', for whether we talk about externalism with respect to mental content (as I am doing) or externalism about knowledge and justification, the Stoics never offered a purely externalist account. I shall soon give reasons against taking Stoics to be pure externalists about mental content. With regard to externalism about knowledge and justification, I accept the arguments of some recent commentators that Stoics are not pure externalists here, either. For more, see Reed (2002) and especially Perin (2005).

[43] The qualifier 'most' is required because, as noted above, Stoics thought that some impressions can have the mind as their source. Cf. DL VII.51 and Hierocles 1.38–9.

[44] I have said nothing about cataleptic impressions yet. I shall discuss them at length in the next section.

[45] Nadler (2006) avoids the use of the concept of representation on the grounds that 'the relationship between the idea and its object is not an external relationship between two distinct things' (157). Della Rocca (1996b) constitutes the counterpoint to Nadler.

[46] In the foregoing, I have omitted mention of the distinction Spinoza makes between confused and non-confused ideas. Some commentators think that Spinoza gives an externalist account of confused ideas and an internalist account of non-confused ones (see, e.g., Della Rocca (1996b), 102). By contrast, my reading holds that Spinoza offers an internalist account of the origin and content of all ideas, whether confused or not. If it proves to be correct that Spinoza is an internalist only about non-confused ideas, then the

Let me cite some authorities to buttress and amplify the claims just made. Earlier, I quoted Bobzien as writing that the impression is 'a function of the external object and the state of our soul'.[47] I find more illuminating Sandbach's statement that 'The presentation, the *phantasia*, "what appears", is at once an impression made through the senses and an interpretation of that impression.'[48] While there are troubling ambiguities to both Bobzien and Sandbach – ambiguities to which I shall turn in a moment – the basic position they describe is plain enough: impressions are a joint product of the world and the soul. Concerning Spinoza, Della Rocca writes that whenever an agent has a non-confused idea, 'the concepts [grasped] . . . are sufficient *by themselves* to determine the particular object of [her] thought'.[49] Here too, the thesis Della Rocca adumbrates is clear: the acquisition of adequate ideas is a product of the agent's intrinsic properties; the role of the environment is nil.

2.1.4   Comparisons (2): the problem of the function

Mention of the role of the environment brings me to the next point of comparison that I want to make. It concerns a weakness in the Stoic theory, a weakness that Spinoza does not suffer. The problem with Stoicism is most plainly displayed by Bobzien's talk of 'function'. A function is a quasi-mathematical notion; it suggests that the product can be determined with a great deal of precision. Yet Bobzien never attempts to quantify and explain how much of the content of the impression is due to the action of the object on the soul versus the soul's interpretation of the impresser's imprint upon it. To be sure, though she may invite criticism by invoking the term 'function', she is not the only guilty party. Sandbach is also criticizable, for he attributes the form of the impression to the physical stimuli of the senses plus the interpretation rendered by the mind of the stimuli without explaining exactly how much each contributes to the end product. Now, it is arguable that the fault is not ultimately the commentators but either the texts as they have been transmitted to us or even the Stoics themselves, who may not have adequately addressed the issue. Moreover, the underlying philosophical problem is vague: it may be impossible to quantify precisely the relative contribution of the stimulus versus the influence of the character of the soul on the formulation of the

contrast between him and the Stoics will have to be modified, for a significant portion of ideas – all those which are confused – would turn out to have external causes. At the same time, since non-confused ideas are more important than confused, there would still be a major difference between Spinoza and the Stoics, for he would insist that their contents must be conceived in fully internalist terms, a point which the Stoics would deny.
[47] Bobzien (1998), 240.   [48] Sandbach (1971), 13.   [49] Della Rocca (1996b), 104.

impression itself. At the same time, if either the texts or the Stoics themselves are to blame, and given the hoariness of the conceptual issue itself, commentators have a responsibility to acknowledge the uncertainty in their commentaries.

Lest it be thought that I may be unfairly singling out Stoicism and Stoic scholars for criticism, I add that the same charges cannot be levelled at Spinozism and Spinoza scholarship because of the difference in Spinoza's views. Given that Spinoza's theory of ideas is so close to being purely internalistic, it is not important to specify the balance between the environment and the mind; the environment plays no role. Even the ideas that the mind forms about the external world are actually ideas of the mind's body. So one's ideas are always acquired independently of any direct relations to external factors and none of their contents are attributable to externalities. The problem of the function is not a problem for Spinoza and his readers, because he does not make ideas out to be functions of the mind and the world.

While the problem of the function is not a problem for Spinoza, it is arguable that he avoids it only at great cost. The reason that he does not owe us an account of how the external world factors into the formation and nature of our mental contents is that he denies that the world plays any role in those matters. Many philosophers nowadays would completely reject this hypothesis, for they think whether we are talking about mental content, representation, knowledge or justification, there must be a causal link between the item in question and the world.[50] So Spinoza may dodge the muddle that Stoicism faces but only to land in the deeper mess of explaining how the mind's mental contents can occur so totally independent of the external world.

2.1.5   Comparisons (3): the mediation of mental contents

Moving on, the remaining point of comparison I want to make concerns the view, held by both Spinoza and the Stoics, that there are no pure, unprocessed mental states. Both parties agree on this. As Long describes the Stoic view, all mental states involve 'the mediation of our own assessments';[51] Bennett says Spinoza thought that 'we don't have a

---

[50] Goldman says when it comes to how we should think of knowledge as being justified, 'internalism is a mirage' and 'we should be thoroughly content with externalism' (Goldman (1980), 58–9). Even Alston, whose rejection of internalism is more tempered, thinks that the only role to be played by purely internalistic factors in the justification of our knowledge is that the agent must have an 'epistemic accessibility of ground for [his] belief' (Alston (1980), 103).

[51] Long (2002), 28. Cf. Frede (1986), 103–4.

cognitive process of bringing propositions into the mind and a further process ... in which they come under propositional attitudes'.[52] Stoics and Spinoza are thus aligned against those like Tyler Burge who argue that the contents of 'perceptual experience ... [are] independent of any one person's actions, dispositions or mental phenomena'.[53]

While they agree on this, Spinoza and the Stoics disagree on a related question. This question concerns the nature of the phenomena found at the earliest stage of a sensation. This is the contracting of the wise man's soul when he is surprised by a sudden sound (Gellius), or the way hair stands on end when one is sprinkled by cold water (Seneca). As we have seen, Spinoza thinks that all ideas – including ideas of mere perceptibles – are assertoric in character. According to the Stoics, though, we only come to assert and believe our impressions after we have assented to them – and assent is conceptually subsequent to the initial acquisition of impressions. Given this difference, their disagreement over primitive impressions/ideas is that Spinoza thinks we are fully committed to even our simplest mental states while the Stoics do not. According to Stoicism, because our impressions are affected by our characters, they do not have the independence alleged by Burge. At the same time, Stoics continue, we do not form full judgments about impressions until a later point in our response to them – namely, until we have assented to them. This shows that there are stages in the evolution of impressions. They can be part of the process which leads to the formation of full-fledged beliefs – as Tad Brennan says, beliefs are defined 'in terms of assent to impressions'[54] – but it would be wrong to equate the two.[55] By contrast, Spinozistic ideas have been glossed as beliefs.[56] There is no division between an initial impression and one's reaction to that impression.

2.2   Typology

2.2.1 The Stoic theory of *phantasia* is marked by a robust and detailed set of distinctions among types of impressions. Just how the different types of impressions are supposed to be related to one another, however, proves complicated. Since this problem summons up the crucial issue of whether and to what extent our impressions are under our control – an issue that came up obliquely in the last section and one which will be addressed directly in the next – I shall now undertake to explore it. My style will be

---

[52] Bennett (1984), 162.   [53] Burge (1986), 125.   [54] Brennan (2005), 62.
[55] I will return to the role of impressions in belief formation in Section 2.3 below.
[56] The case has been argued most strongly by Matson (1994). He draws support from Bennett (1984), 162–7, and Mark (1978).

more dialectical than the last section, as I will move freely between Stoics and Spinoza, contrasting them to advance the discussion and enhance our understanding of both. I start with the Stoics.

In the surviving literature on the early Stoa, a wide range of types of impressions are attested. Stobaeus tells us of hormetic impressions and their opposite, the non-hormetic.[57] In Sextus Empiricus and elsewhere, we read of cataleptic versus non-cataleptic impressions.[58] Diogenes Laertius speaks of the 'persuasive' impression (*pithanon axioma*) as 'one which induces assent' and seems to distinguish it from both the non-persuasive and the hormetic impression.[59] It may be uncertain why Stoics chose to distinguish a ramified range of impressions, including (but not limited to) the three types just mentioned. Most likely, it has to do with a decision they made on how to handle the relationship between the theoretical and the practical in epistemology and action theory. Also unclear is what exactly or even roughly the Stoics meant by some of the types. For example, the persuasive/non-persuasive dichotomy is very poorly attested, with the result being that it is little known and rarely discussed in the scholarly literature.[60] Fortunately, the two types that seem to have been most important to Stoicism – the hormetic/non-hormetic and cataleptic/non-cataleptic – are both comparatively well-attested and the frequent subject of scholarly examination. I shall briefly amplify each of them before moving to Spinoza.

According to Stobaeus, a hormetic impression is of something which is 'obviously appropriate' and capable of stimulating action; a non-hormetic impression would satisfy neither of those conditions.[61] Nothing mysterious is meant by 'obviously appropriate': it is anything that conduces to the health, welfare, enjoyment, happiness, etc. of the agent.[62] As to the requirement that the thing perceived be capable of stimulating action, we may think of it as stipulating that the thing be attainable by an action of the agent. Though an archer may have an impression of a target one kilometre away, it will not be hormetic for him since there is no way he can shoot his arrow that far.[63] And here is a key feature of hormetic impressions: they are

---

[57] See especially *Ecl.* II.9 (= II.86.17–88.7).   [58] See, e.g., *AM* VII.257.
[59] DL VII.75 (my translation).
[60] One discussion can be found in Inwood (1985), 86–8. See also Brennan (2005), 303 n. 4.
[61] *Ecl.* II.86.17–18 (I-G 216).   [62] Cf. Inwood (1985), 56.
[63] As those familiar with the literature will recognize, the example is drawn from ancient texts dealing with the *skopos/telos* distinction (see, e.g., *De fin.* 3.22 and Plutarch, *De comm. not.* 1070f–1017e). To understand the Stoic view, it is crucial to realize that attainability is not solely a function of external states of affairs but rather and primarily a function of the agent's internal intentional and rational states. Such is the upshot of the important *skopos/telos* distinction – the distinction between doing everything one can to

practical, intrinsically tied to action. If an agent is presented with a hormetic impression, then *ipso facto* she has been given a reason to act. Such an impression would entail, practically automatically,[64] a response by the non-rational animal. By contrast, rational animals will always have to accept that reason as valid for them before they act.[65]

Turning to the cataleptic/non-cataleptic distinction, an impression is cataleptic when it 'comes from an existing object, and is stamped and moulded in accordance with the existent thing itself'.[66] Impressions are made cataleptic by their causal origins, content, and impact on the perceiving soul.[67] Though a cataleptic impression differs from a non-cataleptic one by being 'self-evident and striking', it 'all but seizes us by the hair, they say, and pulls us to assent' only when there is no 'impediment' preventing us from appreciating it fully.[68] There is uncertainty about what this implies: does it follow that agents regularly receive cataleptic impressions without appreciating them fully, or does it only follow that, even when agents receive cataleptic impressions (however infrequently or frequently that may happen), circumstances can be such that they might not recognize them as cataleptic? No matter which answer proves correct, it will still be the case that the agent's character must be in a certain state for impressions to be cataleptic to her or him.[69]

As understood so far, then, the hormetic and the cataleptic seem to operate along different axes. Being 'obviously appropriate' and capable of stimulating action, hormetic impressions are action-oriented. As the impression which 'practically . . . drags us to assent' to the truth of what is represented in the impression, cataleptic impressions are alethically oriented. A question which naturally arises is whether any single

---

obtain one's objectives versus actually obtaining those objectives. To continue the example, when an archer takes aim at a target, what matters to the evaluation of his action is that he did everything in his power to hit the target. So long as he took careful aim at his target and flawlessly released the arrow, whether he actually hits the target is relatively unimportant (we would not blame him if a completely unforeseeable gust of wind blew the arrow awry). Impressions are hormetic for us when we perceive them as attainable, not when they actually are attainable, given the condition that the world is in.

[64] I say 'practically automatically', because there appears to be a formal stage (called 'yielding') in the action of non-rational animals analogous to assent in rational ones. See Inwood (1985), 75.

[65] I shall say much more about all of this in Section 2.3 below.

[66] DL VII.46 (I-G 112). See also *AM* VII.248.

[67] This formulation is borrowed from Hankinson (2003), 61. See also Striker (1990), 157.

[68] *AM* VII.257 (L-S 40K3).

[69] I am emphasizing the agent's character but this is not the only factor relevant to the occurrence of cataleptic impressions. The external environment also has to be in the right state. Sextus Empiricus specifies five conditions that must 'concur' (*sundramein*) for cataleptic impressions to happen (see *AM* VII.424).

impression can manifest both properties: to use Stoic terms, can there be hormetic impressions that are also cataleptic? To answer this question, further refinements in the Stoic theory of *phantasia* are needed, but since those refinements are more easily discerned against an early modern backdrop, I want to leave the Stoics for the time being in favour of Descartes and especially Spinoza.

2.2.2 In the third Meditation, Descartes distinguishes three types of ideas: innate, adventitious, and invented or fictitious.[70] Innate ideas are those which derive entirely from principles or other constituents of one's own nature. The adventitious are those caused by things outside oneself, while the fictitious are supposed to have been entirely made up by oneself. As Descartes conceives of them, the three classes are entirely non-overlapping: to say that an idea is innate is to say, inter alia, that it is neither caused by external objects nor made up willy-nilly by the mind. Moreover, the three classes are meant to be exhaustive: since all ideas are caused in one of the three ways, all ideas can be placed under one of the three headings. At the same time, ideas can also be arranged according to different criteria. The most famous Cartesian distinction of ideas – that between clear and distinct versus the not clear and distinct ideas – cuts across the tripartite division just mentioned. Rather than the *origins* of ideas, the clear and distinct / not clear and distinct pairing is about the *epistemic grasp* one has of one's ideas. Descartes certainly thought he had clear and distinct knowledge of some innate ideas; he also probably thought he knew some of his adventitious ideas clearly and distinctly. The relation of the clear and distinct / not clear and distinct dichotomy to the three ways in which ideas are caused is similar to the way the hormetic and the cataleptic are usually thought to be related in Stoicism: in Descartes as in the Stoics, the distinctions cut across each other. With this key difference: whereas Descartes allowed that ideas can be both innate or adventitious *and* clear and distinct, it is uncertain whether Stoics thought impressions can be both hormetic and cataleptic.

Like he did in the theory of emotions, where he accepted Descartes' reductive methodology while simultaneously pruning several of the primitive emotions posited by Descartes, Spinoza also accepts Descartes' claim that there are classes of ideas. In some of his work, he even accepts some of Descartes' proposals about the classes. So for example, as part of the theory of ideas expounded in the *TdIE*, he sharply distinguishes false from fictitious ideas. They do not differ in their content; false and

---

[70] A-T VII: 37–8.

fictitious ideas can both contain the same conceptual elements. Instead, they are differentiated by the way in which the agent commits himself to one versus the other. Spinoza writes, 'between fictitious and false ideas there is no other difference except that the latter suppose assent [*assensum*]; i.e. (as we have already noted), while the representations [*repraesentamina*] appear to him [who has the false idea], there appear no causes from which he can infer (as he who has fictitious ideas can) that they do not arise from things outside him'.[71] Agents receive representations which purport to depict states of affairs in the external world. As it happens, some of those representations are inaccurate – the states of affairs which they depict cannot actually be found in the external world. When agents assent to these representations, they form ideas which are false. If they refuse to assent, they would not accept that the external world is the condition which the presentations allege, and they would not form any false ideas.

While Spinoza seems to have accepted at least part of the Cartesian classification scheme in his early work, he moves to a different typology in the *Ethics*. In that work, there is only one distinction of any import: ideas are either adequate or not. Or, to use another way of putting it, ideas are either clear and distinct or 'mutilated and confused'.[72] The concept of adequate idea is officially defined in IID4: 'By adequate idea I understand an idea which, insofar as it is considered in itself, without relation to the object, has all the properties or [*sive*] intrinsic denominations of a true idea.' Before coming to the notion of adequate idea directly, note its status in Spinoza's theory of ideas. IID4 appears immediately after the official Definition of idea, IID3. Moreover, since IID3 and IID4 are the only Definitions or Axioms having to do with ideas, adequate ideas form half of the entire definitional basis of Spinoza's theory of ideas. When we add the multiple applications of the notion in the middle of Part II, the second half of Part V and elsewhere, it becomes evident that we are plainly dealing with a notion of some importance to Spinoza. The question is – what does it mean?

We can begin by making several preliminary points. First, adequacy is a property that attaches to ideas: if an idea is adequate, then it has the property of having 'all the properties ... of a true idea' (IID4). Second, adequacy is relational: an idea can be inadequate with respect to one mind while adequate with respect to another. For example, an idea might be inadequate in my mind, and yet, for reasons we shall soon encounter, that

---

[71] *TdIE* §66. The bracketed insertions are mine.

[72] See, e.g., IIP35. Since I am not going to discuss what Spinoza might mean by 'mutilated and confused', let me refer interested readers to Bennett (1984), 178–82.

same idea in God's mind would be necessarily adequate. Third and most importantly, adequacy is distinct from, but very closely connected with, truth. In the Explanation attached to IID4, Spinoza explains that when he says adequate ideas have the 'intrinsic denominations' of true ideas, he deliberately wishes 'to exclude what is extrinsic, viz. the agreement of the idea with its object'. So an adequate idea is exactly like a true idea except that the former need not be connected with the world in any way for it to obtain.[73]

The proximity of adequacy to truth leads to a larger issue. A number of commentators have stressed the extent of the propositional content of adequate ideas. So Bennett identifies two different senses of adequacy, each based on different passages from the *Ethics*. According to one, to have an 'adequate perception of x is to have an idea directly of the whole of x'; according to the other, 'to have an idea which is [sic] adequate is to have an idea which is wholly caused from within one's own mind'.[74] Nadler also finds two senses, though operating along different lines from Bennett's. According to the 'strict' sense, God alone has adequate ideas, 'because only God ... can encompass in its ideas the infinite number of conditions that causally determine anything'.[75] According to the 'abbreviated' sense, a human can have adequate ideas, because whether or not one has adequate ideas in this sense depends entirely on 'how ideas are ordered in a person's mind. One's partial knowledge can still be adequate, as long as the idea of the thing is properly situated in its causal/logical nexuses.'[76] While the differences between Bennett and Nadler are obvious and important, they agree on one point: adequacy is to be cashed out in terms of completeness; an idea of x is adequate only in the case that it possesses all the content which is relevant to x.[77] I do not propose to enter into the debate over what exactly it means to say that adequate ideas must be complete; instead, I want to draw attention to *what* is supposed to be complete.

Adequate ideas are adequate precisely because, and only insofar as, they possess content of the appropriate kind. Conversely, inadequate ideas are deficient because they lack the necessary sort of content. This

---

[73] See *Ep.* 60: 'Between a true and an adequate idea I recognise no difference but this, that the word "true" has regard only to the agreement of the idea with its object, whereas the word "adequate" has regard to the nature of the idea in itself.'

[74] Bennett (1984), 177. [75] Nadler (2006), 165. [76] Ibid.

[77] So Spinoza would partially agree with Descartes' statement in the Fourth Replies that 'if a piece of knowledge is to be *adequate* it must contain absolutely all the properties which are in the thing which is the object of knowledge' (CSM II: 155; A-T VII: 220 (his emphasis)). Spinoza would agree with the claim that the adequate idea must contain '*all the properties*'; he would demur, however, at the connection to the 'object of knowledge'.

shows that adequacy – the acquisition of adequate ideas and what makes ideas adequate – is a matter of knowledge: one must know enough of the right concepts, and know those concepts in the right way, before one can claim to have an adequate idea. What this shows, in turn, is that adequacy is knowledge-oriented.

2.2.3 At this juncture, permit me to recall a point established in Section 2.1.2: namely, that ideas are actions. Given that Spinoza thinks that ideas are actions and that adequate ideas in particular are knowledge-oriented, he seems to combine properties which are separated in the Stoic theory of *phantasia*. As we have seen, they theorize the existence of hormetic impressions and cataleptic ones, and like Descartes did with his innate, adventitious, and fictitious ideas, so the Stoics seem to place the two types of impressions in non-overlapping classes. Since Spinoza's adequate ideas combine elements which are not combined in Stoic impressions, it seems to be the case that Spinoza's conception of ideas differs importantly from the Stoics' impressions. Or is it?

This returns us to the question with which we left the Stoics at the end of Section 2.2.1 above: can there be hormetic impressions that are also cateleptic? That is to say, can there be an impression of an apparently appropriate good which is so straightforwardly compelling that it forces the assent of the agent who receives it? If Stoics did think that some hormetic impressions are cataleptic, then their theory of impressions would begin to approach Spinoza's theory of ideas, for in both theories, we would find the existence of impressions/ideas which are both practical and theoretical.

The secondary literature will not be of much use in deciding what the Stoics thought, for commentators sharply disagree. Inwood flatly states, 'it seems certain that no hormetic presentation, whether rational or non-rational, is cataleptic'.[78] Following Inwood, Tad Brennan writes, 'From the standpoint of moral psychology, the most important division of impressions cuts across the distinction between the false, true, and cataleptic ... and characterizes the content of the impression as either practical or theoretical.'[79] On the other side of the aisle Stephen Menn says that practical arts move us to act because 'they contain catalepseis that motivate action'.[80] Steven Strange argues, 'We cannot fail to pursue what we grasp as obviously good or to avoid what is obviously bad, which is to say that there are practical cataleptic impressions as well as theo-retical ones.'[81]

---

[78] Inwood (1985), 76. [79] Brennan (2003), 266. [80] Menn (1995), 11.
[81] Strange (2004), 48.

To find a way forward, we ought to delve more deeply into the basis of the alleged difference between the two types of impressions. All, or nearly all, of the texts about cataleptic impressions from the early Stoa deal with straightforwardly perceptual impressions, such as 'This is a pomegranate.'[82] It is not hard to see how a straightforwardly perceptual impression could be such that, as Sextus says, it practically takes one by the hair and compels assent. Epictetus alludes to the power of such impressions in a passage on the impossibility of assenting to false appearances:

> [Epictetus]: 'Feel, if you can, that it is now night.'
> [Interlocutor]: 'I can't.'
> 'Put away your feeling that it is day.'
> 'I can't.'
> 'Either feel or put away the feeling that the stars are even in number.'
> 'I can't.'[83]

It is also easy to see how a perception could be such that this compulsion is exercised on all normal humans, so that failure to assent to 'it is day' would be proof of abnormality – either severe failure of the senses or downright irrationality. As a result, with abnormal cases being set aside, it is possible to ignore individual variation among sense-perceptions.

Consider now hormetic impressions. When an agent receives a hormetic impression, the entity represented in the impression is good *for him*. An impression of potable water would be hormetic to someone who is thirsty but not for someone who has already drunk to her fill. The individual variability of hormetic impressions – their sensitivity to the states that agents are in – is the exact opposite of the universality of response to sense-perceptions. Because everyone normal receives the same sense-perceptions whereas not everyone normal receives the same hormetic impressions, the two types of impressions are distinct.

Now, catalepsis is a particular property of impressions: it is a property of those impressions that demand an effectively universal response from those who receive them. We can see that this is how catalepsis ought to be interpreted by the interest of sceptics in individual exceptions to general claims. Impressions which are cataleptic are supposed to compel literally all agents to respond in a determinate way. If sceptics are able to find a few exceptions – or even a single one – to a putatively cataleptic impression,

---

[82] The example comes from DL VII.177. For an argument that they *must* be perceptual, see Striker (1974), Appendix.

[83] *Discourses* 1.28.3–4; translation by Oldfather in Epictetus (1928), with modifications from Long (2002), 99. Though he is here describing the necessity of perceptual impressions, the following sections make it plain that he thinks the same necessity can be found in practical impressions – 'in the sphere of actions', as he puts it (1.28.5).

they've shown that that impression is in fact not cataleptic. So what is interesting about cataleptic impressions ought not be something about individual responses to them but rather a feature of their relationship to whole classes of perceivers. For reasons given in the previous paragraph, straightforwardly perceptual presentations can reasonably be expected to be cataleptic in this sense but hormetic ones cannot.

In my opinion, early Stoics would provide an answer along the above lines to the question of whether hormetic impressions can be cataleptic. Because hormetic impressions are not universally efficacious whereas cataleptic impressions are, they are distinct. However, that is not all which can be said on the matter. Two moves can be made which would cast the foregoing into doubt.

The first move does not directly respond to the argument just given but instead erodes the preconditions for that argument. The argument just given takes for granted a theory of *phantasia* which posits precise distinctions among the various types of impressions: it is because the identity conditions for cataleptic impressions are tightly circumscribed that they can be confidently separated from hormetic impressions. Yet it seems that by late antiquity some Stoics no longer utilized these distinctions. In the first chapter of the *Enchiridion*, Epictetus tells his reader to 'Make it your practice ... with every harsh impression, to recite to it straightaway, "You are an impression, and not necessarily its object."'[84] Epictetus' talk of the 'harsh impression', without qualification as to the type of impression, suggests a disinterest in the early Stoa's precise taxonomy of impressions. What matters to Epictetus is whether or not an impression is 'harsh', not whether it is cataleptic or hormetic or persuasive.[85]

Similarly, in his commentary on these lines, Simplicius does not employ the technical language associated with the early Stoa's theory of *phantasia*. He does not speak of hormetic or cataleptic impressions but instead he makes blanket statements about impressions *simpliciter*. For example, he takes Epictetus' descriptions of some impressions as 'harsh' to mean that 'they are irrational and maddening, and genuinely make life harsh by the inconsistency and irregularity of their motions'.[86] Shortly afterwards, he argues that all impressions are ultimately to be classified according to 'one rule': 'the distinction of what is up to us and what is not up to us'.[87] While Simplicius here says that Epictetus posited a rule for

---

[84] Translation by Brittain and Brennan in Simplicius (2002).
[85] I am citing the *Enchiridion* for reasons which will soon be made plain. Similar disinterest in the technical apparatus of the early Stoa's theory of *phantasia* can be found in the *Discourses*; see, e.g., I.27.1–2, II.8.4–8, II.18, etc.
[86] Simplicius (2002), 59 (Dübner 20.7–9).
[87] Simplicius (2002), 59–60 (Dübner 20.36–8).

distinguishing among impressions, this rule is entirely normative in nature; it is not like the epistemological-cum-metaphysical rules of the early Stoa. From both the *Enchiridion* and Simplicius' *Commentary*, then, we learn that Epictetus did not attend to the distinctions drawn by his predecessors among *phantasia*.[88]

The second move differs from the first, in that it does address the argument purporting to deny the possibility of cataleptic hormetic impressions. First it distinguishes between two subtypes of hormetic impressions: those that will elicit the same response from all, and those that will not. Then, it alleges that contrary to what the foregoing argument maintains, some hormetic impressions are such that they will be responded to in exactly the same way by all agents. The contention is not that *all* hormetic impressions will elicit a uniform response – that is clearly preposterous – but rather that *some* will. Epictetus seems to flirt with this view in some texts:

Now just as it is the nature of every soul to assent to the true, dissent from the false, and to withhold judgement in a matter of uncertainty, so it is its nature to be moved with desire towards the good, with aversion towards the evil, and feel neutral towards what is neither evil nor good … The instant that the good appears, it attracts the soul to itself, while the evil repels the soul from itself. A soul will never refuse a clear sense-impression of good [*agathou phantasian enarge*], any more than a man will refuse the coinage of Caesar. On this concept of the good hangs every impulse to act both of man and of God.[89]

We are all moved to act by an impression of the good. Consequently, impressions of the good can be called hormetic: they are capable of moving the agent to act. Moreover, some impressions of the good are so overwhelming as to be universally efficacious: all agents who receive those impressions are moved to act by them. Since impressions are or can be cataleptic when they elicit an effectively universal response from those who receive them, then because some impressions of the good have exactly that effect, it follows that they are cataleptic.

Now, the sole basis for distinguishing cataleptic from hormetic impressions was the universality of response elicited by the former but not the latter. On the assumption that some hormetic impressions will be hormetic for all agents, the scope of that distinction is diminished. It does not disappear totally, as hormetic impressions remain which are not assented to by all agents. So the class of hormetic impressions does not become

---

[88] Let me stress that it is not part of my argument to claim Epictetus was ignorant of those distinctions – only that he did not attend to them. Others have shown how he blurred other pieces of Stoic terminology and concepts. See, e.g., Appendix 2 of Inwood (1985).

[89] *Discourses* 3.3.2–4 (trans. Oldfather in Epictetus (1928), with minor modifications).

identical to the class of cataleptic ones. But for the subclass of hormetic impressions that always stimulate action, there is no reason not to call them cataleptic.

There is more to be said here[90] but let us suppose there is plausibility to the case I have been making – that some Stoic impressions may be both cataleptic and hormetic. Previously, I showed that there is little doubt that Spinoza took ideas to be both alethically sensitive and practical. So to the extent that we buy the case for catalepsis of hormetic impressions in Stoicism, we should also accept that Spinozistic ideas and Stoic impressions are alike in this all-important respect.

2.2.4 A reason for the importance of this issue will become apparent in the next section. For now, I want to conclude Section 2.2 by making one final and purely historical point. At various places, I have suggested that a divide may exist between the early and late Stoa on technical aspects of *phantasia*. This divide is especially apparent in Epictetus: even if he did not deviate from the theory as laid down by Chrysippus, he did largely abandon the complex and precise vocabulary used by the latter to demarcate carefully all the different types of impressions and their epistemological and practical functions. Texts such as the one where Epictetus speaks simply of the 'harsh' impression are evidence of what I mean.[91]

Now, Epictetus may or may not be blamed for the changes he wrought; whether they are philosophically beneficial or pernicious is immaterial. What matters is the influence he exerted over subsequent generations. If it is true that he moved away from complex terminology, then those who came to know Stoicism through an Epictetan filter might well be expected to flatten out the concepts. One of the very few truly Stoic texts in Spinoza's library on his death was an edition of the *Enchiridion*.[92]

---

[90] One reply that can be made to the argument I have mounted is that the Epictetus passage which I have cited works on the level of the good and the true. Agreeing that impressions at that level of description are cataleptic may not settle the issue of whether there are cataleptic impressions of the hormetic variety at a lower and more useful level of description. For just as we never get an impression of the true but only of something we take to be true, so also we do not get impressions of the good but only of what we take to be good. In this respect, Uncle Scrooge's impression of money is shaped by his dispositional belief that money is the good he finds irresistible. It is not veridical, of course, so the appropriate corrective is education. By contrast, one's impression of virtue is shaped by one's dispositional belief that virtue is the (only) good one finds irresistible. This time the impression is correct.

[91] *Enchiridion* ch. 1.

[92] For more on proportionate holdings of Stoic texts in Spinoza's library, see Section 6 of the Introduction.

Moreover, it was the *Enchiridion* bound with Simplicius' *Commentary*[93] and, if anything, Simplicius flattens what nuances remain in Epictetus' epistemology.[94] If Epictetus and Simplicius are some of Spinoza's major sources for Stoicism, he would not have found an epistemology as different from his own as Chrysippus', for it would have been stripped of the Chrysippean apparatus that he himself rejected. This is not to say that he would not have recognized significant differences, including those I have already discussed and more yet to come. Yet some essential similarities might have been more recognizable, since their presence would not have been obscured by the accompanying apparatus. Though I certainly cannot prove this, it is tempting to imagine Spinoza nodding as he read passages such as 'Of existent things, some are up to us, some are not up to us. Up to us are belief, impulse, desire, aversion' (Epictetus[95]), or 'It is clear that what comes first is belief, which is a sort of rational knowledge, and fitting for human beings' (Simplicius[96]). As I said in the Introduction (see Section 3), I have not tried to find source-texts for Spinoza's thought. To the extent that any Stoic texts might have been influential on him, however, I think the edition of Epictetus and Simplicius should be counted among them.

2.3   Contextualizing impressions/ideas

In this section, I place impressions/ideas in the context of the larger philosophical systems which they are parts of and to which they make vital contributions. I start with the place of impressions/ideas in action, after which I spend more time on assent.

2.3.1   The place of impressions/ideas in action

Let me open with the Stoics and this longish passage from Origen:

Ensouled things are moved 'by' themselves when an impression occurs within them which calls forth an impulse. In some animals, impressions which produce

---

[93] It was edited by H. Wolf and published by Birckmann in Cologne around 1595/6. See Brittain and Brennan's comprehensive account of the history of the texts and translations in Simplicius (2002), vol. II, 145.

[94] In the Introduction to their translation of Simplicius' commentary on the *Enchiridion*, Brittain and Brennan write that '[s]ome of Simplicius' comments about Stoicism ... especially concerning their logic, epistemology and moral psychology, suggest a surprising lack of knowledge' (Simplicius (2002), 20). Brittain and Brennan list some of the specific instances where Simplicius is confused, and they include the very issues that I have been discussing, assent and impulse.

[95] *Enchiridion* ch. 1.   [96] *On Epictetus' Handbook* 4, 30–1.

impulse happen when the nature or power of impression immediately stimulates the impulse, as in the spider the impression of weaving occurs and an impulse to weave follows, since the nature or power of its impression immediately produces it to this. It is not necessary to endow the animal with any further nature or power beyond that of impression. The same applies in the case of a bee and the creation of a beehive.

A rational animal, however, in addition to its impressionistic nature, has reason which passes judgment on impressions, rejecting some of these and accepting others, in order that the animal may be guided accordingly ... Rational animals are not able to determine whether a particular external object should appear before them to stimulate in them this or that kind of impression. However, the decision to respond to what appears in this or that way is attributable to nothing other than the reason in them, which moves them [viz., rational agents] in terms of their inclinations which steer them towards the moral and their impulses towards the appropriate, or not.[97]

According to Origen, Stoics think that non-rational and rational animals alike start to act in the same way. For both, action is initiated by the reception of a hormetic impression capable of stimulating an impulse. However, because of the difference between their cognitive and rational capacities, the remaining stages are different. For a non-rational animal, if it receives the kind of impression that is capable of stimulating action – a hormetic impression – then the impulse to act occurs, virtually automatically, upon the reception of that impression.[98] By contrast, when a rational animal receives a hormetic impression, it is not automatically going to act. Before doing so, it must decide whether or not it will respond positively to the impression. If it accepts the impression, then an impulse to act will result; if it rejects the impression, however, there will be no impulse and no action.

Though valuable, Origen's text is unclear in certain respects, one of which deserves mention. When he says that 'reason ... passes judgment on impression', the metaphor of passing judgment is unnecessarily imprecise. The Stoics have a more specific concept which they use to explain how rational animals respond to impressions. To cite two of many texts, Stobaeus writes that 'all impulses are [acts of] assent',[99] and Plutarch says, 'without assent there is neither action nor impulsion'.[100] As these texts attest, when Origen says that the rational judgment is succeeded by impulse, we should cash out the metaphor in terms of assent (*sunkatathesis*). With this addition to Origen in place, we can now state the place of impressions in the thought and action of rational animals: first the rational

---

[97] Origen, *On Principles* 3.1.2–3 (L-S 53A with some additional text translated by me).
[98] See note 64 for an explanation of the qualification 'virtually' automatically.
[99] *Ecl.* II.88.2–3 (I-G 217; the bracketed insertion is I-G's).
[100] *Stoic. Rep.* 1057a (L-S 53S).

animal forms a hormetic impression; then she passes judgment on it, assenting to it or not; if she assents, then her soul issues an impulse to act. Given that such is their theory, impressions are found to be a necessary though not a sufficient condition for action in Stoicism; in addition, rational beings must assent to their impressions before they can be said to act.[101]

Now compare this view to one that appears towards the end of Part II of the *Ethics*. In IIP49Cor, Spinoza asserts the identity of will and intellect. In the Scholium to this Corollary, he raises a number of objections to it, one of which is that

we can suspend our judgment so as not to assent to things we perceive ... E.g., someone who feigns a winged horse – that is, merely entertains the thought of a winged horse – does not on that account grant that there is a winged horse ... Therefore, experience seems to teach nothing more clearly than that the will, or [*sive*] faculty of assenting, is free, and different from the faculty of understanding.[102]

This objection accords to ideas basically the same place in action as impressions are accorded by the Stoics in their account of action: first one forms an idea; then one engages in evaluation of that idea, deciding whether or not to assent to it. Though the text does not go on to say so, it is presumably only after one has assented to the idea that one can be said to act on it.

Spinoza has no time for this Stoical view.[103] He writes, 'I deny that a man affirms nothing in perceiving. For what is perceiving a winged horse other than affirming wings of the horse?' (IIP49CorSch). In Spinozism, the very forming of ideas involves making decisions about the matters implicated in them. There is no sequence of the sort found in Stoicism: first impressions; then assent; then action. As Bennett describes the claim defended in IIP49CorSch, 'it is not the case that in judging or acquiring

---

[101] I am eliding many other issues – examples include impulse (*horme*), the relationship between assent and action, and the precise difference between the 'assent' of non-human animals versus human assent – as they are irrelevant for present purposes. For discussion, see Inwood (1985), ch. 3 and Appendix 4, and Annas (1992), 98–102.

[102] G II, 132: 33 ff.

[103] It is also a Cartesian view, at least in Descartes' later works (whether he held it earlier is debated; see, e.g., Kenny (1998)). In the *Principia*, Descartes distinguishes between the 'perception of the intellect' and the 'operation of the will' (see I.32). The intellect receives input from its environment, which it presents to the will for evaluation. If the will responds positively to the input of the intellect, it will be said to have given its 'assent'. If not, then it will be said to be withholding assent. For Descartes as for the Stoics, the action lies in giving or withholding of assent. It is this alone for which the agent is also culpable. In addition to the above-mentioned passage of the *Principia*, see also Descartes' letters to Princess Elizabeth of 4 August 1645 and 1 September 1645, and the *Passions of the Soul*, Art. 17 ff.

beliefs there is an intellectual process in which material comes before the mind and then a voluntary action of making a judgment about it'.[104] Rather, ideas *are* actions in Spinozism: the very forming of ideas is simultaneously a mental action. This process blends together the elements that Stoicism tries to separate: propositional content and evaluative appraisal are parts of the same package.

2.3.2   *Assent (1): the dominant view*

Because I have already discussed Spinoza's concept of action in this chapter (see especially Section 2.1.2), I do not want to belabour that issue. Instead, I want to come to the notion of assent. Since the comparison will be more easily made by beginning with the Stoics, I shall once again start with them. In this section, I shall present the dominant interpretation of the notion of assent in Stoicism; I shall pose some objections to this interpretation in the next subsection.[105]

The first point concerns what assent is supposed to be. Bobzien nicely states the consensus view: 'The faculty of assent is the power of either confirming the impression, i.e. giving assent (*sugkatatithesthai*) or withholding such confirmation.'[106] This is entirely consistent with what we learned in the previous section. Assent occurs as a response by rational agents to impressions that they receive. Although there are different kinds of impressions (see especially Section 2.2.1), the role that assent places in the case of each kind of impression remains the same. As Bobzien says,

In the case of theoretical impressions, the impression suggests to the human being that assent should be given to it ... but the human being could in principle withhold assent. In the case of an impulsive impression of something desirable, the impression suggests that the human being should give assent ... but again, assent could in principle be refused.[107]

If agents assent to their impressions, then action ensues; if they withhold assent, there is no action. One nuance that may easily be overlooked concerns the range of material that assent is supposed to take into account. When a rational agent entertains an impression, he is primarily

---

[104] Bennett (1984), 160.

[105] By far the most authoritative version of the dominant view is Bobzien (1998). Another powerful case for it is made in Frede (2011), chs. 3 and 4. Other arguments for it can be found in the relevant passages of Annas (1992) and Brennan (2005). References to the alternative will be made in the next subsection.

[106] Bobzien (1998), 240. For another statement of this view, see Annas (1992), 98.

[107] Bobzien (1998), 240–1. For simplicity's sake, I speak of assenting to impressions, though it must be understood that we really assent to *lekta* (or, even more precisely, *axiômata*). Cf. *Ecl.* II.88.1–7 and the discussion in Shields (1994), 209–12.

but not exclusively evaluating its propositional content, asking whether it is true. In addition to doing that, he also considers whether the impulsive dimensions of the impressions are appropriate for him, given his circumstances.[108] If the impression passes both these tests, then the agent will assent to it.

Now, care is needed at this point. From what I have said so far, assent may seem to be something akin to a power of choice. It may seem that agents are free to assent to impressions or not, regardless of how their characters incline them or what the circumstances suggest. However, given the Stoics' acceptance of universal causal determinism (see Section 1.2.5), it is unlikely that this is what they meant by assent. According to the dominant interpretation, which impressions a person will assent to depends entirely on what sort of person she is. Moreover, the sort of person the agent happens to be is enough by itself to determine fully whether or not she will assent to an impression. As one commentator has written,

> The freedom of my assent ... does not consist in my ability to suspend assent from what I believe, as though I could now entertain the impression that two is an even number and refuse to assent to it. My psychology as a whole necessitates my assent; given my beliefs, it is not possible for me not to assent to this impression.[109]

So assent in the technical sense of how rational agents are said to respond to impressions is not a faculty of choice. It is the 'disposition'[110] that agents have to respond in certain determinate ways to their impressions.

Here we encounter a mystery. If that is what the Stoics meant by assent, then how could they also hold that assent is something which is supposed to be in our power (*eph' hêmin*[111])? The answer to this question lies in the special sense that they assigned to the notion of what it is for something to be within our power. To see what they meant by this, it is necessary to bring two new pieces of Stoic doctrine into the discussion.

The first is a distinction between a pair of causes: those which are external to the rational agent, and those which are internal.[112] Assent is the paradigm example of the latter. Being internal, assent is based solely on factors which are internal to the agent: in particular, the agent's assent

---

[108] Cf. Frede (2011), 41.   [109] Brennan (2005), 297.
[110] The word is Bobzien's (1998), 287.
[111] For one of many places where this Stoic expression occurs, see Alexander of Aphrodisias, *De fato* 196.24 ff.
[112] See especially Cicero, *De fato* 39–43 (L-S 62C), and Gellius, *Noct. Att.* 7.2.6–13 (L-S 62D). For discussion, Sorabji (1980), 79–83, and Bobzien (1998), 259–71.

is based on his character.[113] Although it is true that character is affected by external causal factors, since those external causes do not directly affect assent, the primary and immediate cause of assent should still be identified as character. Since character is self-evidently internal to us – who are we if not the dispositions, preferences, aversions, and other traits which make up our characters? – and since character produces assent, it follows that assent is in our power.

If causation is the first answer, modality is the key to the second. Chrysippus believed that 'even if all things happen by fate the possible and the contingent are not eliminated, because that which nothing prevents from happening is possible even if it does not happen'.[114] According to Chrysippus, for it to be possible for a thing S to have a property P, two conditions must be met: (1) the *nature* of S must not preclude its having P; (2) the *situation* in which S exists does not preclude its having P.[115] This conception of possibility led Chrysippus to hold that it is possible for our characters to have different properties than they actually possess. How so? Because there is nothing about the nature of our characters which precludes them from having those properties.

Coming back to the notion of assent, it is true that all events, including all internal events, are determined. So all of our acts of assent are determined. Nevertheless, even though this will never happen, it is possible for our characters to be different. Since character is the basis of assent, it is therefore also possible for our acts of assent to be different. This shows that our acts of assent are up to us. It is possible in the Chrysippean sense of 'possible' for us to refuse to assent to an impulsive impression, even if we actually do assent to it, because there is nothing which prevents us from acquiring the character that would enable us to refuse to give our assent.

Given the foregoing, the early Stoics seem to have had the following in mind when they said that fate does not make it impossible for assent to depend on us.[116] Stoics did *not* interpret the notion of something being within our power in contra-causal terms: when they said that assent is within our power, they did not think it was within our power to go against the determinations of the causal series to which we all belong. Instead, when they took an action to depend on a person, they meant that there is no *external* force making that person undertake that action.[117] The action is the result of the person's giving her assent to an impression that appears

[113] See, e.g., Bobzien (1998), 271.
[114] Alexander of Aphrodisias, *De fato*, 176.14 ff. (L-S 38H). Cf. DL VII.75 and Boethius, *Commentary on Aristotle's De Interpretatione* II, 234–5, 393.
[115] Here I am following Frede (2011), 81–2.
[116] Chrysippus defended this claim in Cicero, *De fato* 41.   [117] Cf. Bobzien (1998), 282.

before herself. She gives her assent because her character determines her to do so. Because she gives her assent based on her character, her assent is said to be within her power.[118] As one commentator glosses the notion of *eph' hêmin*, 'it is up to you to give assent or not in the sense that it depends on you, on the kind of person you are, whether you give assent'.[119]

2.3.3   Assent (2): an alternative view

Though the foregoing account of assent is very widely accepted nowadays, it is not impervious to criticism. Cicero inspires one objection when he writes, 'It is no more possible for a living creature to refrain from assenting to something self-evident than for it to fail to pursue what appears appropriate to its nature.'[120] Here Lucullus seems to deny that it is always within the power of the agent to withhold assent, even in the attenuated sense just adumbrated. There are some impressions so overwhelming as to necessitate our agreement with the states-of-affairs that they represent.[121] Some defenders of the standard interpretation attempt to explain away this text on the grounds that Lucullus is not actually reporting Stoic orthodoxy but instead the ideas of the Academic Antiochus.[122] In any case, they might argue, Lucullus is speaking about mere perception and not full-blown action. While that may be true, there are other texts[123] which suggest a larger point is at issue, one which is not so easily dismissed.

The point can be made by reference to the debate over whether hormetic impressions can be cataleptic (see especially Section 2.2.3 of this

---

[118] As Bobzien says, 'The mere fact that I have and use my faculty of assent, renders my assents in my power' (Bobzien (1998), 290).

[119] Frede (2011), 81.   [120] *Acad.* II.38 (L-S 40H3).

[121] Descartes also took there to be some situations in which the impressions received by the mind are so powerful that it 'could not but judge' they were true (*Meditation* IV; A-T VII: 58). Indeed, there is much that is Stoic about this passage of the fourth Meditation. I would need more evidence to be persuaded by Stephen Menn's claim that 'Descartes is probably taking the theory of judgment as assent chiefly from Cicero' (Menn (1998), 313). However, to understand the Stoics, it may be helpful to consider these lines from Descartes:

> [T]he will simply consists in our ability to do or not do something . . .; or rather, it consists simply in the fact that when the intellect puts forward something for affirmation or denial . . . our inclinations are such that we do not feel we are determined by any external force. In order to be free, there is no need for me to be inclined both ways; on the contrary, the more I incline in one direction . . . the freer is my choice (A-T VII: 57–8).

[122] See, e.g., Bobzien (1998), 323 n.172.

[123] For example, above we read *Discourses* I.28.3–4, in which Epictetus speaks of the ineffability of experience: one cannot refuse to assent to the impression that it is day when it is day. And shortly thereafter, he alludes to the ineffability of normative impressions: a man cannot 'think that something is profitable to him, and yet not choose it' (I.28.6–7).

chapter). There we saw the argument that we always act under the aspect of the good – that is, we always act for what appears to be good to us at the time of acting – and since there are some practical impressions of over-whelming goodness, we cannot help but assent to them. The impossibility here should be construed in Chrysippean terms, since, it is alleged, there is something which prevents our not-assenting from happening: namely, the universality of the catalepsis of the hormetic impression. Because *everyone* who experiences hormetic impressions that are cataleptic will assent to them – and they must, for that is precisely what it means for the impression to be cataleptic – there are no situations in which anyone can not-assent to such an impression. So refusing to assent to them is impos-sible, in Chrysippus' sense.[124]

There is a second criticism of the standard reading, one which is prepared to concede that (in Bobzien's words) 'the human being could in principle withhold assent'. To say that this is true *in principle* is not to say whether it is true *in fact*. Even if it is *possible* for humans to withhold assent to hormetic impressions, does that ever happen? If it does not, what is the significance of that possibility? If humans never actually do withhold assent to hormetic impressions, the compatibilism that the standard reading sees in Stoicism is in serious danger of rigidifying into fatalism. It may be uncertain whose problem this is – the Stoics' (for advertising their theory as compatibilist when it is really fatalist) or their interpreters' (for misreading the Stoics as compatibilists when they are really fatalists). In either case, however, this second criticism holds that the standard interpretation of assent is mistaken, insofar as it implies a compatibilism which the doctrine itself lacks.

Such problems with the standard reading warrant a reconsideration of what the Stoics meant when they said assent is up to us.[125] Let me use an argument from Tad Brennan to offer an alternative account.[126] Suppose

---

[124] So far as I am aware, I am the first person to notice the importance of cataleptic hormetic impressions for the Stoic doctrine of assent. One who comes close is Steve Strange in Strange (2004), 48.

[125] Even among those who support that standard view, doubts seem to creep in. For example, it seems to me that Julia Annas is flirting with a less deflationary concept of assent than Bobzien and Frede want to ascribe to the Stoics in the following passage:

[A]ssent is the point at which things are 'up to' the agent. It is not up to me how the world appears to me; as a result of past habits and so on I cannot help it that some things now appear desirable to me and others not. So I cannot help desiring my bringing about the satisfaction of certain predicates and not others. But what I can help is assenting to the corresponding statements of 'I ought to F'; for without such an assent there may be a mere desire to bring about a certain state of affairs, but there will not be the full impulse to bring it about, and so there will not be the action (Annas (1992), 98).

[126] To be clear, Brennan is a supporter of the standard reading. I am using his argument in a way that he does not.

(as orthodox Stoics did) the agent is 'most essentially his faculty of assent'. If that is the case, then 'it comes to seem that I am essentially something different from my desires'. Now, '[h]aving shed my desires as external, my self has shrunk to a point-like faculty of assent, the free and unconstrained will'.[127]

Now, Brennan holds that though this line of thought may have been present in early, orthodox Stoicism, it was not actually pursued until much later. In fact, he contends that it was not pursued by Stoics at all but instead by their neo-Platonic successors.[128] But if it was part of the orthodox Stoic line to identify the agent with her faculty of assent, then the orthodox Stoics do seem committed to a view of assent as unburdened by any constraining factors, such as the agent's desires.

So an alternative view of assent emerges.[129] It cannot be described as indeterminist or contra-causal, for assent is still caused. The source of the causal efficacy, however, is entirely internal to the agent. Since agency is defined in terms of assent, it follows that assent is self-caused. So when the agent gives her assent to an impression, she is determining herself to act. Since she is causing herself, there is no evident reason why she must be constrained to pick a certain specific course of action. Instead, it seems that there are alternatives available for her to choose from. In particular, she could choose to assent or not. This choice is not determined by her character or desires; it is grounded solely on her free power of assent.[130]

---

[127] Brennan (2005), 301.

[128] For more on the development of assent, see Frede (2011), ch. 5, and Bobzien (1998), ch. 8.

[129] So far as I am aware, there are no published arguments pushing the alternative account of assent that I am about to present. Phillip Mitsis is the one who comes closest. Mitsis has published a couple of pieces going against the claim advanced by Bobzien and others, that there is no contra-causal conception of action in Epicurus (see, e.g., Mitsis (2013), 74–9). If Mitsis is right, then there was a contra-causal conception of action being promulgated at the very time that the early Stoa was formulating its views on assent and action. This is surely significant. Moreover, Mitsis has argued in correspondence that we should understand the Stoic notion of assent, not in contra-causal terms, but rather as requiring a notion of reason with sufficient flexibility to make genuine choices.

[130] This account of assent will seem remarkably similar to Kant's conception of a free will, at least as explicated by Christine Korsgaard. She writes, 'Kant argues: (1) that we must act "under the idea" that we have a free will, where a free will is one which is not determined in accordance with any law external to itself; (2) that a free will, if it is to be a *will* at all, must nevertheless be determined in accordance with some law or other; (3) that it must therefore be determined in accordance with its own law' (Korsgaard (1996), 219). For more on Kant and Stoicism, see especially Engstrom and Whiting (1996).

It is almost time for me to move on to Spinoza. Before doing so, however, I want to make one last point about the Stoics. While there may be uncertainty about how to interpret the Stoic notion of assent, there is no doubt that Stoics believed it was easier to give assent to an impulsive impression than withhold it. There are two reasons for this, the first of which is that great tension (*tonos*) in the *pneuma* of the soul is required to withhold assent from an impulsive impression; to assent to the same impression is to acquiesce to it and does not require much strength. Galen reports Chrysippus as holding that 'we give up right decisions because the soul's tension gives in, and does not persist till the end or fully execute the commands of reason'.[131] A central benefit of experience is that it provides agents with more opportunities to make decisions and strengthen their characters, so that they will have the fortitude to resist problematic hormetic impressions.[132] Second and quite apart from the necessity of strength of soul, there is an epistemic challenge in figuring out which hormetic impressions are truly good for us and which are not. Most of us lack that ability; in fact, only sages possess it to perfection. Because fools are unable to discern the truly good from the only apparently good, they will bend under the pressure of hormetic impressions. While some hormetic impressions will be truly good, others will not be; since fools will not be able to tell the difference between the two, they will give assent when they ought to withhold it.

2.3.4   Spinoza's reactions to the Stoics on assent

Coming now to Spinoza, it is plain that he would have no business with the Stoic notion of assent, no matter how it is interpreted. I will go through just a few of several objections he would make. The first concerns its metaphysics. For Spinoza, the uniformity of nature is absolutely fundamental. This uniformity is all-inclusive, in the sense that both nature as a whole – substance – and everything that is within nature – modes – are governed by the same set of laws and belong to or constitute the same single being. More relevantly for present purposes, Spinoza clearly thinks

---

[131] *PHP* 4.6.2–3 (L-S 65T).
[132] Becker (1998) is good on how the practice of agency can lead to its strengthening; see esp. 62–3. The passage is too long to quote in full but the following gives the gist: 'Stoics hypothesize that agency is very robust, meaning (a) that it is, in any form, highly resistant to extinction through other psychological processes; (b) that when exercised at all, no matter how weakly in relation to our other constitutive powers, it tends to increase its relative strength; and (c) that agency can thus become in material effect, through its own exercise, the most comprehensive and controlling of our constitutive powers' (63).

that all natural phenomena are members of one-and-the-same causal series. This causal series is first described in the second half of Part I of the *Ethics*; Spinoza returns to it in later parts, such as the digression in physics after IIP13Sch and the Preface to Part III. Though the later discussions fill out the theory in various interesting and important ways, Spinoza does not think these refinements amount to the introduction of a totally new kind of causation or causal series. And I think he would regard the Stoics' distinction between external and internal causes as tantamount to the introduction of two distinct, non-interreducible and non-interdefinable types of causal series. If so, he is not alone; commentators today have read them similarly.[133]

That criticism is targeted at both the standard and the non-standard interpretations of the Stoic notion of assent. The next criticism is aimed only at the non-standard reading. Recall that according to this reading, Stoics hold that it is within our power either to assent or not, regardless of how our characters would have us disposed. If such is the nature of Stoic assent, then it seems that humans have the power to resist and even go against the direction of the universal, necessary, and necessitating causal chains of which they are a part. To Spinoza, that is absurd. All of our motions, whether considered under the aspect of extension or of thought, are fully determined by preceding extensional or intensional events. The range of phenomena included in this claim is unqualifiedly universal; as such, it includes even our innermost thoughts and actions. As he writes in IIP48, 'the mind is determined to will this or that by a cause which is also determined by another, and this again by another, and so to infinity'. We do not have the freedom to decide whether or not we ought to assent to our ideas; whether or not we shall do so is determined by the causal forces coming to bear on us.

Insofar as Stoic assent postulates the distinction between internal versus external causes, and insofar as Spinoza would regard that distinction as forcing them from their strict naturalism, then the metaphysical gap just mentioned between Spinoza and the Stoics is unbridgeable. Yet it is slightly narrowed by noting a point from Section 2.3.3 above. Assent may not *always* be up to us, for there are some practical impressions of such overwhelming force as to guarantee that we should embrace them. Spinoza would still regard the metaphysics of assent interpreted in this way with distaste, for he would continue to think that it posits the existence of a supernatural power. Yet he would be pleased by the recognition of absolute limits placed on our power. Such recognition,

---

[133] See, e.g., Inwood (1985), 69–70.

he would think, takes the Stoics closer to the naturalism where they most comfortably belong.

Coming to the next objection that Spinoza would make to Stoic assent, it concerns its modal underpinnings. According to Spinoza, an event or object is possible only in the case that it is compatible with the laws of nature.[134] For Spinoza just as for Chrysippus, the tie between actuality and possibility is not complete: in Spinozism, many more things are compatible with the laws of nature than those which actually come to exist; so in Spinozism as in Stoicism, the set of *possibilia* is larger than the set of *actualitae*.[135] While Spinoza would agree with Chrysippus about the importance of keeping the actual apart from the possible, he would disagree with two other crucial tenets of the Greek's conception of possibility: first, that x is possible iff nothing prevents it from happening; second, that if x is possible, then it could become actual.[136] Regarding the former, Spinoza would say that it is too broad, for it does not specify precisely what could prevent it from happening. To be closer to the truth, Chrysippus ought to have said that x is possible iff *the laws of nature* do not prevent it from happening. On the latter, Spinoza would deny that x's possibility is sufficient to establish that it is a possible *existent*. To say that x is possible is just to say that it is compatible with the laws of nature; to say that x is a possible existent is to assert *both* that it is compatible with the laws of nature *and* that it could be a member of the infinite causal series to which all existent beings belong.

Now, these flaws with Chrysippus' conception of the possible are relevant to assent. Chrysippus' broader conception of the grounds of possibility allows him to think that there is a sense in which we could

---

[134] Spinoza is widely acknowledged to think of possibility in epistemic terms. In addition, I think that he has a metaphysical conception of possibility. I have argued for this in Miller (2001); see esp. 803–10. For another argument that his views on possibility are not solely epistemic, see Newlands (2010). For the next few paragraphs, I shall suppose, perhaps controversially, that a vigorous metaphysical conception of possibility is discernible in Spinoza.

[135] This is admittedly a controversial view. I argue for it in Miller (2001), sections 5–6. Briefly, my argument is this: Spinoza distinguishes the grounds for possibility from the grounds for existing. Something is possible iff it is compatible with the laws of nature, while something exists iff it is compatible with the laws of nature *and* the order of causes. Since more things are compatible with the laws of nature than with the laws of nature *and* the order of causes, the set of *possibilia* is greater than the set of *actualitae*.

[136] Both of these are present in Bobzien's gloss on Chrysippus' conception of the possible: 'A proposition is possible if it is capable of being true, and not hindered from being true by external circumstances' (Bobzien (1998), 112). A few pages later, she explains what it is for a proposition to be possible at a certain moment in time: 'A proposition is possible *now* if and only if it is internally capable of being at some time true and nothing external hinders it from being true at some time from *now* on' (Bobzien (1998), 115).

change our characters and so our assent. But Spinoza would reply that a more careful analysis of the possible, one which simultaneously understands it as delimited solely by the nomological and as distinct from the possibly existent, would reveal that changing our characters is not possible. Given the connection between our characters and the rest of nature – both *Natura naturans* and *Natura naturata* – it follows that any change to our characters would force changes elsewhere in nature.[137] While *perhaps* we might be able to conceive of these changes occurring in *Natura naturata* without transgressing the laws of nature, it is impossible for *Natura naturans* to be changed in any respect. So, because changes in our characters could occur only if there were changes to the nature of *Natura naturans* or substance, it turns out to be the case that changes to our character are impossible.

A connection can be made here to the alternative interpretation of the Stoic theory of assent (see Section 2.3.3 above). There seem to be grounds for wondering whether humans ever *in fact* withhold their assent from hormetic impressions. These grounds do not take away the in-principle possibility that we could withhold assent but they do occasion the introduction of the Spinozistic distinction between possibility and actuality just made. For Spinoza, to say that x is a possible existent is to allege two properties of x: that it is compatible with the laws of nature *and* that it is compatible with the causal series. If Stoics think of assent as a mental action that is only possible in principle, then since assent is unquestionably defined as possible by the Stoics, it seems to be the case that for assent to be both possible and possibly actual, another condition must be satisfied, one which never is satisfied. The remaining condition, it seems to me, would be very similar to Spinoza's requirement about compatibility with the causal series. The upshot is that if the alternative interpretation of the Stoic theory of assent proves correct, then the modal grounds for assent turn out to be very similar to the modal grounds stipulated by Spinoza for the existence of any possible object.

Moving on, I want to make one last and very different point. It relates to the Stoic claim that greater strength of soul is required to withhold assent from impulsive impressions than is needed to give in to them. Of course, Spinoza does not talk about impulsive impressions; nonetheless, there is an interesting parallel between something he does say and the Stoic view. He writes, 'I deny absolutely that we require an equal power of thinking,

---

[137] Indeed, there are plenty of texts where Spinoza makes it seem as if this is not only very likely but definitely his view. As when he writes, 'all things follow from God's eternal decree with the same necessity as from the essence of a triangle it follows that its three angles are equal to two right angles' (IIP49CorSch (G II, 136: 10–13)).

to affirm that what is true is true, as to affirm that what is false is true.'[138]
Spinoza thinks that it is easier to regard a false idea as true than it is to
recognize that a true idea is true. To know the latter, one must know a lot
about the idea and its place in the world; by contrast, saying that a false
idea is true only requires us to utter a falsehood about the idea. For
Spinoza as for the Stoics, resisting the many false yet compelling representations of the world that continually appear before us is difficult
because of the greater strength of mind it requires. And like the Stoics,
Spinoza stresses the physiological grounds required for strength of mind.
He writes in VP39Sch, 'he who, like an infant or child, has a body capable
of very few things ... has a mind which considered solely in itself is
conscious of almost nothing. On the other hand, he who has a body
capable of a great many things, has a mind which considered only in itself
is very much conscious of itself, and of God, and of things.'

2.4   Conclusion

There are few areas in which Spinoza's thought is more different from the
Stoics than on ideas/impressions. Where Spinoza is a strong internalist
with respect to the origins and contents of ideas, the Stoic theory of
phantasia is externalist, even if moderately so. Where Spinoza thinks
that all ideas blend propositional content with propositional attitude,
with the result that they can be construed as beliefs, the Stoics think
that while impressions may be affected by our commitments, genuine
beliefs are formed only after assent is given to impressions. Where
Spinoza's typology of ideas is simple, conceiving of the adequate idea as
both practical and theoretical, the Stoic typology is complex, seeming to
separate impressions which are action-oriented from those which are
truth-sensitive (though there is some uncertainty about this). Most clearly
and perhaps most importantly, where Stoics think of impressions as a
necessary but not sufficient condition for action, Spinoza takes ideas to be
actions and so he takes them to be both the necessary and sufficient
conditions for acting.

   These differences are real and important. This makes the consonance
between the basic metaphysical and ethical outlooks of Spinoza and the
Stoics all the more interesting. That is, despite their widely divergent
epistemologies and action theories, they still conceive the world and our
place in it in highly similar terms. We have already found this to be true
with respect to their monisms; in ensuing chapters, while I will identify

---

[138] IIP49CorSch (G II, 135: 15–17).

and argue for many important disagreements, it will nonetheless emerge that their views on the issues I will discuss stand in close relation to each other. I suspect that if Spinoza were able to comment on the Stoics' epistemology and action theory, he would say that its main problem is that it departs from the thoroughgoing naturalism evident elsewhere in their system.

3   *Conatus* and *oikeiosis*

> Each thing, as far as it can by its own power, strives to persevere in its being.[1]

> [The Stoics] say that an animal has self-preservation as the object of its first impulse[.][2]

The first two parts of the *Ethics* have introduced a quantity of material, including monism and a theory of ideas, which Spinoza requires for building his philosophical system. While potent, those doctrines do not adequately speak to how humans should be understood, for they have only described being in general and not human beings in particular. In *Ethics* III, Spinoza launches his investigation of human nature specifically. He bases his account on the notion that all beings naturally seek their own advantage. This idea, which is often referred to by the Latin word *conatus*, is widely regarded as one of the most important in all of Spinozism. Bennett, for one, thinks that 'Spinoza's substantive morality will be based on [*conatus*]'.[3] Curley goes further, holding that 'The central doctrine which . . . provides Spinoza with a foundation, both for his psychology and for his moral philosophy, is the doctrine of the *conatus*.'[4]

If we recast Stoicism into the mould of the *Ethics* (which I have argued is possible but only to an extent[5]), then our study has so far unveiled a similar amount and calibre of material. Stoic monism and the Stoic theory of *phantasia* are crucial components of the Stoic system. Yet they are not able, or intended, to be the basis for a theory of human nature. For this purpose, the Stoics crafted an elaborate theory of human development, beginning with the infants and continuing through the fully mature adult, which expounds on human nature by identifying the various stages of human life and the different natural ends that humans seek during each of

---

[1] IIIP6.   [2] DL VII.85 (L-S 57A1).   [3] Bennett (1984), 231.
[4] Curley (1988), 87. Della Rocca takes a step beyond even Curley, saying that IIIP6 is 'the central proposition in Spinoza's psychology, ethics, and political philosophy' (Della Rocca (1998), 144).
[5] For discussion of just how this might work, see Section 1.2.5.

these stages. This theory, which scholars usually call by its Greek name *oikeiosis*, is scarcely less important to Stoicism than *conatus* is to Spinozism. As Pembroke says in a piece that remains the standard introduction to the topic, 'if there had been no *oikeiosis*, there would have been no Stoa'.[6]

In this chapter, I shall compare Spinoza's account of human nature with that of the Stoics by studying the relationship between *conatus* and *oikeiosis*. Since *conatus* and *oikeiosis* are broad theories intended to provide explanations for a range of phenomena, my comparison cannot be exhaustive. Instead, I shall focus on the notions of self-preservation and moral progress. By way of conclusion, I shall consider the allegation that Spinoza lapses into incoherence on these issues by being too Stoical.[7]

3.1 *Oikeiosis*, not *horme*

Before commencing, I must address a possible misapprehension. As I have talked about Spinoza and the Stoics through the years, various people have been surprised by my assertion that the true Stoic equivalent to *conatus* is *oikeiosis*, for they had always supposed it was *horme*, a term usually translated into English as 'impulse'. I do not know where this view originates but one influential advocate is H. A. Wolfson. In his seminal study of Spinoza, Wolfson makes two points about the relationship between *horme* and *conatus*, the first of which is philological. Surveying several different classical, medieval, and early modern authors, Wolfson purports to show that while *horme* is sometimes rendered with other Latin words, it 'can also be translated by *conatus*'.[8] After concluding his philological argument, Wolfson goes on to make a second claim. He contends that the philological connection between *horme* and *conatus* has philosophical significance, for it delimits the conceptual possibilities available to Spinoza. Assuming that the Stoic doctrine of *horme* includes a principle of self-preservation, he writes that Spinoza 'developed his own conception of the conatus along the lines of self-preservation as laid down by the Stoics'.[9]

[6] Pembroke (1971), 114.
[7] *Oikeiosis* and *conatus* are occasionally denied to be as important as I have alleged. See, e.g., Brink (1955) on the Stoics and MacIntyre (1998), 190–5, on Spinoza. Following the opinion of the overwhelming majority of contemporary commentators, I will assume in this chapter that they are pivotal to their systems.
[8] Wolfson (1934), vol. II, 196.
[9] Wolfson (1934), vol. II, 199. For more recent discussion of *horme* and *conatus*, see Viljanen (2011), 84–6.

Now, for lack of expertise, I am not able to dispute Wolfson's philology. It may be that *horme* is often rendered into Latin as *conatus*.[10] In any case, that is not the issue. Rather, I disagree with his philosophical claim that the doctrine of *conatus* is paralleled by the Stoic doctrine of *horme*. This is simply mistaken, for it entirely misconstrues the nature of the Stoic concept. A *horme* is a single psychological impulse. As such, it is a dateable event. As a dateable event, it happens at a particular time, which makes it necessarily transient. Moreover, a *horme* plays a technical role in the Stoic theory of action. To use one gloss on this role, a *horme* 'is a mental event that synthesizes a description of a particular determinate state of affairs with an evaluative attitude towards that state of affairs and leads to immediate action'.[11]

To be sure, Cicero does speak of a 'faculty of appetition, in Greek *horme* [*appetitio animi, quae ὁρμή Graece vocatur*]'.[12] This is, however, consistent with my point. There can be a 'faculty' which issues individual *hormai*. What I am presently speaking about is the nature of those things issued by that 'faculty'. Those things are the *hormai*. Taken in themselves, *hormai* are impulses to pursue or not pursue external objects which have stimulated the agent's sense organs.

That is not true of *conatus*. While a being's *conatus* can be roughly described as its impulse for self-preservation, the sense of 'impulse' here is totally different from the Stoic *horme*. We may describe *conatus* as our collective endeavours to remain in and possibly enhance our existence. Alternatively, we may analyse *conatus* as so many 'relatively permanent factors' which determine 'what kind of things we do habitually desire and what kind of things we do habitually shun'.[13] In either case, *conatus* is not a single transient psychological event but rather a perdurable state. Additionally, *conatus* is not relegated a technical role, however important, in a single theory. Far from it. As another commentator says, *conatus* lies 'at the root of a large body of doctrine, presented in *Ethics* 3, in which Spinoza purports to describe and explain many aspects of human

---

[10] I will note, however, that other scholars report different practices. For example, Sarah Byers says that 'Cicero uses *appetitus, appetitio*, and *voluntas* for *horme*. Seneca uses *impetus* and *voluntas* for *horme*' (Byers (2013), 89). In her translation of the *TD*, Margaret Graver says, '*Horme* at IV.11 is rendered, reasonably enough, by *appetitus*' (xxxviii).

[11] Brennan (2003), 267. See also Brennan's discussion in ch. 7 of Brennan (2005). Like so many others, Brennan is indebted to the seminal account of *horme* in modern scholarship, Inwood (1985); see, e.g., 47–53.

[12] *De fin.* III.23 (trans. Rackham in Cicero (1931)). Rackham's translation is rather strong. I-G render the passage thus, 'the impulse in our soul, which is called *horme* in Greek' (I-G 153). Woolf has it this way: 'our mind's desire – termed *horme* in Greek' (Cicero (2001). L-S do not translate this part of *De fin.*

[13] Broad (1959), 25.

behaviour'.[14] Finally, no one claims that Stoics see a *horme* as constituting a being's nature. Yet that is precisely what Spinoza says of *conatus* in IIIP7: 'The striving [*conatus*] by which each thing strives to persevere in its being is nothing but the actual essence of the thing.' For these reasons at least, then, *horme* cannot be identified, even loosely, with *conatus*.

If not *horme*, one might wonder what other Stoic notion has the properties that I have just attributed to *conatus*. Of course, it is possible that there is nothing in Stoicism remotely similar to *conatus*. In the title of this chapter, however, I implied that it must be *oikeiosis*. By the end of this chapter, I hope that my readers will agree.

3.2   Self-preservation

3.2.1   Stoics on self-preservation

As the very word suggests,[15] *oikeiosis* concerns what is appropriate to oneself, what one is oriented to or affiliated with. While the doctrine of *oikeiosis* encompasses all types of animals (and maybe plants[16]) and explains (or is capable of explaining) what is appropriate for any of these beings, its most important applications pertain exclusively to humans. One of these applications is a theory of human development, explaining the various broad stages of moral psychology and intending (among other things) to support the Stoic conception of the end or ultimate goal of all human actions.[17] According to this theory, humans pass through different phases in life, in which they find different ends 'congenial'[18] to themselves. It is not the case that one end drops away as a new end is acquired; rather, the new end assumes a higher position in the

---

[14] Bennett (2001), vol. I, 217–8.

[15] For discussion of etymological issues, see Pembroke (1971), 115–6. I should state upfront that I will draw freely from both of the two main surviving texts on *oikeiosis*: *De fin.* III.5–6, 16–22 and DL VII.85–6. This practice is sanctioned by common (though not universal) belief that they are complementary. For important criticism of the common view, see Engberg-Pedersen (1990), chs. 1–4. Other important texts include Seneca, *Ep.* 120 and 121, a fragment from Hierocles, *Elements of Ethics*, I.34–9 and I.51–7, and other parts of *De fin.* III.

[16] Cf. DL VII.86 and Pembroke (1971), 116–7. The possibility that *oikeiosis* applies to beings besides animals is often missed by non-specialists. To cite Wolfson again: 'There is, however, a difference between the Stoic conception of the conatus for self-preservation and that of Spinoza. To the Stoics the conatus for self-preservation is confined only to animal being' (Wolfson (1934), vol. II, 199).

[17] See Striker (1983), section 2. A different application of *oikeiosis* was to defeat Epicurean claims about the naturalness of the hedonistic impulse. For discussion of this, see Brunschwig (1986), 133 ff.

[18] DL VII.85.

hierarchy and subordinates or subsumes all lower ends to it, so that a lower end is operative so long as it does not conflict with a higher one.[19]

Cicero and Diogenes Laertius both tell us that the first of these ends is self-preservation. Cicero writes, 'every animal, as soon as it is born (this is where one should start), is concerned with itself, and takes care to preserve itself. It favours its constitution and whatever preserves its constitution, whereas it recoils from its destruction and whatever appears to promote its destruction.'[20] And Diogenes: 'They [the Stoics] say that an animal has self-preservation as the object of its first impulse.'[21] The range of self-preserving animals is important: because 'every' animal is self-preserving, then since humans are animals, we, too, have self-preservation as our 'first impulse'.

But what do they mean by self-preservation? I shall make three points. First, when Stoics say that animals have the impulse to preserve themselves, they think that when presented with (external or internal) stimuli of certain kinds, animals will act in a self-preserving manner. This impulse or instinct is a disposition which lies totally dormant when not stimulated, and is activated healthfully when stimulated. Thus, instincts of this sort should not be confused with a Freudian conception of instincts, for as Inwood says, they are 'not to be thought of as dynamic pressures to act in a certain way which demand expression, and which find expression in some sublimated or distorted form if they are repressed'.[22]

Second, we learn from Diogenes Laertius that Nature is responsible for the presence of this impulse or instinct in animals. He writes, 'nature made it [the animal] congenial to itself from the beginning'.[23] Part of making an animal congenial to itself is ensuring that the animal will react to presentations in a self-preserving manner, so it 'rejects what is harmful and accepts what is appropriate'.[24] Chrysippus reportedly argued that this beneficial reaction to danger must be due to Nature, for 'nature was not likely either to alienate the animal itself, or to make it and then neither alienate it nor appropriate it to itself'.[25]

Finally and related to the previous point, self-preservation is not merely an efficient cause – animals are not merely propelled by impulses to preserve themselves. It is an end of their action, a goal for which they strive.[26]

---

[19] If an end acquired earlier in the process of development does conflict with one acquired later on, then it is dropped. Moreover, it may be that something altogether new takes place when the sage becomes perfectly rational (cf. *De fin.* III.22 ff.). I shall return to these issues below.

[20] *De fin.* III.16 (trans. Woolf in Cicero (2001)).   [21] DL VII.85 (L-S 57A1).

[22] Inwood (1985), 190.   [23] DL VII.85 (I-G, 191).   [24] DL VII.85 (L-S 57A2).

[25] DL VII.85 (L-S 57A2). For more, see Pembroke (1971), 116, and Inwood (1985), 189.

[26] Cf. Inwood (1999), 680–2.

Self-preservation regulates responses to stimuli by guiding the animal's decisions, since they are based on the animal's overarching[27] desire to remain in existence.

3.2.2   *Grotius on* oikeiosis

Spinoza will appear soon enough, but for reasons which I will shortly give, I want to digress slightly, into Grotius and specifically his *De iure belli ac pacis*. In the first few pages of the 'Prolegomena' to that work, Grotius sketches the broad outlines of his project. Once he has presented his project, Grotius proceeds to justify it against a certain kind of criticism. Here he writes,

> V. Since our discussion concerning law will have been undertaken in vain if there is no law, in order to open the way for a favourable reception of our work and at the same time to fortify it against attacks, this very serious error must be briefly refuted. In order that we may not be obliged to deal with a crowd of opponents, let us assign to them an advocate. And who better for this purpose than Carneades?
>
> . . . [He argues that] men imposed laws upon themselves for the sake of interest . . . [M]oreover, there is no law of nature, because all creatures, men as well as animals, are impelled by nature to seek their own particular advantage. [C]onsequently, there is no justice at all, or, if such there be, it is supreme folly, since one does violence to his own interests if he consults the advantage of others.
>
> VI. What the philosopher here says . . . must not be admitted for one moment. Man is, to be sure, an animal, but an animal of a superior kind, much farther removed from all other animals than the different kinds of animals are from one another; evidence on this point may be found in the many traits peculiar to the human species. But among the traits characteristic of man is an impelling desire for society [*appetitus societatis*], that is, for the social life – not of any and every sort, but peaceful, and organized according to the measure of his intelligence, with those who are of his own kind; this disposition the Stoics called 'Οικείωσιν. Stated as a universal truth, therefore, the assertion that every animal is led by nature to seek only its own private good must not be granted.[28]

The effectiveness and indeed the exact nature of Grotius' reply to Carneadean scepticism may be uncertain but that need not concern us.[29] Even if there is much that remains unclear about this passage, we can still learn three important points from it.

---

[27] Overarching, that is, until the animal becomes rational (if it is that kind of animal). See the next section.

[28] 'Prolegomena' §§5–6 (trans. Kelsey (modified)).

[29] There is ongoing dispute about what the argument in this passage is supposed to be and hence continuing debate about its power. So Richard Tuck has written, 'Grotius's most powerful and original idea' was to use the principle of self-preservation against Carneades (Tuck (1987), 113). Tuck follows the reading of the eighteenth-century

Two of these are closely connected. First, Grotius' explicit mention of *oikeiosis* shows that this Stoic doctrine did not go unnoticed in the seventeenth century. Second, *De iure belli ac pacis* was very widely read in his day, which makes it not unreasonable to assume that Spinoza encountered the work, even though it is not listed among the books in his library.[30] If he did encounter it, then he would likely have gone through the 'Prolegomena'. If so, then he would have run across *oikeiosis*. As we reflect on how Spinoza's *conatus* compares to Stoic *oikeiosis*, it is worth remembering that he could quite possibly have learned about it from Grotius.

But *what* would he have learned from Grotius? This brings me to the third reason for citing him. My comparison of Spinoza's *conatus* doctrine with the Stoics' *oikeiosis* can be enriched by considering how *oikeiosis* was understood by early moderns. I will not restrict myself to what early moderns took *oikeiosis* to be; as I have done throughout my book, I will provide what I take to be our current best understanding of the doctrine. At the same time, if we have an early modern interpretation at hand, it may be a useful supplement. It would be irresponsible to make universal claims about *the* early modern interpretation of *oikeiosis*. Instead, I will present my reading of one early modern's interpretation – namely, Grotius'.[31]

To ascertain Grotius' interpretation of *oikeiosis*, we may start with a footnote he adds to buttress his argument in §6 of the 'Prolegomena'. In that footnote, Grotius quotes these lines from Marcus Aurelius: '[I]t has long been proved that we are born with a view to community. Or was it not evident that inferior beings are for the sake of the superior, and the superior for the sake of one another?'[32] Nowadays, this text is counted among those which establish Stoic cosmopolitanism – the notion that all rational creatures are members of a cosmic *polis*, which in turn requires them to seek to benefit each other as much as they benefit themselves.[33] This is the linchpin to Grotius' interpretation of *oikeiosis*.

---

translator and commentator on Grotius, Jean Barbeyrac. Against the view of Tuck and Barbeyrac, other scholars question whether self-preservation even features in Grotius' defence against Carneades. For these people, the important work is being done by the inherent sociability that Grotius sees in human nature. See, e.g., Rob Shaver (1996).

[30] The list of these books is reprinted in Alter (1965). Five works either written or edited by Grotius are included in this list. *De iure* is not among them.

[31] Admittedly, my interpretation is truncated; I cannot cover the topic in full. For more on *oikeiosis* in Grotius and its relation to Cicero's notion of *appetitus societatis*, see Straumann (2003/2004). Grotius' broader relations to Stoicism are explored in Blom and Winkel (2004).

[32] Marcus Aurelius V.16 (L-S 63K6–7).   [33] See, e.g., Schofield (1999), 760–1.

As Grotius seems to understand *oikeiosis*, it combines two elements: the desire for self-preservation with the innate need for other people.[34] Like the Stoics did, Grotius credits Nature for establishing both impulses in us. He writes,

[T]he very nature of man, which even if we had no lack of anything would lead us into the mutual relations of society . . . The law of nature nevertheless has the reinforcement of expediency; for the Author of nature willed that as individuals we should be weak, and should lack many things needed in order to live properly, to the end that we might be the more constrained to cultivate the social life.[35]

Because Nature made us beings who seek both our own self-preservation and the society of others, we seek to establish just states where we can thrive together.

One final point. As Grotius understands *oikeiosis*, it originates in the concern that Nature (or, as he calls it, 'God') exhibits for us. Grotius writes, 'the law of nature of which we have spoken . . . proceeding as it does from the essential traits implanted in man, can nevertheless rightly be attributed to God, because of His having willed that such traits exist in us'.[36] Grotius explicitly names 'Chrysippus and the Stoics' here and quotes a line from Chrysippus: '"There is no other or more appropriate way of approaching the theory of good and bad things or the virtues or happiness than from universal nature and from the administration of the world."'[37]

3.2.3 *Introducing* conatus

With that background in place, we can come to Spinoza. Let us begin with some key Spinozistic texts.[38] The core text is IIIP6: 'Each thing, as far as it can by its own power, strives to persevere in its being.'[39] Every word in this proposition needs careful consideration. For our purposes, the term 'striving' is especially important. How it should be taken will affect our understanding of how *conatus* relates to *oikeiosis*. We will return to this below.

In the Demonstration to IIIP6, Spinoza cites two earlier propositions from Part III.[40] One of these is IIIP4: 'No thing can be destroyed except

[34] As one commentator writes, 'We are indeed self-seeking, but we are sociable as well' (Schneewind (1998), 72).
[35] 'Prolegomena' §16.   [36] 'Prolegomena' §12.
[37] The line is preserved by Plutarch, *Stoic. Rep.* 1035c (L-S 60A1).
[38] Because I am merely introducing the texts here, I will expound on them only very briefly at this point. More sustained exposition will occur below, once I begin comparing *conatus* with *oikeiosis*.
[39] *Unaquaeque res, quantum in se est, in suo esse perseverare conatur* (trans. Curley (modified)).
[40] He also cites IP25Cor and IP34, which concern how particular things relate to God and how God's power is his essence. I will not discuss them here, as they are more distant to *conatus* than the material from Part III.

through an external cause.' This proposition has been glossed as Spinoza's 'no-self-destruction thesis'.[41] It is normally taken to hold that a thing's destruction will never follow from that thing's essence alone; instead, as one commentator says, 'Factors beyond the essence must be brought in to explain the destruction of the thing.'[42]

The other proposition from Part III cited in IIIP6Dem is IIIP5: 'Things are of a contrary nature, that is, unable to subsist in the same subject, to the extent that one can destroy the other.' Part of what IIIP5 holds is that one thing, x, can destroy another thing, y, if and only if x is unlike y in some respect. But that is not all. In addition, it maintains that if x can destroy y, then x and y cannot be coinstantiated by one thing. There is, however, a size limitation. If the object (call it z) in which x and y are supposed to co-exist is small, then x and y cannot be parts of it. On the other hand, if z is very large relative to x and y, then they may be coinstantiated. After all, all things are ultimately part of the universe. So even if some things are mutually destructive, they may be able to co-exist so long as they do not exist in proximity to each other.[43]

If IIIP4 and P5 provide crucial argumentative support for IIIP6, the pair of propositions immediately after IIIP6 offers invaluable clarification of the meaning of that proposition. In IIIP7 we are told that 'The striving by which each thing strives to persevere in its being is nothing but the actual essence of the thing.' The tie between a being's *conatus* and its 'actual essence' is of critical importance for many reasons. One of these is spelled out by the next proposition, IIIP8: 'The striving by which each thing strives to persevere in its being involves no finite time, but an indefinite time.' Because a being's essence is constituted by its *conatus*, then so long as the being has an essence, it must strive to maintain whatever degree of being it possesses.

3.2.4   Descartes' first law of motion

So those are the key Spinozistic texts for *conatus*. I shall soon compare them with what we find in Stoicism and Grotius but first, I need to mention Descartes. In his *Principles of Philosophy*, Descartes advanced three laws of motion, the first of which reads as follows: 'that each thing

---

[41] The words are Bennett's (see Bennett (1983), 160). Many other commentators use similar language.

[42] Della Rocca (2008), 139.

[43] Here I am indebted to Garrett (2002). Garrett holds that there are degrees in which one thing, x, can be in another thing, y. This notion that there are degrees in which one thing can be in another is vital to the correct interpretation of IIIP5, Garrett argues; see esp. 142–3.

[*unamquamque rem*], as far as is in its power [*quantum in se est*], always remains in the same state; and that consequently, when it is once moved, it always continues to move'.[44] This law was not unnoticed by Spinoza. When he wrote his commentary on Descartes' *Principles*, Spinoza provided a close gloss on it: 'Each thing, insofar as it is simple and undivided, and it is considered in itself alone, as far as it can by its own power, always perseveres in the same state.'[45] It is almost incontestable that Spinoza was being influenced by Descartes when he formulated IIIP6 of the *Ethics*, which I shall quote again for ease of reference: 'Each thing, as far as it can by its own power, strives to persevere in its being.' The wording is just too close to be mere coincidence. As one commentator has written, 'Spinoza's definition of *conatus* and, indeed, his use of that term, is very likely an intentional reference to or borrowing from Descartes.'[46]

So what am I to make of the importance of Descartes' first law of motion for Spinoza's *conatus* doctrine? Two things. First, I cannot deny that Descartes factors at least as much and probably more into Spinoza's *conatus* than Grotius or the Stoics. Second, even though Descartes was so important, Spinoza did not hesitate to depart from him when he deemed it necessary. It is likely that Spinoza fuses Stoic or Grotian elements with Cartesian ones, and adds his own new thoughts, in the final presentations of *conatus* in the *Ethics*. Because I am trying to determine the extent of Spinoza's affinity to Stoicism, I shall not try to specify just which elements of *conatus* may have come from Descartes.[47]

3.2.5 Stoics and Spinoza on self-preservation

Let me return now to Spinoza. Certainly, additional texts and more discussion of the texts gathered in Section 2.2.3 could be provided. At the same time, I think we have enough material to begin comparing *conatus* to *oikeiosis*. So let us start that comparison.

A natural place to begin is with a point made in the last paragraph of Section 2.2.3. The *conatus* instinct is a disposition or tendency to behave in a self-preserving manner; it is always (i.e., constantly) active. This differs subtly from the Stoic view of self-preservation. For the Stoics, the individual may not always (i.e., constantly) have its actions guided by a self-preservation instinct; Stoic theory allows for other motivations for action

---

[44] Part II, Art. 37 (trans. CSM I: 241) (trans. modified).
[45] *Unaquaeque res, quatenus simplex, et indivisa est, et in se sola consideratur, quantum in se est, semper in eodem statu perseverat* (*PPC*, IIP14).
[46] Marshall (2013), 78, n. 31.
[47] I am grateful to an anonymous referee for pressing me to include Descartes here.

besides self-preservation. Most importantly, Stoics thought that rational beings are motivated by rational concerns, which are not reducible to the concerns of self-preservation.[48] The difference between Spinoza and the Stoics on the constancy of the self-preservation impulse surfaces in their differing attitudes towards suicide. As we saw above, Spinoza thinks self-destruction is impossible. Hence he argued that suicide, defined as the act of self-destruction, is impossible.[49] By contrast Stoics took suicide to be not only possible but also, in certain circumstances, morally justifiable.[50]

Yet there is a wrinkle here. Stoics allowed for and enjoined suicide but only by the sage. In his case, he may and should commit suicide if he foresees the deterioration of that most valuable aspect of his self: namely, his reason. For example, if a sage recognizes that he is in the early stages of dementia, he may conclude that he ought to end his life. The question is whether he is actually acting in a self-destructive manner. Perhaps the sage is not truly destroying himself. Perhaps he is preserving the only part of his self that matters, his reason. By ending the life of his physical body, he may keep his rational capacity from being undermined by changes in his physical states. If so, then the Stoics will say that the individual should and does act in a self-preserving manner whenever a threat to its existence arises. This suggests that in the absence of any additions to the Stoic view of self-preservation, there may be little practical difference between it and Spinoza's. At the moments that matter the most – the moments when the self's existence is actually at risk and self-preserving actions are needed – Stoics (just like Spinoza) believe that animals will take those actions.[51]

The next contrast concerns the ultimate source of the self-preservation impulse. Let me begin here with the different sorts of explanation that could be given for *conatus*. According to one of these, any being's *conatus* can be explained in simple mechanistic terms: each being strives to persevere in its being because it was caused to do so by preceding members of the causal series to which it belongs.[52] Given the activities of those

---

[48] See Seneca, *Ep.* 71.1–2.   [49] See IVP40Sch and *Ep.* 23.

[50] See, e.g., Cicero, *De fin.* III.60 (L-S 66G1–2). For more on suicide in Spinoza and the Stoics, see Miller (2005).

[51] I shall return to this issue in the next section. For now, I will note that Andrew Youpa has found a more complex theory of motivation in Spinoza than I have allowed (see Youpa (2007)). According to Youpa, Spinoza does indeed think that most of our actions are driven by our desire to preserve our being. However, Youpa argues, there are some situations in which our value judgments and not our *conatus* produce motivations. If Youpa is right, then Spinoza is closer to the Stoics than I have granted. The source of motivation may be different in Spinoza than the Stoics: it is *conatus* and value judgments in Spinoza, as opposed to self-preservation and reason in the Stoics. Still, both parties think our actions are motivated in two distinct ways.

[52] See IApp (at G II, 80: 35 ff.).

beings, and that *conatus* is 'the supreme law of nature',[53] it follows that the being in question must strive to remain in existence. Those antecedent beings brought it into existence; once in existence, *conatus* requires that it strive to remain in that state. With this kind of explanation, then, we remain in the infinite causal series of which all modes are members. Since we stay on this level, there is no place for Nature; we are on the wrong side of the substance-mode division for Nature to appear. Given that this is the case, Spinoza would disagree with the Stoic notion that Nature 'made [the animal] congenial to itself'.[54] It is not Nature who makes animals (and other beings) self-preserving; this instinct is solely the result of the (efficient) causes that produced these beings.

So far, so good. Trouble arises only when we seek a second-order explanation for why the members of the causal series exhibit their self-preserving behaviour. Here the answer must involve Nature. We cannot appeal to other modes, for we are now asking a question about the modes themselves: namely, why they are all governed by *conatus*. Since, apart from modes, there is nothing outside of Nature, there is nothing outside of Nature that could be invoked to account for everything's striving to remain in existence. Thus whatever explanation is provided of this phenomenon must inevitably appeal to Nature.[55] Further, if (as some have argued[56]) general laws of Nature like *conatus* are Nature's infinite modes, then the appeal to Nature will be fairly direct. It is not merely that Nature is responsible for everything's *conatus* because Nature is ultimately responsible for everything. In addition, by acting in a self-preserving manner they are manifesting a property of Nature itself and any attempt to understand such actions must draw upon Nature. IIIP6Dem says that 'singular things are modes by which God's attributes are expressed in a certain and determinate way (by IP25C), i.e. (by IP34), things that

---

[53] See *TTP* ch. 16: 'it is the supreme law of Nature that each thing endeavours to persist in its present being, as far as in it lies, taking account of no other thing but itself' (G III, 189: 25–7).

[54] DL VII.85.

[55] An interesting example of a similar appeal to God can be found in ch. 4 of the *TTP*. After introducing the distinction between laws which depend on Nature versus those which depend on 'human will' (G III, 57: 23–7), Spinoza acknowledges that this distinction can be made to collapse. He writes, 'I grant that, in an absolute sense, all things are determined by the universal laws of Nature to exist and to act in a definite and determinate way' (G III, 58: 6–8). In an 'absolute sense', God is ultimately responsible for both kinds of laws – natural and human – because in an 'absolute sense' God is ultimately responsible for everything. At the same time, this passage also contains two *different* reasons for why explanations and theorizing should not simply invoke God to settle matters (ibid.). Spinoza is not an explanatory reductionist; he believes that different explanations may be needed for the same phenomena.

[56] Notably Curley (1969), 59 ff.

express, in a certain and determinate way, God's power'. It is because modes are modifications of substance, and substance is fundamentally self-preserving,[57] that modes are self-preserving. For these reasons, then, Spinoza would agree with the Stoics that Nature is responsible for the instinct animals (not to mention other beings) have to preserve themselves.

Yet this agreement seems somewhat trifling; it largely follows from the identification of God with Nature. I have skirted the deeper metaphysical issue, which is just how and why God acts in both systems. I just argued that Stoics and Spinoza both attribute the self-preservation impulse to an action or actions by God. But what does it mean to say that God acted to make animals (and other beings) self-preserving? In both Stoicism and Spinozism, God's actions are rooted in his nature, so to understand God's actions, it is necessary to know something about the relationship between his nature and his actions. Let us look into this relationship, starting with Spinoza.

Spinoza's God is powerful – 'omnipotent', as he says in IP17Cor2Sch1. In Spinoza's metaphysics, power is necessarily productive: it is of the essence of power to produce what it can, for that is what power does.[58] Since God is powerful, and power is productive, God is productive. In fact, God is supremely productive, in keeping with his status as the supreme power. As IP16 says, 'From the necessity of the divine nature there must follow infinitely many things in infinitely many modes (i.e., everything which can fall under an infinite intellect).'[59] Now, power does not produce for the sake of anything; it produces just because that is its nature.[60] Since God produces only because he is powerful, he also does not produce for the

---

[57] This is implied by IIIP4: 'No thing can be destroyed except through an external cause.' Since there is nothing external to Nature, there is no cause by which Nature can be destroyed. Since there is no cause by which Nature can be destroyed, it is the most enduring, most preserved of all beings.

[58] Cf. IP11Sch: 'For since being able to exist is power, it follows that the more reality belongs to the nature of a thing, the more powers it has, of itself, to exist. Therefore, an absolutely infinite Being, or [*sive*] God, has, of himself, an absolutely infinite power of existing. For that reason, he exists absolutely.' Cf. also IP16Dem: 'This Proposition must be plain to anyone, provided he attends to the fact that the intellect infers from the given definition of any thing a number of properties that really do follow necessarily from it (i.e., from the very essence of the thing); and that it infers more properties the more the definition of the thing expresses reality.'

[59] Cf. also his gloss of IP16 in IP17Cor2Sch1: 'But I think I have shown clearly enough (see P16) that from God's supreme power, or [*sive*] infinite nature, infinitely many things in infinitely many modes, i.e., all things, have necessarily flowed.'

[60] My thoughts on Spinoza's conception of power owe much to Viljanen (2011), 59–67. I disagree with Viljanen's modal claims about the isomorphism of the actual and the possible in Spinoza (see, e.g., 63) but I very much like his assertion that '*Spinoza's God is, in essence, a power – the ultimate dynamic force behind all existence*' (71 (emphasis his)).

sake of anything. Rather, the things he produces follow from his nature 'by the same necessity and in the same way as from the nature of a triangle it follows, from eternity and to eternity, that its three angles are equal to two right angles'.[61] One of the things God produces is *conatus*. Like everything else, *conatus* is not produced for the sake of anything; it is produced just because God is powerful and power produces. On this analysis, then, God's nature as a powerful being gives rise to *conatus*, and since God *qua* producer does not produce for the sake of anything, *conatus* is not produced for the sake of anything. Further, the divine creation of *conatus* and hence of our self-preservation impulse did not require anything specific of God; he did not have to engage in any sort of deliberation and special series of actions. Rather, just by existing, God gave rise to self-preservation as the fundamental impulse.

The comparison of Spinoza's views on God's action with the Stoics' may be complicated by two somewhat different strands of Stoic thought concerning God's nature.[62] Some Stoics such as Chrysippus assumed a thinner God with fewer native properties and tended to rely on other principles or concepts for their philosophical explanations.[63] On the other side Stoics like Cleanthes believed in a more robust God, with greater powers and properties, and they understandably saw fit to use their God more frequently in philosophical argument and analysis.[64] With its inflationary conception of God and the theocentric orientation it gives to philosophy, Cleanthes' version of Stoicism is closer than Chrysippus' to Spinoza's God and his conception of philosophy. And just as Spinoza's method begins with an analysis of God's nature and proceeds to extract from it truths about the mind and morality, so Cleanthian Stoicism places the study of *phusis* or God ahead of logic and ethics.[65]

However, although inflationary Cleanthian Stoicism is closer to Spinozism than deflationary Chrysippean Stoicism, the distance of even Chrysippean Stoicism from Spinozism should not be overstated. As in

---

[61] IP17Cor2Sch1. I do not take the necessity Spinoza speaks of here to be self-evident. But it is not important for my argument to specify precisely – or even roughly – the modalities involved in God's production. What matters is that God produces 'blindly', without 'looking' to an end for guidance. For more on Spinoza's notions of necessity, see Carriero (1991).

[62] My identification of these two strands is admittedly speculative. Those who do not find it convincing may just proceed to the next paragraph.

[63] Hence the difficult work that Chrysippus undertook in logic and semantics, where 'God', 'Zeus', and other cognate terms never appear, and for good reason. To make progress in logic and semantics, Chrysippus had to think about logical and semantical problems, wherein there is no place for God.

[64] See above all the devotional opening lines to Cleanthes' *Hymn to Zeus* (L-S 54I1).

[65] See DL VII.41.

Spinozism, both strands of Stoic thought made God a centrepiece of philosophy. While Chrysippus may have recommended the study of logic before that of *phusis*,[66] he agreed with Cleanthes that *phusis* is one of the three subjects of philosophy. Furthermore, Chrysippus followed inflationary Stoics in regarding God as the repository of all real metaphysical powers and properties and holding that it is only in virtue of his Being that other creatures are individuated, gaining their essence and existence.[67] In this respect too, then, Chrysippean and Cleanthian Stoicism resembles Spinozism. Finally, and most importantly for present purposes, both strands of Stoic thought agree with Spinoza's answer to the question of how God acts: viz., by drawing on his own innate, infinite capacity for activity.[68]

The contrast between Stoics and Spinoza on the issue of God's responsibility for the presence of the self-preservation impulse in animals (and other beings) thus cannot be found in the source of God's actions or how he acts. While Stoics may have quibbled over the exact specification of God's nature, they all endowed him with tremendous powers similar to those of Spinoza's God and agreed that God acts from these powers. Instead, the contrast lies primarily in the reasons for his actions.

Even on the deflationary Chrysippean account of God and his place in philosophy, God exhibits concern for the universe and for us in particular, and this concern leads him to act in certain ways.[69] While it may be possible for God's concern for the universe not to bear at all upon his decision to make his creatures self-preserving, in fact Stoics rule out this possibility. Indeed, Chrysippus' argument (from Diogenes Laertius VII.85, cited above) proving God's responsibility for the self-preservation impulse makes this clear. Nature (which can be taken as a synonym for God in this context), it was said, is responsible for the creation of animals. Having created them, Nature (or God) would not then also not instil in them the resources necessary for their survival, such as the impulse to self-preservation. Although the reason why Nature would not do this is left unstated, it is clear that this must be because of its concern for their welfare. In answer to the question, 'Why does God act to do so-and-so?', then, Stoics would say it is because of his concern for the welfare of his creation. As we have seen, this is how Grotius interprets Stoicism. He is undoubtedly correct. As the Stoic spokesman Balbus states in *ND*, 'I

---

[66] See DL VII.40. [67] See, e.g., DL VII.134. [68] See, e.g., Plutarch, *Stoic. Rep.* 1052D.
[69] The universal agreement among Stoics over God's concern for the universe and its members is of course very well attested. Among the more interesting sources: Plutarch, *De comm. not.* 1075E (where God's 'benevolence' and 'care' are said to be 'preconceptions'); Cicero, *ND* II.73–4; DL VII.147; Epictetus, *Discourses* III.24.3.

therefore assert that it is by the providence of the gods that the world and all its parts were first compounded and have been governed for all time.'[70]

In sum, then: both Spinoza and the Stoics think that God's actions are rooted in his nature, such that because of his nature, he acts in the ways he does. Although Stoic opinion on God's nature is not undivided, all of them think that whatever else God is, he is by nature providential and cares for the well-being of his creation. His providential nature affects his actions by causing him to act in ways that best ensures the well-being of the universe and everything in it. One of the requirements for well-being is the existence of his creatures. Because of this requirement, his nature led him to instil the impulse for self-preservation in us and this is why – it is through his action – we (and other creatures) are self-preservers. By contrast, Spinoza's God acts simply because he is powerful and power by nature is productive. There are numerous products of God's actions, one of which is *conatus*. Because God acted and through his action gave rise to *conatus*, we are self-preservers. No other reason is cited to explain *conatus* besides God's power; in particular, there is no need to cite his supposed care for his creation.[71]

The next contrast follows close on the heels of the previous one. Although Spinoza agreed that animals (and other beings) are self-preserving, he did not think that they have this impulse because they desire to remain in existence. Instead, because they have a self-preservation instinct, they come to desire to remain in existence. And because they come to have this desire, they come to regard self-preservation as good. The core of the argument for the first of these propositions is given in IIIP9Sch:

---

[70] II.75 (L-S 54J1).

[71] In an interesting passage from the *Short Treatise*, Spinoza does connect providence to *conatus*. He says,

> The second 'attribute' which we call a *Proprium* is Providence, which according to us is nothing but that striving we find both in the whole of Nature and in particular things, tending to maintain and preserve their being . . . So according to this definition of ours, we posit a universal and a particular Providence. The universal is that through which each thing is produced and maintained insofar as it is a part of the whole of Nature. The particular Providence is that striving which each particular thing has for the preservation of its being insofar as it is considered not as a part of Nature, but as a whole. (Book I, Chapter V (G I, 40: 1–4, 10–16))

> Displaying his penchant to appropriate traditional concepts for use in his own philosophy, Spinoza here grants that God is providential, only that his providence is the *conatus* of Nature and its parts to remain in and preserve their being. The hollowness of this notion of providence might have made it seem ridiculous to Spinoza, for he dispenses with it entirely by the time of the *Ethics* and instead makes direct appeal to *conatus*. For more on Spinoza's treatment of providence, see Lloyd (2008), ch. 6.

When this striving is related only to the Mind, it is called Will; but when it is related to the Mind and Body together, it is called Appetite. This Appetite, therefore, is nothing but the very essence of man, from whose nature there necessarily follow those things that promote his preservation. And so man is determined to do those things.

  Between Appetite and desire there is no difference, except that desire is generally related to men insofar as they are conscious of their Appetite. So *desire* can be defined as *Appetite together with consciousness of the Appetite.*[72]

IIIP9 itself states, 'Both insofar as the Mind has clear and distinct ideas, and insofar as it has confused ideas, it strives, for an indefinite duration, to persevere in its being and it is conscious of this striving it has.' The Mind must have its *conatus*, because its *conatus* is its 'actual essence'.[73] Because the Mind has its *conatus*, then because the Mind is conscious of itself,[74] it is conscious of its *conatus*. From this consciousness of its *conatus*, it follows as a matter of definition that the mind desires to persevere in its being: for desire is the consciousness humans have of their appetite to remain in existence – i.e., of their *conatus*.[75]

  The second proposition – that the desire for self-preservation gives rise to the valuation of self-preservation as good – also appears in IIIP9Sch, in one of the more celebrated passages of the *Ethics*: 'From all this, then, it is clear that we neither strive for, nor will, neither want, nor desire anything because we judge it to be good; on the contrary, we judge something to be good because we strive for it, will it, want it, and desire it.'[76] The full story about how value is extracted from the fact of *conatus* is not told until Part IV and I shall postpone detailed investigation of it until my next chapter. For now, let the following suffice. The traditional relationship between physical or psychological concepts such as 'striving' and 'desire' and normative ones such as 'good' has to be inverted. Rather than define our strivings and desires in moral terms and the terms of our value judgments, we have to define our moral concepts and value judgments in terms of our strivings and desires.[77]

  The primacy of strivings and desires, and derivativeness of moral concepts, is evident from their very essences. As we learn from the opening arguments of Part III, strivings and desires are real members of the world; we cannot understand the way things are and act unless we posit the *conatus* principle. On the other hand, folk moral concepts and the value

---

[72] Spinoza's emphasis. [73] IIIP7. [74] IIIP9Dem. [75] Cf. IIIP9Sch.
[76] The language of IIIP9Sch is echoed by that of IIIP39Sch. For discussion of the significance of this, see LeBuffe (2010), 153.
[77] As Irwin puts it, 'we do not desire our own continuance, or anything else, because we take it to be good. On the contrary, desire is prior to belief about goodness' (Irwin (2007–9), vol. II, 195).

judgments based on them are not part of the furniture of the world but are hauled in by humans. As Spinoza says in the Appendix to Part I,

> After men persuaded themselves that everything that happens, happens on their account, they had to judge that what is most important in each thing is what is most useful to them, and to rate as most excellent all those things by which they were most pleased. Hence, they had to form these notions, by which they explained natural things: *good, evil, order, confusion, warm, cold, beauty, ugliness.*[78]

Moral concepts and value judgments (which come to be as a result of belief in final causes and teleology) are artificial, 'nothing but modes of imagining'.[79] Nevertheless, it is not necessary to dispense with them entirely, especially if they are found to have some use or value (as indeed they will in Parts IV–V). Instead, they need to be given a new grounding and place in philosophy. Their proper position is sketched in the passage of IIIP9Sch just quoted; they are to be defined in terms of *conatus.*[80]

For the past few pages the contrast between Spinoza and the Stoics' notions of self-preservation has been sharpened. To conclude this section, two important commonalities between them will be mentioned. Self-preservation is an odd beginning or basis for a moral system. We may be self-preserving animals, but such behaviour is hard to describe as *moral.* Usually, when we act in a purely self-preserving manner, we think of such actions as driven by necessity or cold-hearted self-interest; we do not think of them as *moral.* Such actions do not involve a regard for others that is often taken to be essential to morality, nor can they be interpreted as structured with the principles that, in the cognitivist tradition at least, seem necessary for morality. In the words of one commentator, 'ethics is concerned not only with the actual power or efforts of man for self-preservation, but also and primarily with the nature and validity of the ideals and norms of human character'.[81] Nevertheless, neither Spinoza nor the Stoics were deterred by these problems. They attempt to surmount them by displaying the principles implicit in self–preservation and arguing that, if determinism is true, then all actions are, in some sense, necessary, and that this cannot count against the morality of self-preserving actions. Since it is possible to categorize philosophical systems according to how they handle major philosophical problems or issues, then if self-preservation is one of these watershed issues, the fact that both

---

[78] G II, 81: 25–30.   [79] IApp (G II, 82: 17).

[80] Spinoza forcefully states the connection between *conatus* and morality in IVP18Sch. He writes, 'the foundation of virtue is this very striving to preserve one's own being' [*virtutis fundamentum esse ipsum conatum proprium esse conservandi*].

[81] Bidney (1962), 409.

Spinoza and the Stoics make self-preservation part of the foundation of their ethics gives us reason for thinking of them as alike.

The second commonality is inspired by Grotius. As we saw, he took *oikeiosis* as combining two desires: the desire for self-preservation with the desire for living in society. According to his reading of the doctrine, *oikeiosis* makes us seek out the company of others, for we realize that we cannot accomplish all that we need for our existence on our own.[82] This impulse for society forms the basis of all social orders, both local and global. In the ideal world, where truly rational agents are able to act without interference from non-rational forces, it would result in a society encompassing all rational agents everywhere. To use the parlance of the ancient Stoics, the entire *cosmos* can be a single *polis*.[83]

There is much here that Spinoza would accept.[84] In the so-called Dictates of Reason given in IVP18Sch, Spinoza declares that the 'foundation of virtue is this very striving to preserve one's own being'. Because we want to preserve our being but we realize that we are not perfect enough to succeed in this quest by acting on our own, we are led to seek the assistance of other beings.[85] Because nothing is 'more excellent' for us than those things 'that agree entirely with our nature', we are led to seek the assistance of human beings in particular.[86] The best living arrangement we could be in is one in which we live in complete harmony with other human beings like us. This living arrangement would transcend all political and geographical boundaries; it would unite us with all like-mannered human beings, no matter where they happen to live. Spinoza may not have used the word 'cosmopolitan' but his ideal living arrangements bears a striking resemblance to it.[87]

---

[82] Cf. Irwin (2007–9), vol. II, 95.

[83] See, e.g., Plutarch, *On the Fortune of Alexander* 329a–b (L-S 67A) and Seneca, *De otio* IV.1 (L-S 67K).

[84] As I shall describe it, Spinoza's cosmopolitanism is rooted in his philosophical psychology. To preserve our own being we must create a living arrangement encompassing all like-minded creatures. This grounding of his cosmopolitanism is different from one which places it on his conception of a social contract (if he has such a conception). Since there is nothing in Stoicism remotely analogous to a social contract, there can be no similarity between the Stoics and Spinoza here.

[85] IVP18Sch (at G II, 223: 1–3).

[86] It is here that Spinoza makes his declaration, 'To man, then, there is nothing more useful than man' (IVP18Sch (at G II 223: 8–9)).

[87] So far as I am aware, Spinoza's cosmopolitanism has not been extensively discussed in the secondary literature. One mention of it appears in Feuer (1958), 69. See also DeBrabander (2007), ch. 4, and Huenemann (2014), ch 5. There is an interesting clash between DeBrabander and Huenemann. DeBrabander thinks that Spinoza differs from the Stoics in that he (unlike the Stoics) attached great importance to politics. By contrast, Huenemann argues that while Spinoza was ready to engage in politics, he would

At the same time, I think we ought to acknowledge a difference in Spinoza. He was more hard-bitten than either Grotius or the Stoics. He plainly does not think that most human beings are rational most or even much of the time.[88] To be sure, Grotius and the Stoics took most humans to be irrational. When the Stoics called the great run of humans 'fools', they meant precisely that they are irrational. The difference between Spinoza and the Stoics/Grotius lies in the possibility for progress towards rationality. The Stoics thought all or almost all humans were irrational and foolish; at the same time, they believed strongly that all humans could become rational and wise.[89] Spinoza did not share this optimism.

3.3   From self-preservation to . . .?

The general injunction in Stoicism is to live in accordance with nature, both one's own and universal Nature.[90] Under this injunction, there is no reason why beings cannot find themselves with patterns of appropriate behaviour that vary over time. While Nature will not change, its demands on their actions may, if something should change about their own individual natures. If this happens – if, say, their natures come to have new properties – then it is possible that behaviour which counts as appropriate will change, too. Unless the new properties are very akin to older ones, the beings which possess them will have to adjust their behaviour in response to their presence. Since humans in particular, as they grow and develop, come to have a property radically dissimilar to any they had in their early years, they have to add a new end on top of the original ones. Diogenes tells us what this property is when he writes, 'When reason has been given to rational animals as a more perfect governor [of life], then for them the life according to reason properly becomes what is

---

do so only when the *polis* is rational. Otherwise, 'the philosopher retreats to a world where reason rules: the world of the mind, or the world created by a book of philosophy' (130).

[88] This idea is best explored in Den Uyl (1983).

[89] I assume that Stoics, including early Stoics, allowed for the possibility of moral progress. This is sometimes denied. For a very helpful overview of the notion of moral progress in Stoicism, including a list of the primary and secondary as well as the main conceptual difficulties, see Ramelli (2009), l–liv.

[90] In Diogenes Laertius, we find something different reported: 'By the nature with which our life ought to be in accord, Chrysippus understands both universal nature and more particularly the nature of man, where Cleanthes takes the nature of the universe alone as that which should be followed, without adding the nature of the individual' (VII.88 (trans. Hicks in Diogernes Laertius (1972)). While the disagreement between Cleanthes and Chrysippus should not be overlooked, it should also not be over-emphasized. There is total agreement between one's individual nature and that of Nature. When it is necessary to forego what one wants to do in favour of what Nature has ordained, then the rational agent will do so without hesitation.

natural for them.'[91] For humans and other rational animals (if such there be), when they become rational, the impulses under which they were previously acting become secondary to their rationality. Since the most important component of their natures is now reason, the general injunction to live according to nature becomes (for humans) an injunction to live according to reason.

Such is the Stoic account of human development that I want to compare with Spinoza's. There are two issues that I shall discuss: one, about the identity of the individual herself or himself; the other, about the character of the changes involved in becoming rational. Let me deal with these in turn.

3.3.1   Individual identity

Before getting to their theories on individual identity, a few words on both the Stoics and Spinoza's theories of substance are in order. I have touched on this in Chapter 1 but since their views on individuals are heavily influenced by their views on substances, I want to rehearse the material again.

Stoics assign ontological primacy to the corporeal – they hold that only bodies exist – and in keeping with this, they confine substance to the physical realm alone. Thus, whatever things turn out to be substances, they will at minimum be bodies. Now, in one sense of the word, 'substance' refers to one of the four basic categories or genera of Stoic ontology (the other three being the qualified, disposed, and relatively disposed). Since Plutarch tells us that each individual entity belongs to all four categories,[92] it follows that each individual entity (that includes humans) is a substance. There is another special sense in which 'substance' refers only to God. However, this need not detain us here, since that distinction does not operate on the level of basic metaphysics but rather on the level of cosmology. Because individual entities like human beings are substances, the challenge of the Stoic theory of individuals is not so much to explain how individuation is possible as it is to explain what individuation consists in.

By contrast Spinoza famously insists that there is one and only one substance, God. Since there is one and only one substance, everything else in the universe must somehow be related to it, by a kind of dependency relation. Of course, Spinoza uses the words 'mode' and 'modification' to describe this relation. Lest he be accused of saying everything

---

[91] DL VII.86 (the bracketed insertion is I-G's). [92] *De comm. not.* 1083D.

except God is illusory, it is important for him to explain how individual beings such as you and I can be modes of God and yet still have some degree or kind of reality. This challenge is one of the main ones his theory of individuals and individuation must address; it must explain how individuation is possible, given that there is only one substance.

Bearing in mind their notions of substance and the different demands they place on their theories of individuals and individuation, let me now begin an examination of the Stoic theory. A theorem of the Stoic conception of individual identity is that the individual is analysable into two parts, one enduring, the other transient.[93] Cicero writes in *De fin.*, 'every animal, as soon as it is born (this is where one should start), is concerned with itself, and takes care to preserve itself. It favours its constitution and whatever preserves its constitution [*commendari ad se conservandum et ad suum statum*]'.[94] When the animal seeks to preserve 'itself', it is seeking to preserve a combination of body and soul that roughly corresponds to our notion of the self. When it seeks to preserve its 'constitution', on the other hand, it is seeking the preservation of a narrower part of itself, its arrangement at a particular stage in its development.

In an important letter, Seneca puts a definition of this notion of 'constitution' into the mouth of an imagined opponent: '"According to you, the constituition [*constitutio*] is the leading part of the soul in a certain disposition relative to the body."'[95] The phrase 'in a certain disposition relative to the body' [*quodammodo se habens erga corpus*] is technical, used to speak of members of the fourth category or genus of Stoic ontology. Members of this category or genus are relatively disposed things (*pros ti pos echon*), characterized by an extrinsic (*not* an intrinsic) relation. Simplicius tells us that relatively disposed things are 'all those whose nature it is to become and cease to be a property of something without any internal change or qualitative alteration' in the thing of which they are properties.[96] As a 'relatively disposed' thing, then, one's constitution will reside neither in the body nor in the soul but in a relationship between them. So stated, there is no reason why one cannot have different constitutions: disposed one way relative to the body at time t, the leading part of one's soul (the *hegemonikon*) can be disposed another way relative to the body at t + 1. And if it is so disposed, then one has a new constitution.

---

[93] I take the standard Stoic conception of individual identity to be something like that described by Sedley (1982).
[94] *De fin.* III.16 (trans. Woolf in Cicero (2001)).
[95] *Ep.* 121.10 (trans. Inwood in Seneca (2007)).
[96] Simplicius, *On Aristotle's Categories* 166.17–19 (L-S 29C1).

In fact, Seneca proceeds to argue that this is exactly what occurs:

He [i.e., his hypothetical interlocutor] objects, 'You say that every animal has a primary attachment to its own constitution, but that a human being's constitution is rational and so that a human being is attached to himself not *qua* animal but *qua* rational. For a human is dear to himself with respect to that aspect of himself which makes him human. So how can a baby be attached to a rational constitution when it is not yet rational?'
    There is a constitution for every stage of life, one for a baby, another for a boy, <another for a teenager>, another for an old man. Everyone is attached to the constitution he is in. A baby has no teeth – it is attached to this constitution, which is its own. Teeth emerge – it is attached to this constitution. For even the plant which will one day grow and ripen into grain has one constitution when it is a tender shoot just barely emerging from the furrow, another when it has gotten stronger and has a stem which though tender is able to carry its own weight, and yet another when it is ripening, getting ready for harvest and has a firm head: but whatever constitution it has reached, it protects it and settles into it.[97]

Take the plant example. It will progress through many different stages in life: a seed, a shoot, an unripe adult, a fully mature specimen ready for harvesting. In each of these stages it has a separate constitution which 'it protects it and settles into it'.
    Yet at the same time as a being has a 'constitution', it also has other qualities. Seneca says in the sentences immediately following those just quoted:

A baby, a boy, a teenager, an old man: these are different stages of life. Yet I am the same human as was also a baby and a boy and a teenager. Thus, although everyone has one different constitution after another, the attachment to one's own constitution is the same. For nature does not commend me to the boy or the youth or the old man, but to myself.[98]

There is an underlying self which seeks different ends as it undergoes development; the different constitutions it possesses are incapable of this search, since they do not exist from one stage of development to the next. Although Seneca does not invoke this terminology, this 'underlying self' is the 'peculiarly qualified' thing which makes up one half of the second of the Stoic categories, the 'qualified' (*poion*). Taken broadly to include both common and peculiar qualifications (*koinos poion* and *idios poion*), the qualified covers all inherent distinguishing characteristics. Common qualifications are describable with common nouns and adjectives, whereas the peculiarly qualified are qualitatively unique individuals denoted by rigid designators. Any being's peculiar qualification is a conjunction of

---

[97] *Ep.* 121.14–15 (trans. Inwood in Seneca (2007) – the bracketed insertion is mine).
[98] *Ep.* 121.16 (trans. Inwood in Seneca (2007)).

enduring common qualifications. So, for instance, Seneca's peculiarly qualified quality might include man, Roman, cautious, etc. Other properties that he might possess – e.g., teacher of Nero or subject of Tacitus – are not peculiar qualifications, technically speaking, since they are relational and whatever qualifies him peculiarly is intrinsic.

Now, among other things, the theory of individual identity was probably intended to explain how it is possible for the same individual to have different ends. If the same individual is to have different ends, then since the individual's ends are conditioned by or dependent on his nature, changes must be transpiring within the individual's nature. So individuals can have different ends only if it is possible for their natures to undergo genuine change. But as David Sedley[99] has pointed out, it cannot be the case that the individual's nature undergoes a *complete* change. If the individual completely changed identity, then since real change requires that the same individual exist after the change as existed before, it would not in fact be the case that the individual was changing at all. When a change occurred, the being that previously existed would cease to exist and would be replaced by a new one. Sedley argues that it was precisely the need to explain how the individual's nature changes, but only partially, that led Chrysippus to devise the Stoic theory of categories. He argues that Chrysippus showed with the theory of categories how 'a unitary object may under different descriptions have different and even incompatible things truly said of it'.[100] Under some descriptions (say, described in terms of our relative dispositions or 'constitutions'), we will not endure through time, cannot be said to grow or shrink, and therefore cannot be said to experience real change. Under other descriptions, however (say, as 'peculiarly qualified individuals' of the second category), we will endure through time, be proper subjects of growth and shrinkage, and thus experience real change.

The question I now want to ask is: does Spinoza possess a notion of an individual that allows for real change? The answer, I shall argue, is no.

The closest definition to an individual given by Spinoza occurs at IIP13SchDef.[101] There are many elements to this definition, one of

---

[99] Sedley (1982), 257–8. [100] Sedley (1982), 260.

[101] At G II, 99: 26 ff. Two provisos. First, here and throughout I will be speaking of composite individuals, of which humans are one important instance. Second, IIP13SchDef is technically just his definition of a bodily individual. Yet along with other commentators, I think it can be used to obtain one of his most complete accounts of an individual *simpliciter* and so I will treat it as such (by 'individual *simpliciter*' I mean the combination of mind and body that Spinoza thinks makes up each human; see IIP13Cor). The reasoning is as follows: IIP13SchDef tells us what Spinoza takes a bodily individual to be. Since the body is identical to the mind, this definition must also, in some way, be telling us what a mental individual is. It cannot be literally applied to the

which comes out in IIP13SchLemma4Dem. There he writes, 'bodies are not distinguished in respect to substance; what constitutes the form of the individual consists [only] in the union of the bodies (by the preceding definition [i.e., IIP13SDef])'.[102] By the 'union' of the (composite) individual's bodies, Spinoza means the composition which results when those bodies either 'lie upon one another, or if they so move . . . that they communicate their motions to each other in a certain fixed manner'.[103] These two means of forming a union – lying upon one another or communicating motion via a certain fixed manner – are the same two means he later glosses as 'rest and motion'.[104] Thus in IIP13SchLemma4Dem Spinoza stipulates that an individual is unified and attains a 'form' only in the case that its constituent members maintain the same proportion or ratio of activity relative to one another. Now, as other scholars have argued, this proportion or ratio serves at least two functions: individuation (since the individual is differentiated from other beings just because its parts act together[105]) and continuity of existence (since the individual exists just so long as its parts act together in the same way[106]). Clearly, these are two crucial parts of a concept of what makes an individual. So the constant proportion or ratio of motion and rest (*motus, et quietis ratio*) that IIP13SchLemma4Dem says an individual's members must maintain in order for the individual to come into and remain in existence plays an essential part in Spinoza's notion of an individual.

Now, because his conception of the 'form' of the individual essentially involves the idea of a certain constant proportion or ratio of motion-and-rest,

---

mental individual; terminological and conceptual changes must be made to reflect the fact that it is now speaking of the individual *qua* mental (and not physical) being. These changes are readily achievable, however, due to mind–body parallelism. So II13SchDef can also be made into a definition of a mental individual. The legitimacy of this application of IIP13SchDef follows from IIP11 and IIP13, and is confirmed by IIP15 (about the nature of the human mind) and IIP21Sch (where he says that 'the Mind and the Body, are one and the same individual, which is conceived now under the attribute of Thought, now under the attribute of Extension'). For more, see Morrison (1994), 32–3, and Rice (1975).

[102] The first bracketed insertion is Curley's, the second mine. The bracketed 'only' given by Curley appears in NS edition of the *Ethics*, but not the OP. I think that Curley is right to include it in his translation, as it helpfully accents a key part of the Demonstration.

[103] IIP13SchDef.   [104] IIP13SchLemmas5–7.

[105] As Rice (1975) puts it, an individual is individuated by 'this fixed relation of motion and rest (or interchange of energy) among its parts . . . It is the relation among its parts, and not the parts themselves, upon which Spinoza fixes in order to characterize an individual' (202).

[106] In Bennett's words, 'the same individual persists so long as its parts "preserve towards one another the same proportion of motion and rest"' (Bennett (1984), 107). See also Garrett (2008), 11.

Spinoza's conception of an individual is intrinsically quantitative or mathematical.[107] Alan Gabbey has argued,

> To talk of bodies maintaining among themselves 'the same proportion of motion and rest', or communicating motion to each other 'in a certain fixed proportion', is to say nothing effective, unless a mathematical account is provided of those proportions and of the measures of motion and rest from which they are formed, and unless there is some account of the laws that ensure the claimed invariance in proportionality.[108]

Spinoza never supplied the mathematics that Gabbey says is necessary for his account of an individual to be effective. This does not, however, necessarily imply that he himself was unaware of the need for this account; rather, he could have thought the *Ethics* not to be the appropriate place for it.[109] In any event, one important consequence of Spinoza's mathematical conception of an individual is that it incorporates a very strong theoretical bias against real change. If the two sides of a ratio such as 4:3 are multiplied by 3 to get 12:9, it is hard to see how the ratio has really changed at all. The numbers are different, but the relationship between the numbers is not, and it is precisely that relationship which constitutes the ratio itself. Likewise, Spinoza's individual may undergo metabolic change (IIP13SchLemma5) or change in posture or position (Lemmas 6 and 7), but since its essential feature – the ratio of motion and rest among its parts – is not changing, it seems that the individual is not, either.[110]

By contrast, as we learned from our foray in the Stoic notion of an individual, it is capable of undergoing very real changes; it must, since, if it is a potentially rational being, the transition from potential to actual

[107] The mental counterpart to the physical ratio of motion-and-rest cannot be expressed in terms of motion, of course, since ideas do not move. I suppose it could consist in the conceptual relations that exist among all the mind's ideas. So long as a certain set of conceptual relations is maintained, the mind remains in existence; once that relation is lost, so, too, is the mind. Whatever the intensional equivalent to the extensional ratio discussed in this paragraph turns out to be, all the terms and concepts I am applying to the ratio would have to be translated into intensional ones. For economy's sake, I will not undertake this task here. Let me just say that I do not think there is any reason why it could not be completed. However, others disagree. For example, Steven Barbone thinks that Spinoza's conception of an individual is ultimately physicalist. For him, 'Individuals are composed of matter that operates on their environments' (Barbone (2002), 102). If Barbone is correct, then it would not be possible to provide an account of an ideational or intensional individual, because individuals are physical entities.

[108] Gabbey (1996), 168.

[109] He does write at the end of IIP13SchLemma7Sch, 'If it had been my intention to deal expressly with body, I ought to have explained and demonstrated these things more fully. But I have already said that I intended something else, and brought these things forward only because I can easily deduce from them the things I have decided to demonstrate.' See also Gabbey (1996), 168–9, and Rice (1975), 197.

[110] Steven Barbone emphasizes the physicalist bent of Spinoza's conception of an individual.

rationality involves a transformation of the self. Since Spinoza's individual may undergo the appearance of change but cannot undergo genuine transformation, and since the Stoic individual can undergo real transformation, it follows that a Spinozistic individual differs fundamentally from her or his Stoic counterpart. This is an important conclusion; among its implications is that Spinoza's account of human development and moral progress must differ fundamentally from the Stoics. As we develop and progress in Spinozism, our natures do not undergo any changes; any changes we experience must take place on another level.[111] These differences in their notions of individuals force Stoics and Spinoza to hold different notions of development and moral progress.[112]

3.3.2   *The change involved in becoming rational*

In Stoicism, one of the self's constitutions (if it is this kind of self) is that of a normally developed adult human. Many things are 'congenial' to the normally developed adult human; one of these is reason. Since reason is congenial to the adult human, reason is an end to be pursued. But reason is not like any other end; it is special – so special, in fact, as to be unique. As Epictetus colourfully exclaims, 'What, then, is a philosopher's matter? Not a ragged coat, surely? No, it is reason. What is his end? Surely it is not wearing a ragged coat? No, it is keeping his reason right.'[113] Rather than be concerned with wealth or health or family, we ought to focus our efforts on our reason. If we do, we can attain the highest good for humans – sagacity. This much is well known; what actually happens to us as we become rational is less familiar.

When we become rational, our natures change: whereas we previously had the property of being merely potentially rational beings, with the advent of reason we acquire the property of actually being rational. Since there is no obvious reason why this change must occur in only one way, it behoves us to hear the story Stoics tell about it. There are several points about this.

First, from Aetius we learn how it is that humans *acquire* reason, which they do not possess at birth:

---

[111]   To be precise: I am urging here that Spinoza's *motus, et quietis ratio* cannot be mapped on to the Stoics' *idios poion*. The fundamental difference between the two is that Spinoza's *ratio* is mechanical and hence quantitative whereas the peculiarly qualified is a special kind of property and hence qualitative.

[112]   It is sometimes doubted that Spinoza consistently hewed to the conception of an individual just outlined and that he shifted covertly to a more Stoic conception. This would of course undermine the conclusion for which I have just argued. I will attempt to show that he made no such shift in Section 3.4.

[113]   *Discourses* IV.8.12 (L-S 31J).

When a man is born, the Stoics say, he has the commanding-part of his soul like a sheet of paper ready for writing upon. On this he inscribes each one of his conceptions. The first method of inscription is through the senses. For by perceiving something, e.g. white, they have a memory of it when it has departed. And when many memories of a similar kind have occurred, we then say we have experience. For the plurality of similar impressions is experience. Some conceptions arise naturally in the aforesaid ways and undesignedly, others through our own instruction and attention. The latter are called 'conceptions' only, the former are called 'preconceptions' as well. Reason, for which we are called rational, is said to be completed from our preconceptions during our first seven years.[114]

Stoics apparently entertained two notions of reason. One, preserved for us by Aetius in the above text, is that reason (*logos*) is 'completed from our preconceptions [*prolepseis*]'. Another, attributed by Galen to Chrysippus, is that 'Reason is a collection of certain conceptions [*ennoiai*] and preconceptions [*prolepseis*].'[115] Whichever definition one prefers – that reason develops out of our preconceptions and is apparently separate from them, or that it is a collection of conceptions/preconceptions – it must be the case that humans are not rational at birth, since the conceptions (and preconceptions) on which reason relies are not present in infants but are only accumulated by experience.[116] That is why Stoics maintained that humans become rational by a certain age, be it seven or fourteen.[117] Once we have lived long enough, we have the material necessary to be rational; until we have crossed that threshold, we are merely potentially rational beings. Thus the change from potential to actual rationality can be said to occur gradually, over the course of time and with increasing experience. At the same time, however, there may be a sharp transition at the actual moment one becomes rational. While Stoics disagreed over the number of years required for humans to accumulate the conceptions (and preconceptions) necessary for rationality, they agreed that at a definite age, humans are suddenly rational. This picture of gradual progress followed by abrupt change mirrors the transition said to occur when humans become sagacious.[118]

---

[114] Aetius IV.11.1–4 (L-S 39E). My interpretation of this text is much indebted to Scott (1995), ch. 8.

[115] Galen, *PHP* 5.3.1 (L-S 53V).

[116] Cf. Frede (1994): 'The Stoic view is not that we acquire reason in addition to something we already have at birth, but rather that something we already have at birth, namely the hegemonikon of the irrational soul, is transformed into something else, namely reason' (51).

[117] The age fourteen is attested by DL (among others) at VII.55.

[118] So Pembroke (1971): 'There is a definite emphasis on the continuity of childhood with maturity, just as there is elsewhere on that of animal behavior with human life and even on that of the man who makes moral progress with the man who has actually attained to wisdom. In each case the continuity is offset by a violently sharp break' (120–1).

As depictions of the Stoic sage attest, there is a period when sages move slowly towards their goal of full rationality. The *techne* that sages possess can only be acquired through practice and experience, as proven by the fact that a *techne* is a *hexis*, and a *hexis* admits of degrees. Thus Olympiodorus writes,

> Cleanthes says that expertise [*techne*] is a tenor [*hexis*] which achieves everything methodically. This definition is incomplete. After all, nature also is a tenor which does everything methodically. That is why Chrysippus added 'with impressions', and said that expertise is a tenor which advances methodically with impressions . . . Zeno says that an expertise is a systematic collection of cognitions unified by practice for some goal advantageous in life.[119]

At the same time, skill in utilizing preferred indifferents and performing proper functions is not sufficient for sagacity. Stobaeus writes,

> Chrysippus says: 'The man who progresses to the furthest point performs all proper functions without exception and omits none. Yet his life', he says, 'is not yet happy, but happiness supervenes on it when these intermediate actions acquire the additional properties of firmness and [stability] and their own particular fixity.'[120]

Though the sage is rational before becoming sagacious, he or she is not fully rational; at the moment of full rationality she or he metamorphoses into true wisdom. This transfiguration is depicted as sudden and complete: 'the wise man has changed in a moment from the greatest possible worthlessness to an unsurpassable virtuous character, and has suddenly shed all the vice of which he failed to remove even a part over a considerable time [when he was still foolish]'.[121] The final point of transition from foolishness to sagacity is so immediate and total because the sage is moving between the contradictories of vice and virtue. In his description of the Stoic sage Diogenes Laertius makes the point that 'nothing is in between virtue and vice, though the Peripatetics say the progress is in between these. For as, they say, a stick must be either straight or crooked, so a man must be either just or unjust . . . and likewise with the other virtues.'[122] The relationship of foolishness to sagacity – why it is that they are opposites – can perhaps be more easily grasped with an analogy to the Stoics' two-valued logic. Just as (simple) propositions are either true or

---

[119]   *On Plato's Gorgias* 12.1 (L-S 42A).   [120]   *Ecl.* V.906.18–7.5.

[121]   Plutarch, *On Moral Progress* 75C (L-S 61S1–2 (my brackets)). Plutarch seemed especially provoked by this aspect of Stoic philosophy; for some of his more hyperbolic ridicule, see especially *Conspectus of the Essay, 'The Stoics talk more paradoxically than the Poets'*, 1057E–8C.

[122]   DL VII.127 (L-S 61I1).

false and nothing else,[123] so humans are either sages or fools and nothing else. And just as the true and the false have nothing in common, so with the sage and the fool.

Underscoring and providing a basis for their views on the move from non-rationality to rationality is the Stoics' belief that the physical make-up of the individual alters as he or she becomes rational. In Stoic terms, the *pneuma* of rational souls attains a higher degree of 'tension' (*tonos*) than that of non-rational souls; the more rational the soul, the higher the degree of tension. This is most clearly reflected in various Stoic doctrines about the sage. For example, most (but not all) Stoics held that only the souls of the wise survive death and last until this cosmic cycle ends in conflagration.[124] Eusebius reports, 'They [the Stoics] say that the soul is subject to generation and destruction. When separated from the body, however, it does not perish at once but survives on its own for certain times, the soul of the virtuous up to the dissolution of everything into fire, that of fools only for certain definite times.'[125] To cite another, less exotic example, a principal reason for the errors fools make regarding which appearances to assent to is that our (material) souls are not properly configured. Julia Annas explains,

Appearances, on this view, will be the same for everyone in the journey from object to sense organ; but in the further journey from sense organ to mind they will be affected by the perceiver's overall state, which expresses itself in pneumatic tension. The ignoramus assents to a vague or wrong statement because only a vague or wrong appearance has made its way to the *hegemonikon*; information has been lost en route from sense organ to *hegemonikon* which in a person with more coherent and firmer beliefs, and thus stronger tension, would have been retained. Thus my perceptions, and hence my perceptual beliefs, are a function of two factors: the way the world impinges on me, and my overall psychic state.[126]

Finally, in their theory of the emotional behaviour of humans, Stoics looked on passions as movements in the (material) soul, and offered as one explanation for the dispassionate behaviour of sages that their souls were in a different physical condition than the souls of fools. As Annas argues, because emotions are weaknesses in the (material) soul, when a human achieves sagacity, '[l]ooked at from the physical point of view, the result is a literally strengthened character, with stronger pneumatic tension'.[127]

---

[123] Cf. Cicero, *De fato*, 38: 'How can that which is not true not be false? Or how can that which is not false not be true? We will hold fast to the position, defended by Chrysippus, that every proposition is either true or false' (L-S 34C).

[124] Cleanthes was one of the dissenters; he thought that all souls lasted until conflagration (see DL VII.157).

[125] *Evangelical Preparation* 15.20.6 (L-S 53W).   [126] Annas (1992), 83.

[127] Annas (1992), 107.

It should be evident by now that the change undergone by the human who becomes rational and, if he or she is so fortunate, sagacious, is complex. Rather than attempt to catalogue all it involves, it is more useful to step back from these individual trees and view the whole forest. In essence, when the individual becomes rational, she or he is transformed. And in essence, reason does the transforming. Whatever the transformation consists in, and however reason brings this transformation about, these are the notions that comprise the forest we have been exploring. Let us turn now to Spinoza, to see how much of this is true for him.

The present issue is not what the sage's sagacity consists of, nor how the person *qua* sage relates to her or his non-sage self; rather, it is the change itself that the individual experiences as he or she becomes wise. Unlike in Stoicism, where this change is discussed almost ad nauseam (hostile commentators such as Plutarch fasten on it as an instance of Stoicism's absurdity), Spinoza and his discussants have little to say about it. This is a case of silence speaking volumes. The fact that neither Spinoza nor his friends or foes bothered to examine the issue suggests that they did not think there was much of an issue to be examined. Either his views were obvious and unobjectionable, or he had no views and had no need of any (or, at any rate, was perceived as not needing any). Either way, it seems as if the issue of what happens when someone becomes a sage is a non-issue. If so, then there is, at the least, a difference between Spinozism and Stoicism over whether the transition to sagacity is philosophically interesting and controversial: in Spinozism, it seems not to be; in Stoicism, it seems that it is.

Nevertheless, even if the change is philosophically uninteresting, we might try to determine what it is. Since Spinoza himself says virtually nothing about it, a certain amount of speculation is necessary. The penultimate paragraph of the *Ethics* spurs one thought:

With this I have finished all the things I wished to show concerning the Mind's power over the affects and its Freedom. From what has been shown, it is clear how much more the Wise man is capable of, and how much more powerful he is than one who is ignorant and is driven only by lust. For not only is the ignorant man troubled in many ways by external causes, and unable ever to possess true peace of mind, but he also lives as if he knew neither himself, nor God, nor things; and as soon as he ceases to be acted on, he ceases to be. On the other hand, the wise man, insofar as he is considered as such, is hardly troubled in spirit, but being, by a certain eternal necessity, conscious of himself, and of God, and of things, he never ceases to be, but always possesses true peace of mind.[128]

---

[128] VP42S.

Notice the qualifier 'insofar as he is considered as such' (*quatenus ut talis consideratur*) in the last sentence. Spinoza is fond of such expressions; think of the 'insofar as it is conceived to follow necessarily' of ID8, the 'as far as it can by its own power' of IIIP6, the 'insofar as we are a part of Nature' of IVP2, etc.[129] While commentators understandably find these expressions beguiling, one thing is clear enough: they indicate Spinoza's comfort with the notion of perspective. In the present instance, 'insofar as he is considered as such' tells us that the sage is being considered in VP42S as a sage. Insofar as he is a sage, all that VP42S says will be true of him. But this is just insofar as he is a sage. From another perspective, VP42S might not be true at all. For instance, if he is considered not as a sage but as an ordinary human, he will be seen to be subject to the passions, limitations on power of acting, ignorance, and other woes afflicting the rest of us (see, e.g., IVP4Cor). Now, both of these perspectives are valid or applicable; the sage is both sagacious and ordinary. What happens when one becomes sagacious is that one becomes the subject of a new set of descriptions – the set describing the sage. It is not the case that the old descriptions no longer apply; it is rather that one is now capable of being described in more ways – in particular, as a sage. This is one change that occurs when one becomes sagacious.

At first, one might be tempted to think that something similar goes on in Stoicism. For Gellius writes, 'When some terrifying sound . . . or anything else of that kind occurs, even a [Stoic] wise man's mind must be slightly moved and contracted and frightened – not by a preconceived opinion of anything bad but by certain rapid and involuntary movements which forestall the proper function of mind and reason.'[130] If this were all, perhaps the Stoics' sage would be like Spinoza's; perhaps it could be said of him, too, that he is simply the subject of a new set of descriptions when he becomes wise. However, Gellius adds in the very next sentence: 'Soon, however, the wise man does not . . . assent to such impressions nor does he add an opinion to them, but he rejects and belittles them and finds nothing in them that should be feared.' The Stoic sage is still a human being and so subject to human impulses. His refusal to assent to false and inconclusive impressions, however, separates him from ordinary humans. Furthermore, unlike ordinary humans, he cannot be described as passionate at all; his unhealthy passions have been extirpated.[131] Given these remarkable abilities, it can seem that the Stoic sage is almost

---

[129] Don Garrett also draws attention to Spinoza's use of '*quatenus*' in Garrett (2008), 19 n. 20.
[130] *Noct. Attcc.* 19.1.17–18 (L-S 65Y1 (L-S's brackets)).
[131] Of course, he still experiences healthy passions (*eupatheiai*).

non-human,[132] that the Stoic sage *qua* sage has little or nothing in common with his non-sage persona. Stoics reinforce this impression by calling their sage 'godly' and the non-sage 'godless'.[133] Rather than allow the set of descriptions applicable to the non-sage to be expanded when he or she becomes a sage (in the way that Spinoza does), Stoics insist that the old set be replaced by a new set.

The change that the Spinozistic agent undergoes as she becomes sagacious cannot be abrupt because the sage is not moving between the contradictories of vice and virtue (as in Stoicism) but rather is progressing along a continuum from ignorance to knowledge and understanding. This is one place where Spinoza's emphasis on knowledge differentiates his philosophy from Stoicism. Unlike Descartes and, to a lesser extent, the Stoics, for whom knowledge is merely an instrument to the end of happiness, Spinoza makes knowledge itself constitutive of happiness. He writes in IVP26Dem, 'this striving for understanding . . . is the first and only foundation of virtue, nor do we strive to understand things for the sake of some end'. Again, with IVP28 he proves, 'Knowledge of God is the Mind's greatest good; its greatest virtue is to know God.' Since the increase of one's body of knowledge is gradual, occurring as one engages in the study recommended by the *Ethics*, Spinoza refuses to say that at time t one is foolish and at t + 1 wise. For him, at a certain stage in the progression of one's knowledge, one will know enough to be considered wise. But one can always learn more. Since it is only by knowing that we overcome our limitations, and since, as finite beings, we can never know everything, we will always be subject to the passions and other limitations on our action.

Moving on to the question of the origins of our reason, there are both theoretical and textual grounds for thinking that Spinoza took reason to be innate and not acquired. The theoretical grounds are these: the mind is the 'idea of the body'.[134] As such, at least two different types of ideas will comprise the mind. Some of the mind's ideas will be adventitious or derived from the body's experiences (e.g., those ideas derived from the senses). But others will not. Included in the latter are ideas about the general principles and laws of nature pertaining to the body, which apply to the body regardless of what happens to it. For example, the law of inertia always governs the body; since the mind is the idea of the body, it

---

[132] On the other hand, Stoics might say that non-sages are the ones who are non-human. As Margaret Graver argues, because the sage is the perfect human, 'becoming like the sage would be becoming more human, not less; it would be recognizable as human maturation' (Graver (2007), 51).

[133] DL VII.119 (trans. Hicks in Diogernes Laertius (1972)).   [134] IIP15Dem.

will have an idea of the law of inertia. Now, reason concerns this type of idea – the idea which is independent of adventitious experience.[135] Since these ideas are innate in us, and reason consists in the 'perceiving' of these ideas and 'forming notions' from them, the capacity to reason must also be innate, and not acquired.[136]

It would be tendentious to recount all of the textual grounds in support of this conclusion, so I shall just draw upon the *TdIE*. In general, the project of the *TdIE* is to teach the mind how to utilize properly its native endowments so that it might attain the highest good of which humans are capable.[137] As a result, it is critical for the mind to have certain ideas and abilities, since it is only by properly exploiting them that it can achieve happiness. In numerous places Spinoza ensures that the mind can reach its potential by explicitly endowing it with various ideas and abilities. For example, in §33 he writes, 'we have a true idea'. In §39, 'before all else there must be a true idea in us, as an inborn tool'. In §86, 'a true idea and other perceptions . . . arise from the very power of the mind'. And in §91, 'The aim, then, is to have pure and distinct ideas, i.e., such as have been made from the pure mind, and not from the fortuitous motions of the body.'

As with Descartes,[138] Spinoza took the mind to be embedded with assorted ideas (such as ideas of the laws of nature) and abilities (such as reason). This means not only that the mind is capable of developing these ideas and abilities but also that they are literally present in it from birth. We can find evidence of this in his reply to the following criticism of the *TdIE*'s basic project: 'Here, perhaps, someone will be surprised that, having said that a good Method is one which shows how the mind is to be directed according to the standard of a given true idea, we should prove this by reasoning. For that seems to show that this is not known through itself' (§43). To this objection Spinoza replies,

if, by some fate, someone had proceeded in this way in investigating Nature, i.e., by acquiring other ideas in the proper order, according to the standard of the given true idea, he would never have doubted the truth he possessed . . . and also everything would have flowed to him of its own accord. But because this never or rarely happens, I have been forced to lay things down in this way[.][139]

People are unaware of the presence in their minds of certain ideas and abilities because people are not good at self-examination and do not know

---

[135] IIP44Cor2.
[136] Surprisingly little has been written about innate ideas in Spinoza. My thoughts have been influenced most by tantalizing remarks in Wilson (1996), esp. 115–6 and n. 36.
[137] See, e.g., §§13–16, 18, 25.
[138] See especially *Meditation 3* (A-T VII, 37–8; CSM II, 26) and *Comments on a Certain Broadsheet* (A-T VIIIB, 358–9; CSM I, 303–4).
[139] *TdIE* §44.

the correct way to pursue knowledge. That is the point of the *TdIE*: to teach people how to use their native faculties correctly so that they can be their best.

Next, consider what Spinoza might make of the Stoic thesis that humans experience physical changes in their (material) souls as they become rational. Interpreted a certain way, the Stoic thesis is not laughable. If the Stoic 'soul' is equated with the brain and central nervous system, then since the brain and central nervous system do undergo substantial development from infancy to adulthood, the Stoic belief that the emergence of rationality corresponds to and depends upon a series of changes in the human body may seem quite reasonable. Caution is needed, then, in identifying the specific Stoic doctrine that is being examined. For it is one thing to criticize the literal original doctrine based on science which now seems quaint, ludicrous, or worse; it is another to attempt to keep the basic insight and update it (to the extent possible) so that it meshes with the best current understanding of the relevant data.[140] Of course, even if our sympathies incline us to the latter, more charitable approach, the Stoics may still come in for some criticism. They may seem to have constructed a defensible theory, but to have done so without justification, since they lacked the data necessary to support that theory.

Now, it is hard to imagine Spinoza embracing, warts and all, the original Stoic doctrine about the *pneuma* of the (material) soul increasing in tension as it becomes more developed and rational. For one reason, neither the concept of *pneuma* nor that of *pneuma*'s tension is defined purely extensionally. Since, in the Cartesian physics that Spinoza adopted, matter is simply extended substance, any conception of matter that attributes non-extensional properties to it is suspect. Further, Spinoza might have thought that *pneuma* and its tension are wedded to a science outmoded and inferior to the new mechanistic one. Stoic science may be preferable to Aristotelian, since it studiously avoids the obfuscations of substantial forms. But it does not start with the right first principles, and so cannot hope to reach unblemished conclusions. For these reasons and more, then, Spinoza would have been unlikely to endorse without reservation the concepts of *pneuma*, etc.

---

[140] I think that Annas (1992) – which balances careful, critical reading of the original texts against informed understanding of contemporary philosophy of mind to show the *philosophical* (and not just historical) interest in Stoic and Epicurean views of the mind – is proof of the viability of this admittedly very difficult project. Becker (1998) does something similar in ethics, ridding Stoic ethics of its unacceptable (to us) teleological components while retaining and updating its naturalism, rationalism, and other features.

At the same time, he *might* have endorsed these concepts *with* reservation. Some scholars have argued that the Stoic concept of *pneuma* has a counterpart in what came to be called 'aether' during the early modern period. Sambursky is one of these. He writes,

[certain texts suggest that] it was the Stoic theory of pneuma which led to the change in the usage of the term 'aether' which became of such historical significance. During the Middle Ages, when Aristotle reigned supreme, aether again became the element confined to the celestial spheres, but from the beginning of the seventeenth century on, the term was generally used to express the universal substance imbued with all the properties attributed to it by the Stoics . . . There are of course some important differences between the pneuma of the Stoics and the aether of the physicists at the beginning of the modern era . . . But the similarities are nevertheless striking . . . [141]

To the best of our knowledge, Spinoza never explicitly discusses *aether*. Since he accepted so much else of early modern physics, however, it is possible that he did this as well. To the extent that *aether* resembles *pneuma*, then, Spinoza would likely accept it, too.

There is one curious text that lends some support to this conclusion. In the *Treatise on the Emendation of the Intellect*, Spinoza writes,

For example, some of the Stoics heard, perhaps, the word *soul*, and also that the soul is immortal, which they only imagined confusedly; they also both imagined and at the same time understood that the most subtle bodies penetrate all others, and are not penetrated by any. Since they imagined all these things at once – while remaining certain of this axiom – they immediately became certain that the mind was those most subtle bodies and that those most subtle bodies were not divided, etc. (§74)

In the passage from which this excerpt is taken, Spinoza has been arguing for the importance of pursuing knowledge in a certain way. Even if one has ideas that are true, unless one uses those ideas correctly, one is prone to make mistakes.[142] As illustration, Spinoza invokes the Stoics. Rather than distinguishing 'the distinct [ideas] . . . from the confused' and considering 'all our perceptions according to the standard of a given true idea', Stoics employed ideas that were half-'imagined' and half-'understood'.[143] Failing to analyse them correctly and not doling them out in the right order, Stoics may have reached conclusions that were true, but they were certainly not justified, since they were not based on clear and distinct foundations.

To be sure, it is true that Stoics are criticized here; indeed, the only reason for their mention is that they provide fodder for his treatise on

---

[141] Sambursky (1959), 34–5. See also Long (1986), 158.   [142] *TdIE* §74.
[143] *TdIE* §§74–5.

method because they have breached proper epistemological protocol. It is also true that Spinoza runs together several different Stoic ideas or doctrines (the notion of the soul, its immortality, the theory of total blending, the soul's materiality), so it is unlikely that he had much of a grasp of Stoic physics. Neither of these considerations matters so much, however, as the awareness that Spinoza evinces of the Stoic thesis of the soul's materiality and his regard for it as meritorious. In his words, Stoics believed that the mind was 'subtle bodies', and this belief has some value, being based on ideas that are 'imagined and at the same time understood'. This text suggests that Spinoza might have applauded Stoic materialism and the attempt to explain the soul's development in physicalistic terms. Stoics got the physics wrong, and they reasoned crudely, but they were approaching the topic in roughly the right manner and may deserve credit for that.

Whatever the above passage from the *Treatise on the Emendation of the Intellect* may reveal about Spinoza's views on *pneuma*, it says nothing about Stoicism's beliefs on the physical *development* of the soul. Thus it cannot be used to speculate about Spinoza's views on this issue. There are, however, other grounds for thinking that Spinoza might have been sympathetic to them. Namely, given parallelism and given that the sage has more ideas in his mind than he did when he was a non-sage, it must be the case that the sage's body is changed. A text near the end of the *Ethics* seems to confirm this:

And really, he who, like an infant or child, has a Body capable of very few things, and very heavily dependent on external causes, has a Mind which considered solely in itself is conscious of almost nothing of itself, or of God, or of things. On the other hand, he who has a Body capable of a great many things, has a Mind which considered only in itself is very much conscious of itself, and of God, and of things.[144]

In this passage, Spinoza is relying on parallelism to go in the opposite direction from the one just stated: that is, he makes an inference about the nature of the mind of the person who has made progress towards happiness on the basis of the condition of this person's body. But it does not matter which way he goes – from mind to body, or body to mind – because parallelism sanctions inferences in either direction. It does seem that Spinoza believed the mind and the body of the person who advances towards sagacity are different – as he might say, they are more 'powerful' – than they were beforehand.

---

[144] VP39S.

3.4   Conclusion

It is time to wrap things up. This wide-ranging chapter has dealt with a number of issues. In Section 3.1, I corrected the long-standing belief that the closest Stoic equivalent to Spinoza's *conatus* was their concept of a *horme*. This is wrong because a *horme* is a single impulse issued on a particular occasion in response to specific stimuli which the agent receives from the world. Rather than a *horme*, the doctrine of *oikeiosis* is in fact more akin to *conatus*.

The rest of the chapter tried to determine just how akin *oikeiosis* is to *conatus*. In Section 3.2, I looked at the place of self-preservation in *oikeiosis* and *conatus*. I did not try to say whether there was more to *oikeiosis* and *conatus* than self-preservation; rather, I just wanted to know what self-preservation amounts to in each doctrine and how it is that each system establishes the existence of the self-preservation impulse. The question of whether self-preservation exhausts each doctrine was deferred to Section 3.3. For the Stoics, when an agent reaches the age where she could be wholly rational, then her end changes. It is no longer merely self-preservation; in addition, she seeks a greater self, the self defined by pure reason. By contrast, Spinoza does not think the agent acquires a different kind of end as she progresses towards sagacity. For her, the end is always maximizing her power. Spinoza does allow, however, that the agent progressing towards sagacity may realize that her power is best realized through living the life of reason. In this way, she may be said to understand her end in terms which are different from how she had previously conceived them.

Appendix: on the (in)coherency of Spinozism

The chapter could end at this point. As an appendix, though, I want to deal more with an issue that arose above. As I repeatedly stated, Stoicism holds that if the individual is successful in his quest for wisdom, he is somehow transformed, and that reason is the agent responsible for this transformation. At various points, I have argued that the same cannot be said of Spinoza. This, however, is contentious. In particular, it is sometimes said that Spinoza inconsistently argues both ways – that the agent who achieves sagacity is transformed and that he or she is not. Since this is such an important question, both for our understanding of Spinoza as well as for the comparison of his system to that of the Stoics, the matter ought to be pursued further. One of the best proponents of the inconsistency thesis is David Bidney. As an appendix to this chapter, I will present and evaluate his arguments. This material is clearly labelled

'Appendix', to indicate that is extraneous to the main argument and hence something that the reader may bypass if she wishes.[145]

In his book, Bidney emphasizes the debt of Spinoza's psychology and ethics to Plato, Aristotle, the Stoics, Scholastics, Jewish philosophers, Descartes, Hobbes, and others, while highlighting his innovations and pointing out where the weight of this ambitious project results in its collapse. He argues,

> Spinoza's greatness and vitality as a thinker . . . lie primarily in the fact that he more than any previous thinker attempted to combine together all the great philosophical traditions. If, as is the general theme of this study, his synthesis was not logically coherent, it should be remembered that no one has ever accomplished in systematic form what he failed to do.[146]

Bidney thinks that deep problems lurk in virtually all of Spinoza's important doctrines; in some cases, they are plagued by problems on several levels. Nowhere is this more true than with *conatus*.

When *conatus* first appears, Spinoza is commencing his study of human psychology proper. At this stage, Bidney says, 'his professed approach is a thoroughly naturalistic one. Human emotions are to be understood according to the same universal laws and rules as the rest of nature.'[147] It may also be the case that *conatus* as interpreted later in the *Ethics* is also 'thoroughly naturalistic'; but if so, Bidney argues, its naturalism would be very different from the naturalism of the other *conatus*. It is 'naturalistic in the radical sense of being in accord with all naturalistic *human* desires and aspirations . . . a naturalistic ethics [of the later *Ethics*] is one that is in accord with the laws of *human* nature as a whole'.[148] I have emphasized the word 'human'; the point is to stress the difference between this naturalism and the other. Here, ethics is still being conducted as a naturalistic science: Spinoza is still attempting to deduce ethical conclusions from metaphysical and other 'natural' premises; or, if you prefer, he still takes the job of ethics to consist in stating or describing certain 'natural' facts.[149] But the set of premises – or the set of facts that ethics

---

[145] I am grateful to an anonymous referee for helping me to recognize the distant connection between the Appendix and the main body of Chapter 3.

[146] Bidney (1962), 368.   [147] Bidney (1962), 23.

[148] Bidney (1962), 414 (my emphasis).

[149] Eisenberg (1977) identifies these two different kinds of ethical naturalists (see esp. 146–7). Unlike Frankena (whom he is criticizing), Eisenberg denies that Spinoza is either of these kinds of naturalists. I am not as convinced as Eisenberg that there is no overlap between these kinds (at least in Spinoza's case), so I state them both as different, possible, and not necessarily mutually exclusive, ways of being an ethical naturalist. The issue of naturalism arose in Chapter 2 (Section 2.4). It is taken up again in Chapter 4 (Section 4.5).

takes as its raw material – is more restricted. Whereas the naturalism of the early *conatus* pertains to the strivings of all beings, this *conatus* deals only with 'human desires and aspirations' and 'the laws of human nature'. That is, unlike the early *conatus*, it isolates humans from the rest of nature and, after setting them apart, applies to them and their attempts at self-preservation. In essence, the procedure or method by which Spinoza's psychology and ethics operate is constant throughout; it is the premises or data which he employs that change. According to Bidney, numerous problems ensue from this change.

On one level, Bidney links it to an ambiguity clouding the notion of self-preservation itself. The problem can best be seen as pertaining to the self that is being preserved. In Bidney's view, this shifts as the *Ethics* unfolds. He writes, '*In the first place he means the preservation of the individual considered as a psychophysical organism. In the second instance he means the preservation of the intellect which is the real or true self and principle of being and activity.*'[150] Elsewhere he elaborates:

[Spinoza] was the first of the moderns to identify the virtue of man with his power of self-preservation and hence anticipated the Darwinian doctrine of the 'survival of the fittest' . . . For Spinoza, as we have seen, self-preservation is the end of life; there is no transcendent good for the sake of which one lives . . . Spinoza, however, did not consistently hold to his biological naturalism . . . Man, he admitted, is not only a creature of emotions but also a rational animal that endeavors to understand the order of nature apart from any practical consequences for survival. Hence he modified his original thesis by saying that man's real or true efforts for self-preservation consist in his efforts to understand adequate ideas of which man alone is the adequate cause[.][151]

The alleged shift in the notion of self-preservation is problematic, because if the arguments that support *conatus* in Part III are valid at all, it is only under a certain interpretation of that doctrine. If Spinoza illicitly replaces that interpretation with another, then he either should also offer new arguments for it or show that the old arguments still apply. Since he fails to do either (probably because he is not aware of the alleged shift), one might wonder whether the later *conatus* has received adequate justification.

As bad as the alleged equivocations in the notion of *conatus* are, it is only when we move to another level of analysis and look at applications of *conatus* that (according to Bidney) the situation becomes truly dire. For example, Bidney thinks that Spinoza inconsistently argued both against and for the possibility of suicide. In keeping with his earlier conception of *conatus*, which made preservation of the (biological) self the impulse behind all action, Spinoza denied suicide's possibility in some texts

[150] Bidney (1962), 347 (his emphasis).   [151] Bidney (1962), 408.

(such as IVP20Sch). In others (such as IVP72Sch), however, he was influenced by his later conception of *conatus* and so argued not only for its possibility but also for its rectitude.[152] More broadly, Bidney argues that different conceptions of *conatus* led Spinoza to hold different (and inconsistent) interpretations of central moral concepts such as good and evil:

> Insofar as Spinoza regards the effort of self-preservation as the foundation of all virtue he defines the good in relation to this conatus. Whatever one regards as helping or hindering his power to exist is good or evil accordingly; the knowledge of good and evil is nothing but the perception of pleasure and pain (IVP8). Life is but a brief struggle for existence in competition with other modes . . . On the other hand, insofar as the essence of man is identified with the perfection of his intellect, we find Spinoza defines the true good (*verum bonum*) as primarily that which is useful for or conducive to understanding.[153]

Finally and most generally, Bidney thinks that these lesser inconsistencies led Spinoza to have different conceptions of the *summum bonum*. In some passages, he seems to argue that it consists in 'the effort of self-preservation'; in others, in 'the intuitive knowledge of the intellect'; in yet others, 'in the joy arising from [one's] power of activity'.[154]

While Bidney's arguments are interesting in themselves, my motivation for bringing them is that they are illustrative of a common response to Spinoza. Many commentators think that there is a deep tension in Spinoza, especially between the earlier parts of the *Ethics* and the later ones. Commentators cast this tension in different terms. For Bidney, the tension is between Spinoza's attempts to explain human action and norms in terms of efficient causality and his elevation of reason and knowledge as the greatest goods which humans can achieve. Bidney thinks these two commitments lead Spinoza into confusion and contradiction from the middle of Part IV onwards.[155]

For others, the tension centres on Part V, where Spinoza begins his notoriously difficult excursus into 'those things which pertain to the Mind's duration without relation to the body'.[156] Margaret Wilson could be speaking for these commentators when she writes, 'up until now Spinoza has consistently maintained the complete inseparability of mind from body: They are, after all, said to be "one and the same thing"

---

[152] Bidney (1962), 316–7.   [153] Bidney (1962), 343–4.   [154] Bidney (1962), 347.

[155] Other commentators who find roughly the same problem are Allison (1987), 149, and DeBrabander (2007), ch. 2. As DeBrabander puts it, 'Spinoza's description of blessedness in *Ethics* V seems to stray from his original account of virtue. Accordingly, he appears to arrive, like the Stoics, at an unabashed intellectualism, which would contradict the monism of his metaphysics' (39).

[156] As he puts it in VP20Sch.

[IIP7 S]. In [IIP8] (concerning "the ideas of non-existing modes") Spinoza even appears specifically to tie the duration of the mind to the duration of the body.'[157] Given his acceptance of these ideas, Wilson says, 'many have found [the end of Part V] a baffling fundamental departure from all that has gone before in the *Ethics*, even amounting to direct contradiction of previously stated doctrines'.[158] What response can be mustered to Bidney, Wilson, and others who think there is a deep tension, even incoherence, in the *Ethics*?

Because I have been dealing with Bidney, I will focus on him. His single greatest charge in support of his claim that the *Ethics* is incoherent concerns *conatus*. According to Bidney, Spinoza either severely modified or entirely abandoned *conatus* in the later *Ethics*. On Bidney's reading, he did so in favour of the idea that humans can be impelled by different forces: sometimes preservation of the (biological) self, sometimes a desire for knowledge and understanding that is not connected with self-preservation. Another way to state Bidney's interpretation is that Spinoza saw humans as having different ends. Bidney is not clear on whether these ends emerge as humans develop or whether they always obtained. That does not matter, however, since on the two crucial questions of whether humans can have singular or multiple ends, and what the higher-order end(s) might be, Spinoza gives Stoical answers. According to Bidney, his answers are: yes, they can; and, conformity with reason. Thus, if Bidney is right, some of the major grounds that have been identified for distinguishing Spinoza from the Stoics are washed away. So is Bidney right?

Here are two responses. First and very briefly, even if Bidney is right on all counts, self-preservation is still the force behind actions. We are driven at first to preserve ourselves as biological beings. Then, we are driven to preserve our intellects. Thus there is no acquisition of a new end: it is always preservation. Just as I argued in the earlier parts of this chapter, then, Spinozism differs from Stoicism in this respect.

Second, it is probably the case that Bidney misreads Spinoza if he thinks that it begins with one basic objective and ends with another. It may be that the *conatus* of the later *Ethics* is modified or defined in different terms than the *conatus* of IIIP6. But it does not follow that they are unrelated. In fact, Spinoza explicitly links them in certain texts, especially IVP26, where *conatus intelligendi* appears for the first time. IVP26 states, 'What we strive for from reason is nothing but

---

[157] Wilson (1996), 129.
[158] Wilson (1996), 129. Others who share Wilson's befuddlement include Bennett (1984), 7, and Curley (1988), 84.

understanding; nor does the Mind, insofar as it uses reason, judge anything else useful to itself except what leads to understanding.' Here and in the Demonstration, Spinoza attempts to deepen *conatus* – endowing it with properties it previously lacked – and he does so by tying *conatus intelligendi* with *conatus, simpliciter*. Consider a few lines from the Demonstration:

The striving to preserve itself is nothing but the essence of the thing itself (by IIIP7), which, insofar as it exists as it does, is conceived to have a force for persevering in existing (by IIIP6) . . . But the essence of reason is nothing but our Mind, insofar as it understands clearly and distinctly . . . Therefore (by IIP40) whatever we strive for from reason is nothing but understanding.

Next, since this striving of the Mind . . . is nothing but understanding (by the first part of this demonstration), this striving for understanding (by P22C) is the first and only foundation of virtue, nor do we strive to understand things for the sake of some end (by P25). On the contrary, the Mind, insofar as it reasons, cannot conceive anything to be good for itself except what leads to understanding (by D1), q.e.d.

Whereas *conatus* has hitherto been analysed in relation to the mind and body together, beginning with IVP26 it is related to and dissected in terms of the mind's striving to persevere in existence, what that means or consists in, and what is required for its success. This focus on the mind's *conatus* allows Spinoza to achieve a depth of analysis that previously was unavailable – not theoretically unavailable, but practically, since it would have been inordinately difficult to describe the *conatus* of mind and body simultaneously. Let me mention two of the results of this more specialized investigation.

First, as he shifts away from *conatus* of the mind–body combination, he begins his argument for reason's special value. This is connected to the *conatus* of the mind, because the mind not only utilizes reason in its quest for persevering in existence, but also is partly constituted by reason, insofar as reason is the mind's power of acting. Genevieve Lloyd nicely expresses how the awareness of reason's special value arises and what it amounts to:

Reason is an expression of human nature, and it arises from the complexity of bodily structure that distinguishes human bodies. It strengthens human powers, especially when pursued in collaboration with other rational beings . . . Cartesian minds rest their self-esteem on [the transcendence of the mind] and the prospects of control which go with it. Spinozistic minds rest their self-esteem on knowing their status as ideas of bodies of a sufficiently complex structure to allow the formation of the common notions of reasons.[159]

[159] Lloyd (1994), 158 and 159.

Whereas reason was previously valued primarily as an instrument (see, e.g., IVP17Sch), now Spinoza says that 'man's highest happiness, *or* [*sive*] blessedness' consists in the 'perfection' of 'our intellect, *or* [*sive*] reason' (IVAppIV).

Second, the discussion of *conatus* after IVP26 consists, in Yirmiyahu Yovel's words, in a 'striving not only to exist and enhance our power, but also to interpret our existence, to make sense of it, to endow it with *meaning*'.[160] As mentioned above, Bidney rightly points out that humans often seek knowledge and understanding, irrespective of whether such things contribute directly to their well-being and survival. The dimension of *conatus* identified by Yovel accommodates this impulse by incorporating the desire for seemingly impractical knowledge into *conatus*. It is not an unjustified expansion of *conatus*, for two reasons. First, because it is often difficult to predict what knowledge and understanding will be practically beneficial at some future point. So it may be that knowledge and understanding appeared impractical when acquired at time t but turn out to be practical at t + 1. Second, because even if knowledge and understanding never directly contribute in any practical way to the mind's well-being, they are sure to do so in indirect ways. As the old dictum states, 'knowledge is power'; for no one is this truer than Spinoza, who both equated the mind in important respects with its knowledge, and also believed that action follows knowledge and understanding.

All of Bidney's criticisms and misgivings about the coherency of Spinoza's project cannot be resolved here. So let me conclude this appendix with a simple assertion: the more one is attracted by Bidney's interpretation of Spinoza, the more Stoical Spinoza is likely to appear. One need not be persuaded by Bidney's arguments about the incoherency of Spinozism; one could think that Spinoza was Stoical, through-and-through (not just in the later parts of the *Ethics*). But if one does hold such a view, one will likely explain it in Bidney's terms.

---

[160] Yovel (1999b), 54 (his emphasis).

4   Value

> By good I shall understand what we certainly know to be useful to us.[1]

> The Stoics, sticking fast to the common conceptions so to speak, define the good as follows: 'Good is benefit or not other than benefit'[.][2]

As philosophical systems, Stoicism and Spinozism are practically oriented. The ultimate aim of each is to articulate and defend a conception of the nature of happiness and how it can be attained. Given that they took happiness to lie in conformity to nature – the happy life is the fulfilled life, which in turn is the life that possesses everything one needs to flourish, which is to say that it is the life fully agreeing with nature – they were required to explore the nature of value as such.[3] They could explain what it is for a life to conform to nature only if they could explain what is valuable about nature and why. This task required them to classify bearers of value as well as draw distinctions among types of value. Proof of the importance they attached to understanding the nature of value abounds in their writings.

For example, Spinoza writes:

After experience had taught me that all the things which regularly occur in ordinary life are empty and futile, and I saw that all the things which were the cause or object of my fear had nothing of good or bad in themselves, except insofar as [my] mind was moved by them, I resolved at last to try to find out whether there was anything which would be the true good, capable of communicating itself, and which alone would affect the mind, all others being rejected – whether there was something which, once found and acquired, would continuously give me the greatest joy, to eternity.[4]

In these opening lines of the *Treatise on the Emendation of the Intellect* (*TdIE*) – among the most stirring in all his corpus – Spinoza asks what, if anything, is

---

[1] IVD1.   [2] Sextus Empiricus, *AM* XI.22 (L-S 60G1).
[3] I argue that conformity to nature is the main tenet of Spinoza's ethics in Miller (2014). For the Stoics, see, e.g., Frede (1999), 79–80. I return to the idea that the best life is one lived in accordance with nature in Section 5.7 of Chapter 5.
[4] *TdIE* §1.

truly valuable. He returned to this question in many of his works, from the early *TdIE* and *Short Treatise* to his mature masterpiece, the *Ethics*.

For their part, the Stoics devoted just as much effort to axiology as Spinoza. Among many texts which could be cited as illustration is this passage from Stobaeus:

All things in accordance with nature have value and all things contrary to nature have disvalue. Value has three senses: a thing's contribution and merit *per se*, the expert's appraisal, and thirdly, what Antipater calls 'selective': according to this, when circumstances permit, we choose these particular things instead of those, for instance health instead of disease ... Disvalue, they say, also has three senses analogous to these.[5]

The twin problems of disambiguating value and arguing for the Stoa's preferred conception of the nature of value occupied Stoics, from the early Stoa to the end of the ancient school.[6]

In this chapter, I compare Spinoza's value theory with that of the Stoics'. My project begins by explaining what I mean by 'value theory'. Then I proceed through specific aspects of their theories. As I go through the issues, I will have in mind the notion that Spinoza differs from the Stoics more on axiological matters than on most other issues.[7] There are differences but if we understand both parties properly, I contend that their axiologies are often closer together than is sometimes allowed.

4.1   Value theory

Let me begin, then, with remarks concerning the subject matter before me.[8] The broadest questions facing value theory concern value *simpliciter*: what is value? What is it to be of value? What (if anything) is special about value claims, separating them from other claims? Because value theory when unqualified in any way is the inquiry into the nature of value as such, a theory of value can encompass much more than moral value. As we shall see, this is true of Spinoza. When he talks about value, he talks about value *tout court*.[9] At the same time, I shall argue in Section 4.3 that his theory of

---

[5] Stobaeus *Ecl.* II.83 (L-S 58D).
[6] For a succinct overview of this history, including mention of deviants from the Stoic orthodoxy (like Aristo), see Inwood (1999), 691–9.
[7] Such is Bidney's claim (see Bidney (1962), 317). It is also the view of DeBrabander (2007); see, e.g., 36.
[8] The following remarks make no claims to originality. Among the sources I have consulted are Hurka (2006) and Schroeder (2012).
[9] To be more accurate, Spinoza talks or writes about good and bad, not about value *per se*. I would argue, however, that his comments on good and bad can be retooled to be about value. So even if he does not use the word or cognate terms, we can discern a theory of value in what he does say. Thanks to an anonymous referee for pressing me on this point.

value distinguishes two broad types of values: non-moral and moral.[10] I shall argue that not only did he recognize the difference between the two types of values but also he defended the existence of each. On the other hand and unlike Spinoza, it is possible to conceive of value so that the only kind of value is moral value. That was the Stoic view.[11] So we shall find Spinoza and the Stoics clashing here.

Now, in the process of examining the nature of value, philosophers commonly find it necessary to draw distinctions among types or kinds of value. The most familiar distinction would be between intrinsic versus instrumental value but many others are also promulgated (e.g., instrumental values as the causal means to intrinsic values are sometimes distinguished from constitutive values, which are supposed to amount to intrinsic values).[12] In Section 4.2 and elsewhere, we shall find Spinoza and the Stoics engaged in this enterprise. Indeed, I shall argue in Section 4.4.1 that the key to understanding Spinoza's so-called relativistic theory of value is a previously overlooked distinction he draws between two kinds of unconditional value.

Mention of relativism takes me to the next preliminary point I wish to make. A key axiological problem concerns whether there are any bearers of value, in the strict sense of that word, and, if so, what they must be. One obvious dichotomy presents them as either (1) mental entities or (2) entities that exist outside the mind. Here, the opposition is between the view that the objects of value are (1) mind-dependent or (2) mind-independent. Now, if the objects of value are mind-dependent, then value proves to be relative, for it is only in relation to the mind that things can be said to be valuable. At the same time, however, if the objects of value are mind-dependent, it does not necessarily follow that value becomes 'subjective', in the sense of being dependent on the whims of individual mental agents. If value is mind-dependent in such a way that it is a feature of mentality as

---

[10] What I mean by 'moral' should hopefully become clearer in the pages that follow (see, e.g., the end of Section 4.3.2). Briefly, a good can be said to be of moral value iff it either benefits our ability to live a life according to nature (in which case it is morally good) or hinders our ability to live such a life (in which case it is morally bad). By contrast, a good is of non-moral value iff it neither benefits or hinders our ability to live a life according to nature.

[11] See, e.g., Epictetus, *Discourses* I.6.12–20. It is true that the Stoics mark a class of objects which, while not valuable strictly speaking, still have selective preference (see DL VII.101–3). This is a source of dispute among the school, which led some (notably Aristo of Chios) to deny that goods such as health or friends possess any kind of value. For Aristo, since the only value is moral value, and this is constituted by virtue alone, everything else possesses literally no value whatsoever. See, e.g., Sextus Empiricus, *AM* XI.64–7. I shall return to this in the next section.

[12] See Schroeder (2012), section 2.1, for more.

such, then there would be no variation from mind-to-mind, for all minds would find it to be the same.

Turning to (2), if the objects of value are mind-independent, value does not necessarily become non-relative, for value could exist only in relation to something else (perhaps a structural feature of the universe or, more commonly, God). Moreover, even if value is mind-independent, it could still be 'subjective' in the aforementioned sense. This would be the case if valuable things were valuable in relation to God. Indeed, this provides the impetus for a common objection to divine command theories of ethics. If moral properties such as 'good' are relative to God's will, then the content of the good could differ radically from its actual form. These considerations serve to undermine the assumption that theories of value which make it mind-dependent are contingent and variable psychological states while theories that take value to be mind-independent make it, *ipso facto*, to be necessary and immutable. The complex relation between the two opposed poles is vital to understanding how Spinoza's 'relativism' compares to the Stoics' 'absolutism'. I deal with this especially in Section 4.4.

The final issue that I wish to flag is connected to the foregoing. Are values factual or not? Given his identification of a certain kind of value as a consequence of human nature, and given his necessaritarianism, I shall argue in Section 4.5 that Spinoza regarded some values as facts. The same is true of the Stoics, though for different reasons.

While value theory can address many more issues than those that I have just adumbrated, I will content myself with an examination of them. So I will start by looking for evidence of whether the theories advanced by either Spinoza or the Stoics differentiate moral value from other kinds of value. Then I shall argue for the existence of a distinction in Spinoza between two kinds of unconditional value and I shall ask whether we can find anything analogous in the Stoics. This will lead me to the next major comparand: viz., Spinoza's value relativism with the Stoics' absolutism about value. I will wrap up with the facticity of values.

4.2   Three categories of value

Let me begin with a basic but crucial distinction both Spinoza and the Stoics make between three categories of value.[13] In IVP31Dem Spinoza

---

[13] Indeed, this distinction is so basic that many others have advanced their own versions. Two ancient examples are Plato and Aristotle. For Plato, see, e.g., *Laws* 697a–b and DL III.81. For Aristotle, see, e.g., *Nicomachean Ethics* I.8 and the pseudo-Aristotle text *Divisiones Aristoteleae* I.1. In the middle ages, it was advanced by many philosophers.

says, 'Insofar as a thing agrees with our nature, it cannot be bad (by P30). So it must be either good or indifferent.' According to Spinoza, bivalence does not apply to the value that goods might have for their possessors. Instead of things being either good or not good, there are three categories of value: good, not-good, and neither good nor not-good. To use his terminology, things are good (*bonus*) when they 'agree with our nature'. If a thing disagrees with our nature, it is bad (*malus*). If it neither agrees nor disagrees, it is indifferent (*indifferens*).

The same distinction is accepted by most Stoics.[14] For example, we read in Diogenes Laertius, 'They [the Stoics] say that some existing things are good, others are bad, and others are neither of these.'[15] The value granted to a thing is determined by whether it accords with the nature of the being who possesses it. As Stobaeus says, 'All things in accordance with nature have value and all things contrary to nature have disvalue.'[16] This division of goods into three values is completely general; it would reveal which kind of value a good has for any kind of creature, whether it is a bird or a human. Of course, its most important application is to us. Since our nature is reason, then any good that accords with reason is valuable and any which clashes with reason has disvalue or is bad.

One difference between Spinoza and the Stoics is that the latter have more fully developed this tripartite division of value.[17] This shows especially in the work they did on the middle category of goods, those which are neither good nor bad. Here some Stoics offer a further tripartite division. As Stobaeus says, 'Some [indifferent things] are in accordance with nature, others are contrary to nature, and others are neither of these.'[18] Because goods such as health or wealth are not part of reason, they are not truly good. At the same time, they address our primary needs and so should be

---

See, e.g., Aquinas, *Commentary on Aristotle's Nicomachean Ethics*, Lecture XII (on *NE* 1098b9–1099a7), section 142, and Giles of Rome, *On the Instruction of Rulers and the Governance of Kings*, I.3. It was also articulated in the early modern period by Descartes, among others. See, e.g., his letter to Elizabeth of 1 September 1645. My point in mentioning these various sources is to underscore that there is nothing special about the distinction itself. What matters is how the distinction is explained.

[14] Not all. As I noted above (see n. 11), Aristo of Chios is one exception who argued that there are just two categories of value: good and not-good, or bad. I will set him aside as outside the Stoic orthodoxy.

[15] DL VII.101.   [16] *Ecl.* II.83.10–11.

[17] Orthodox Stoics are normally said to hold a tripartite division of value whereas heterodox ones such as Aristo are said to have a bipartite division. A different description is also available. According to this, Aristo and other heterodox did have a threefold division (good, bad, absolutely indifferent) while the others had a fourfold division (good, bad, indifferent-but-preferred-or-dispreferred, absolutely indifferent). This description is entirely consistent with what I say in the text and so I will not unnecessarily complicate my task by adding it to the comparison I am making.

[18] *Ecl.* II.79.18–19.

thought of as preferred to their opposites (illness and poverty). While some goods in this middle category of goods are preferred and others dispreferred, still others are truly indifferent. Our ability to flourish is not at all affected by whether there is an odd or even number of hairs on our heads,[19] so this good is absolutely indifferent.

Indeed, the existence of indifferents was so important to Stoics that they offered a variety of ways of understanding it. Just now I mentioned Stobaeus' report; it is of the early Stoa. In Epictetus (a late Stoic), we find a different take. For Epictetus things are divisible into two categories: those which are 'up to us' (*eph' hēmin*) and those which are 'not up to us' (*ouk eph' hēmin*). He opens his *Enchiridion* by declaring, 'Some things are up to us and some are not up to us. Our opinions are up to us, and our impulses, desires, aversions – in short, whatever is our own doing. Our bodies are not up to us, nor are our possessions, our reputations, or our public offices, or, that is, whatever is not our own doing.'[20] It is consistent with Epictetus' account that some things which are not up to us would be more preferable than their opposites; he does not say, for example, that there is no difference between having possessions and not. At the same time, he thinks that our focus ought to be things that are up to us.[21]

Now, Spinoza would agree with the Stoics on the status of indifferents. In one passage, he even offers a distinction which is reminiscent of Epictetus':

> But human power is very limited and infinitely surpassed by the power of external causes. So we do not have an absolute power to adapt things outside us to our use. Nevertheless, we shall bear calmly those things that happen to us contrary to what the principle of our advantage demands, if we are conscious that we have done our duty, that the power we have could not have extended itself to the point where we could have avoided those things, and that we are a part of the whole of nature, whose order we follow.[22]

For Spinoza as for Epictetus, there is a basic difference between things that are 'outside us' and those that are inside us. Given our frailties and the overwhelming power of the causal system we inhabit, our desires for

---

[19] The example comes from DL VII.105.

[20] *Enchiridion* I.1 (trans. White in Epictetus (1983)).

[21] Michael Frede argues that there is a further significance to Epictetus. He writes, 'In classical Stoicism the phrase "up to us" (*eph' hēmin*) is used in such a way that an action is up to us if its getting done is a matter of our giving assent to the corresponding impulsive impression . . . But Epictetus uses "up to us" in a much narrower way. He insists on taking account of the fact that no external action in the world is entirely under our control . . . This had been assumed by the Stoics all along, so Epictetus' narrowing of the use of "up to us" hardly constitutes a change in doctrine but rather a shift in emphasis or focus' (Frede (2011), 45).

[22] IVAppXXXII.

external goods will inevitably be frustrated. However, we need not be bothered by this, so long as we keep what is inside us in good order.[23]

So Spinoza creates the same conceptual space for indifferents as the Stoics. He seems aware of the difference among indifferents, for he takes some to be more valuable than others.[24] He also acknowledges different ways in which indifferents can be valuable.[25] He even provides robust lists of indifferents, lists which can help to expand his notion of indifferents.[26] Though he does all of this, he does not directly theorize about the nature of indifferents in the way that the Stoics do. There may be good reason why the Stoics did so whereas Spinoza did not: the Stoics were vigorously attacked on this very issue whereas (so far as I am aware) no one ever pressed Spinoza on it. Still, whatever the reason, we ought to acknowledge that this aspect of Stoic axiology (i.e., the notion of indifferents) is much more articulated and hence sophisticated than Spinoza's.[27]

4.3   On the normativity of the good

4.3.1 Be that as it may, let me turn attention now to notion of the truly good. In Stoicism, a thing is placed in this category based on whether it benefits its possessor (for simplicity's sake, let us make the possessor be a human).[28] A good can benefit a human only by impacting her ability to lead a life according to nature.[29] The ability to lead a life according to nature is the greatest accomplishment that any human can hope for.[30] It constitutes a full flourishing of human nature. Since human nature is

[23] As I noted in Section 6 of my Introduction, a copy of the *Enchiridion* was in Spinoza's library; it is tempting to think he was drawn to it. I might also note that Descartes says something very similar in his 1645 correspondence with Elizabeth. See, e.g., the letter of 4 August 1645. I shall return to the notion of what is up to us, and the implications which follow from how a philosopher answers that question, in Chapter 5, Section 5.6.3.
[24] For example, he singles out health and 'mechanics' as particularly important indifferents in *TdIE* §15.
[25] See, e.g., the footnote to *TdIE* §4. In the body of the text he writes, 'The mind is also distracted not a little by the pursuit of honours and wealth, particularly when the latter is sought only for its own sake.' In a note attached to this sentence Spinoza says, 'I could explain this more fully and distinctly, by distinguishing wealth that is sought for its own sake, or for the sake of honour, or for the sake of sensual pleasure or for the sake of health and the advancement of the arts and sciences. But I reserve this for its own place; such an exact investigation is not appropriate here.'
[26] See, e.g., IVP45Cor2Sch.
[27] There is more to say about this. I shall return to it in the next chapter.
[28] See, e.g., Sextus Empiricus, *AM* XI.22.   [29] See, e.g., Stobaeus *Ecl.* II.83.10.
[30] Stoics use the eudaimonistic parlance, describing living a life in accordance with nature as 'the end, for the sake of which everything is done, but which is not itself done for the sake of anything' (Stobaeus *Ecl.* II.77.16–17 (L-S 63A1)).

reason, the life according to nature is the rational life and nothing more.[31] The virtues are those means by which one can conform to nature.[32] By contrast, insofar as one is vicious, one is opposed to nature. Everything else apart from virtues and vices is strictly speaking indifferent to one's ability to follow nature. This explains why virtue, and virtue alone, is good, vice, and vice alone, is bad, and all other goods are indifferent.

One recent commentator has called the Stoics 'value monists' precisely because they hold that the only good is virtue.[33] For Stoics, if they are speaking literally, to say that a thing is good is just to say that it is morally good. I shall not belabour this point. Instead, I shall ask whether the truly good and truly bad are, in Spinoza, things of *moral* value.

4.3.2 At the onset, I should note that in the opinion of some Spinoza commentators, there is also a value monism in Spinoza. However, it is the exact inverse of the value monism found in Stoicism, for while Stoics are value monists in the sense that they think all goods are *moral* goods, some Spinoza commentators hold that for Spinoza, all goods are *non-moral* goods. As William Frankena has written, 'one has only to look at Spinoza's official definition of "good" to see that it is a nonmoral term'.[34] According to Frankena, Spinoza allows there are good things but all good things prove to be those which are useful aids to one's power of acting. As such, the value that they possess is merely prudential value; it is not moral. Frankena says, 'Spinoza is in effect giving up moral talk except for the multitude who do not live by the dictates of reason as he sees them.'[35] I think Spinoza's position is more nuanced than this, which I shall now try to show. To make my case, I need some texts.[36]

In an important passage from IVPref Spinoza writes,

As far as good and evil are concerned, they also indicate nothing positive in things, considered in themselves, nor are they anything other than modes of thinking, or [*seu*] notions we form because we compare things to one another. For one and the same thing can, at the same time, be good, and bad, and also indifferent. For

---

[31] See, e.g., Seneca *Ep.* 76.9. I shall return to this passage in the conclusion of this chapter.
[32] See, e.g., DL VII.89.
[33] Shields (2012), 182. Shields is aware of the notion of preferred indifferents and the value attached to them. In calling Stoics value monists, Shields is emphasizing the enormous gulf between virtue and other so-called goods such as health and wealth.
[34] Frankena (1975), 95. More recent commentators who would side with Frankena and who offer more subtle readings of Spinoza include Garrett (1996b), at 286, and Steinberg (2013), section 2.3.
[35] Frankena (1975), 96.
[36] In addition to the texts from the *Ethics* that I quote, there is also a prolonged discussion in the *Short Treatise* (Part I, ch. X). I omit it here on the grounds that the views expressed there differ significantly from those of the *Ethics*.

example, Music is good for one who is Melancholy, bad for one who is mourning, and neither good nor bad to one who is deaf.

But though this is so, still we must retain these words. For because we desire to form an idea of man, as a model of human nature which we may look to, it will be useful to us to retain these words with the meaning I have indicated. In what follows, therefore, I shall understand by good what we know certainly is a means by which we may approach nearer and nearer to the model of human nature that we set before ourselves. By bad, what we certainly know prevents us from becoming like that model.[37]

Shortly after, he introduces IVD1 and D2.

IVD1: By good [*bonus*] I shall understand what we certainly know to be useful to us.

IVD2: By bad [*malus*], however, I shall understand what we certainly know prevents us from being masters of some good.

Finally, there's IVP8:

IVP8: The knowledge of good and bad is nothing but an affect of Joy or Sadness, insofar as we are conscious of it.

DEM: We call good, or bad, what is useful to, or harmful to, preserving our being . . .

The notions of good and bad are important to Spinoza, so I could cite many more texts. Rather than extend the quotations, however, let me provide some observations about them.

People do use the words 'good' and 'bad'; unfortunately, they use them incorrectly. Part of Spinoza's programme is therefore revisionary, urging his readers to drop the vulgar usage in favour of the correct one. This point is important, as it shows that Spinoza's value theory is not merely descriptive.[38] He is not merely telling us how the words are used. He takes this as a goal but in addition, he wants to argue for the *right* way to use them. The right way to use the word 'good' is to apply it to whatever 'we know certainly is a means' to becoming more like the ideal human being. 'Bad' is to be applied to whatever impedes our progress towards that goal.

Now, it is helpful to know the abstract nature of goodness and badness. As a practical matter, however, we might want more concrete guidance, we might want to be told what things can help us become more perfect. Spinoza provides this guidance. Insofar as we are bodies, the things which are useful and hence good for us are those things 'which bring about the preservation of the proportion of motion and rest that the human Body's parts have to one another'.[39] To make sure his meaning is not lost, Spinoza provides examples of such things a few pages later:

---

[37] G II 208: 8–22.   [38] For more on this, see Eisenberg (1977), 148.   [39] IVP39 (part).

It is the part of a wise man, I say, to refresh and restore himself in moderation with pleasant food and drink, with scents, with the beauty of green plants, with decoration, music, sports, the theatre, and other things of this kind, which anyone can use without injury to another. For the human Body is composed of a great many parts of different natures, which constantly require new and varied nourishment, so that the whole Body may be equally capable of all the things which can follow from its nature, and hence, so that the Mind also may be equally capable of understanding many things.[40]

If we consider ourselves under the attribute of thought, then we are minds. The mind is made up of ideas.[41] Because Spinoza takes 'idea' to be synonymous with 'knowledge', the mind must be comprised of knowledge. Given that the mind is knowledge, knowing or understanding must be its peculiar power.[42] Now, because the mind is an aggregate of related knowledge and its peculiar power is knowing or understanding, what is useful to the mind will be knowledge or understanding. As Spinoza says, 'What we strive for from reason is nothing but understanding; nor does the Mind, insofar as it uses reason, judge anything else useful to itself except what leads to understanding.'[43] Since what is useful to the mind is 'what leads to understanding' and given that useful things are good, things are good (or bad) for the mind only insofar as they further its capacity for knowledge or understanding. As Spinoza says, 'We know nothing to be certainly good or bad, except what really leads to understanding or what can prevent us from understanding.'[44]

Of course, there are many possible objects of knowledge or understanding: we could spend our time learning hockey statistics or how to play a video game. However, the basic justification for the acquisition of knowledge or understanding must be, for Spinoza, that it will increase our power of action, for this is how we approach our goal of being a model human. We might increase our power of action in certain respects or contexts by knowing more about hockey, but the effects of such knowledge are bound to be limited. For knowledge to be more versatile, useful in a wider range of circumstances, it must be about an object that itself has a richer nature. In general, the rule for determining the utility of an item of knowledge would be: the greater the propositional or conceptual content of the essence of the thing being known, the more the useful knowledge or understanding of such a thing will be. Since nothing has a richer essence

---

[40] IVP45Cor2Sch.
[41] For more on how ideas make up the mind, see Alanen (2011). I shall return to the nature of the mind in Section 4.4.1 below.
[42] As Spinoza says, 'the power of the Mind is defined only by understanding' (VPref (at G II 280: 22)).
[43] IVP26.   [44] IVP27.

than God, 'the greatest thing the Mind can understand is God'.[45] That is, 'Knowledge of God is the Mind's greatest good; its greatest virtue is to know God.'[46]

So that is the nature of the good for a human. Something is good if and only if it helps us approach our conception of a model human being. Nourishing food is therefore good; junk food is bad. Understanding (especially understanding God) is good; whatever blocks understanding is bad. Now that we are clear on this, we can return to the question raised above. According to Spinoza, what is the normative status of things that are good?

To simplify matters, I shall set aside those things that are good for us *qua* extended beings.[47] Instead, I shall focus solely on those things that are good for us *qua* thinking beings. This is knowledge or understanding. Now, I do not deny that much knowledge or understanding will be useful for instrumental reasons. While there may be some intrinsic value to knowing how to read a map, there is also instrumental value, as it helps me reach my destination. At the same time, there is other knowledge that is solely of intrinsic value. In IVP26Dem Spinoza writes, 'nor do we strive to understand things for the sake of some end (by P25)'. It is true that Spinoza speaks of understanding without qualification. In this part of the *Ethics*, however, he is specifically addressing the value of understanding God. So I take it he has that particular kind of understanding in mind. If so, then he is saying that understanding God is something we strive to possess solely for its own sake. If that is correct, then it seems that knowledge or understanding of God is a good that has value not for prudential or instrumental reasons. Rather, it is of direct value, in itself.[48] As such, it seems that knowledge or understanding of God is a good that has moral value. As Spinoza says in the *Theological–Political Treatise*, 'our supreme good [*summum nostrum bonum*], not merely depends on the knowledge of God but consists entirely therein'.[49]

There is another way to put the difference between knowledge or understanding that is good but not morally good, versus knowledge or understanding that is good in the moral sense. Knowledge or understanding that

---

[45] IVP28Dem.   [46] IVP28.

[47] I will return to this in Chapter 5, Section 5.6.2–3. Though I disagree with it, there is an interesting discussion of the good for us *qua* extended beings in Kisner (2011), 78–9.

[48] Commenting on this passage, Michael LeBuffe places Spinoza directly in the *eudaimonic* tradition to which the Stoics belong. He writes, 'Understanding then is for Spinoza a complete good in the traditional sense of a good that is to be sought for its own sake, and the best among complete goods, the summum bonum, is the knowledge of God' (LeBuffe (2010), 164).

[49] *TTP* ch. 4 (at G III, 60). I shall return to this passage in the conclusion of this chapter.

is good in the moral sense is constitutive of our perfection.[50] Knowledge or understanding of God is good and it is morally good, because when we know God, we are attaining the highest degree of flourishing possible for us as human beings. No other knowledge or understanding does this for us.[51]

Given the foregoing, we have an answer to the question posed above. The good of the mind is knowledge or understanding, and some knowledge or understanding does have moral worth. So just like the Stoics, when Spinoza speaks of the good for the mind, he can be taken to mean the *morally* good.[52]

4.3.3 I have just argued that Spinoza's conception of the good is similar to the Stoics, insofar as (like the Stoics) he thinks that the good can be morally good. To conclude this section, I want to note how Spinoza's theory of value differs from the Stoics. According to Spinoza, a good is valuable for its possessor only in the case that it is useful to that person or thing. Such is what he takes value to be. This holds whether we are talking about seemingly factual matters (fuel is valuable for a ferry because it provides energy for the engines) or seemingly normative ones (knowledge of God is valuable because we find in it our best condition). All value is in its essence the same. Some goods can have moral value, however, because of the way in which they are of use to their possessors. In particular, those goods which have moral value are useful because they constitute our perfection.

It seems, then, that Spinoza acknowledged two kinds of value: non-moral and moral. In this he differs from the Stoics. At the end of Section 4.3.1 I borrowed the term 'value monism' to describe Stoic axiology. It seems that Spinoza is not a value monist. Instead, he is a value dualist.

---

[50] Irwin writes similarly, 'Once we grasp the connexion between happiness and intellectual perfection, we can reject Hobbes's purely instrumental attitude to the moral virtues. Spinoza believes that virtue deserves to be chosen for its own sake. He disagrees . . . with Hobbes, who believes it is worthwhile only for its natural consequences . . . All those who take an instrumental attitude toward moral virtue fail to see that, as Spinoza understands it, it is the greatest happiness' (Irwin (2007–9), vol. II, 199).

[51] I shall return to knowledge of God below.

[52] To be clear, I am not only asserting that knowledge of God is of moral value but also that it is different in kind from all other types of knowledge. So I disagree with those like Kisner, for example, who think that (as Kisner nicely puts it), 'Spinoza does not recognize a category of peculiarly moral goods: being just, moral or fair is valuable in the same way as a nice car, a cup of tea or a vacation. Any distinction among these goods must be one of degree, rather than kind' (Kisner (2011), 81). I don't know about the difference between being just versus having a nice car. However, I maintain that there is a difference in kind between the value attached to knowledge of God versus everything else. Because knowledge of God is always and necessarily useful, it is qualitatively different on Spinoza's own terms from all other goods.

4.4   Relativism versus absolutism

In his magisterial *The Psychology and Ethics of Spinoza*, David Bidney notices the affinities between Spinozism and Stoicism. While he thinks that Spinoza's Stoical proclivities are often fully compatible with his own presuppositions, Bidney argues that sometimes Spinoza's Stoicalness comes at great cost to his system. Nowhere is this truer than on the matter of value. Summing up the problem, Bidney writes, '*Spinoza's Stoic rationalism with its acknowledgment of absolute moral standards is incompatible with his biological naturalism which teaches the complete relativity of all good and evil, virtue and vice, to the requirements of self-preservation.*'[53]

Though he does not bring in the Stoics, Steven Nadler has more recently echoed Bidney's concerns. There is, Nadler says, 'a notorious problem in interpreting Spinoza's ethical theory'.[54] On the one hand, Nadler says, Spinoza speaks of 'good' and 'evil' as 'only relative to our conceptions of things, and they do not denote anything real about things in themselves', while on the other hand, he talks about 'the "true knowledge of good and evil"', thereby suggesting that there is something real about things which can make normative statements about them truth-susceptible.[55]

In this section, I want to address this problem. My strategy is simple. I want to show that Spinoza's axiology is more absolutist than Bidney allows while that of the Stoics contains more relativistic elements. I will start with Spinoza.

4.4.1   Spinoza's non-circumstantially variable relativism

Given the importance that Spinoza assigns to value in his writings, it should not be surprising that his answers have been the subject of a number of studies.[56] For all their differences, however, there is a common theme to these studies: that Spinoza was a relativist about value. Disputes about how, precisely, his relativism ought to be understood have kept the ink flowing but there has been essential agreement among most commentators that value obtains solely in relation to us.

As noted below, there are texts in support of a relativistic interpretation. Yet there are others which suggest that Spinoza was not an unqualified relativist. He speaks in the *TdIE* of the successful completion of his quest

---

[53] Bidney (1962), 317 (his emphasis).   [54] Nadler (2001b), 69.
[55] Ibid. I should note that Nadler thinks the problem has a solution, which he seeks to argue for in his piece.
[56] These include: Wolfson (1934), esp. 437 ff.; Bidney (1962), esp. ch. XV; Curley (1973); Frankena (1975); Bennett (1984), ch. 12; Garrett (1996b); Jarrett (2002).

for a 'true good' (and, in addition, a 'highest good').[57] In the *Ethics* he says that some things are 'certainly good or bad' (IVP27) and something is 'necessarily good' which 'agrees with our nature' (IVP31). Texts like these (and others to be cited below) are hard to fit into an unqualified relativistic framework, where value is not obviously thought of as 'true' or 'certain' or 'necessary'. Indeed, texts like these have led some of the best Spinoza commentators to conclude that his thoughts on value are incoherent. *Vide* Bidney and Nadler, op. cit.

Now, I do not disagree with the relativistic interpretation but I do maintain that, for it to do justice to Spinoza's thought, a distinction previously unnoticed must be acknowledged. Taken broadly, relativism about value may be defined as the view that a good x is valuable iff x is valuable to or for some subject S. Within this definition, we may distinguish between non-circumstantial versus circumstantial relativisms.

(1) Non-circumstantial relativism: the view that a good x is valuable iff x is valuable for some subject S, irrespective of S's actual or possible circumstances.

(2) Circumstantial relativism: the view that x is valuable iff x is valuable for S, given S's actual or possible circumstances.

The significance of the distinction between (1) and (2) lies in the relevance of S's circumstances to the value that x has for S. According to (1), S's circumstances are irrelevant to x's value, with the result that x will always have value for S, whereas (2) stipulates the relevance of S's circumstances to x's value: x may or may not have value for S, depending on her or his circumstances. Even though they differ in this respect, (1) and (2) are still relativistic theories of value, since both of them make value relative to the subject S.[58]

Most relativistic interpretations of Spinoza are circumstantial because they link determinations of value to the agent's circumstances. This is true of Jarrett, who argues that value is derived from or determined by the actions of a particular agent pursuing a particular goal at a particular time.[59] On Jarrett's account, if you change any of the circumstantial factors – the agent or the goal or the time – you might get a different

---

[57] *TdIE* §13.

[58] Though there are certain affinities between them, non-circumstantial relativism must be distinguished from an absolutist or non-relativistic theory of value. Like the former, the non-relativistic theory does not tie value to circumstances. In addition, however, non-relativism takes the significant extra step of severing *all* ties between value and the subject. While non-circumstantial relativism holds that goods can only have value for the subjects who possess them, non-relativism contends that there are goods which have value, *simpliciter*.

[59] See Jarrett (2002).

value-determination. Consider the music example from IVPref. In some circumstances music will be good whereas in others it will not: it may help distract one person from her headache and so be good for her while causing a headache in another person and so be bad for him. What makes music valuable, Spinoza says here, is not something innate to music itself; rather, its value is entirely dependent on the conditions and natures of those who hear it. Texts where Spinoza made value dependent on circumstances can be multiplied to such an extent that it is impossible to deny that he took many goods to have their values circumstantially determined.[60] The only real question is whether this is true for *all* goods.

An important passage of IVP18Sch forces this question on us. In the passage in question, Spinoza writes that reason demands everyone should seek 'what is truly useful to him' (*quod revera utile est*). Because reason does not issue demands which cannot be achieved, there must be things which are 'truly useful' to us. The question to be answered is – what does Spinoza mean by 'truly'? Two interpretations suggest themselves. First, a good x can be truly useful to someone if and only if it helps him obtain his goals, given the exigencies of his circumstances. For example, water may be truly useful to a thirsty person, or a new friend may be truly useful to a lonely person, just because of the thirst or loneliness. To someone who is not thirsty or lonely, it is possible that neither water nor new friendship would be truly useful. The second interpretation takes the 'truly' to mean that the good x is not possibly not useful. If x is not possibly not useful, it is necessarily useful. To say that something is necessarily useful is to say that it is useful without condition or regardless of circumstance. To say this is to say that it is non-circumstantially valuable.

Now, when this passage from IVP18Sch is taken out of context, it must be admitted both interpretations can be given of it: there is nothing in the wording or ideas which favours one reading over the other. Placed in context, however, it seems to me that the second is more natural. For in this part of the Scholium Spinoza is emphasizing the unconditionality or (as he calls it) 'absoluteness' of the demands that reason places on rational agents. Given that reason's demands are unequivocal – they apply across circumstances – it seems natural to suppose that at least some of the goods which might help us to meet those demands will also be available in all circumstances.

Though IVP18Sch seems to imply that there are non-circumstantially relatively valuable goods, the implication is not incontestable. Other texts are less ambiguous. For example, Spinoza writes in IVP27, 'We know

---

[60] See, e.g., IIIP39S, IIIP59S, IVP65Dem, IVP68.

nothing to be certainly good or bad, except what really leads to under-standing or what can prevent us from understanding.' The key word here is certainly (*certò*): that which leads to understanding is certainly good. Some things – say, water or friendship – may not be certainly good; they may be only uncertainly good, because they may be useful only at specific times. But anything which does certainly aid our quest for understanding is certainly good. There is no need to consider what is going on in our lives: if something increases our body of knowledge, it is sure to be useful and hence valuable; if it impedes knowledge acquisition, it is definitely harmful. The irrelevance of circumstances to the utility and value of epistemically beneficial goods places them in a different axiological cate-gory from non-epistemic goods.

Other problematic texts for the circumstantially relative interpretation could be cited[61] but it will be more instructive to build a positive case for a non-circumstantially relative reading. Essentially, the positive case sees Spinoza as believing in some non-circumstantially relatively valuable goods because of his views on human nature. The argument is this:

(1) Human nature can be properly conceived in terms of the nature of the human mind.
(2) The human mind is, by nature, knowledge.
(3) Knowledge is benefitted by knowledge.
(4) Because that which benefits is valuable, knowledge is valuable.
(5) Because of how our *conatus* is constructed, there is some knowledge which is always useful.
(6) So this knowledge is non-circumstantially valuable.

Since this forms the core of the non-circumstantially relative reading, let us go through it systematically, examining each step and its connection to the others.

The first premise relies on parallelism, which sanctions the perception of individual modes under any of the attributes of substance: one and the same mode can be perceived as a thinking being or as an extended being. Regardless of which way the mode is perceived, an account can be given of its nature in the terms provided by that perception. So when a mode

---

[61] For a subtle attempt to read the passage of IVPref quoted above in terms favourable to the non-circumstantial relativist, see Curley (1988), 122–4. Curley himself is not arguing for a non-circumstantial relativistic reading; he shows no sign of being aware of the distinction between circumstantial versus non-circumstantial relativism, and in any case his purpose is to defend the claim that the notion of a human exemplar plays an important role in Spinoza's ethics. Nonetheless, although this was not his intention, it would be a substantial blow to the circumstantial relativists if Curley succeeds in explaining how IVPref can be read in a way that is compatible with non-circumstantial relativism (and I think he does), because that text is a key piece of evidence in the circumstantial relativists' case.

which is a human being is perceived as thinking, an account can be given of this mode which construes its nature in thinking or mentalistic terms. When such an account is given, the nature of the human being turns out to be its mind.

Now, the question arises as to the nature of the mind. There are two points to be made here, the first of which can be obtained from IIP11Cor:

[T]he human mind is a part of the infinite intellect of God. Therefore, when we say that the human Mind perceives this or that, we are saying nothing but that God, not insofar as he is infinite, but insofar as he is explained through the nature of the human Mind, or insofar as he constitutes the essence of the human Mind, has this or that idea[.]

Here the dependency of the human mind on God is forcefully stated. Also forcefully stated is the idea that the human mind is comprised out of one type of thing: at bottom, the mind is made up of God's infinite intellect. That's the first point: in Spinoza's metaphysical psychology, only one kind of material forms the contents of the mind. The second point concerns the nature of those contents. On this issue we are told different things: for example, Spinoza writes in IVP36Sch that 'the very essence of man ... is defined by reason' whereas in VP36Sch he says that 'the essence of our Mind consists only in knowledge'. There is no conflict between these statements, however, since reason and knowledge are both cognitive, active, intentional states and as such, they can be read as synonymous. Because the mind is monistic and because its single component is knowledge or reason, it follows that it is by nature knowledge (or reason).

The third and fourth premises – concerning what benefits knowledge – draw upon the thesis that only like benefits like. For a good x to be of use and hence of value to a subject S, x and S must share something in common. As a possible example, we possess the enzymes to digest corn kernels but lack the ones needed to digest cornstalks. Because we have the enzymes to digest the former but not the latter, we have something in common with the one but not the other. Because we have something in common with corn but not cornstalks, corn is useful to us as a nutrient while cornstalks are not. In general, Spinoza thinks that the more a good x has in common with S, the more valuable it is to S (IVP31Cor).[62] Since and insofar as knowledge shares its nature with other knowledge, knowledge is the most useful and so most valuable good for knowledge.

The fifth premise is the one most likely to incite controversy. Understood properly, however, it should not. The core idea is this: *qua*

---

[62] For further discussion of IVP31Cor, see Garrett (1990), 223 ff.

thinking beings, our nature is knowledge. Because our nature is knowledge and because of the principle that like benefits like, our nature will be benefitted by knowledge. Much knowledge will be circumstantially relatively beneficial: it will be useful in some circumstances and for some people but not others. Such knowledge is therefore circumstantially-relatively valuable. Other knowledge, however, will *always* benefit us: no matter who we are or what our circumstances, it is useful for us to know certain truths or propositions. The reason that such knowledge is always beneficial has to do with our natures or *conatus*: such knowledge will always serve to preserve and increase our power of acting. If our *conatus* or natures were different, perhaps such knowledge would not be beneficial to us. But it is impossible for our *conatus* to be different from what they are and given their actual content, it is beneficial. And it would be beneficial to any being with a *conatus* like ours. As a result, because of how our *conatus* is, there is some knowledge which is valuable irrespective of our circumstances.

To put the matter in a different way, for some knowledge, there will be circumstances in which it is useful and others in which it is not; because use determines value, such knowledge will sometimes be valuable, and other times, not. For example, it will sometimes be useful for us to know the weather forecast; at other times, it will not. As a result, knowledge of the weather will sometimes be valuable, and sometimes not. Most of the knowledge that we can possess will be relatively valuable in this way. However, there is some knowledge which it is always useful for us to know: viz., rational knowledge and especially knowledge of God's nature. This knowledge is always useful because of our natures as essentially rational or knowledgeable beings. If our natures were different, perhaps this knowledge would not be unwaveringly useful; but our natures necessarily being what they are, it is. As a result, such knowledge is always valuable. It is still relatively valuable, because it is valuable for us, but it is non-circumstantially relatively valuable.

From the fifth premise, the sixth follows immediately. Given that some knowledge is always useful, that same knowledge must be always valuable. This is because of the connection between use and value: that which is useful is valuable and so that which is useful always is valuable always.

Such is the argument which proves that some goods – more precisely, one good, knowledge of God – are non-circumstantially relatively valuable. While the reasoning which leads to it may be somewhat opaque, the truth of the conclusion can be seen by stepping back and viewing Spinoza's normative project from afar. Whether in the *Treatise on the Emendation of the Intellect*, the *Short Treatise*, or the *Ethics*, Spinoza's overarching concern is to explain what happiness is and how we can become happy. This goal would be incoherent if the value of the goods which are essential to happiness were totally dependent on circumstances. In such a case, no general or universal statements could be made regarding happiness; rather, they would have to be tailored to particular circumstances. It would make no sense to talk generally about 'the greatest satisfaction of Mind' (VP27), for there would be no truly general satisfaction holding across or for all minds. Rather, there would be an indefinite disjunction of greatest satisfactions, just as there is an indefinite disjunction of greatest satisfactions of the body.[63] If the good of the mind were relative to the subjective conditions of individual minds in the way that the good of the body is dependent on the physical states of individual bodies, there would be no single state of happiness holding for all minds. That there is such a state implies that there must be a single, non-circumstantially relative good.

4.4.2   Stoic 'absolutism'

Spinoza's value theory is a peculiar sort of relativism, for it holds that there is and never will be a circumstance in which certain goods do not possess value for us. The constancy of the value of such goods makes them seem absolutely good. This helps to account for why Spinoza occasionally employs stronger language when speaking about them. Yet for all that, Spinoza's value theory remains relative. What about the Stoics?

Recall the rationale for categorizing goods as good/bad/indifferent. If a good benefits its possessor's quest for perfection, then it is good; if it impedes that quest, it is bad; if it neither benefits nor harms, then it is indifferent.[64] So understood, it is apparent that goods do not possess value absolutely. To use a trivial example, while hay would be good for a horse because it helps the horse actualize whatever potential it possesses to be a perfect horse, it would be harmful for a human, since it would make her sick. This shows the relativity of the value of hay to the nature of the agent consuming it. The same is true of other goods, such as the virtues. A horse cannot be kind, magnanimous, or courageous because it lacks the necessary and sufficient condition for those conditions, reason. For us, however, the virtues do have value since we are rational beings.

It is not merely that the value of goods hinges upon the nature of those possessing. The relativity of value is stronger than that. For the Stoics, the very *possibility* of the being of some goods depends on the nature of those

---

[63] This is assuming that there is in fact no single non-circumstantially relative good for the body. In Chapter 5, Section 5.6.3, I address this issue.

[64] For more, see Section 4.2 above.

whose good it would be. In relation to horses, there are no virtues, in the strict sense of that word. Sure, we can speak of a horse as brave or sensitive (if we regard sensitivity as a virtue) but at best, such traits are analogous to the true virtues of bravery and sensitivity. Genuine virtue requires knowledge of the relevant factors, the ability to assess changing conditions and respond appropriately, the physical strengthening of the tenor of the soul, and more. Horses are unable to engage in any of these activities for the simple reason that they are non-rational. As a category of value, then, the virtues just do not exist for horses.

We can learn what is going on from Cicero: 'The Stoics say that that is "valuable" (for we may use this term, I think) which is either itself in accordance with nature or such as to bring about that state of affairs.'[65] As he explains, the value of any good is wholly constituted by reference to nature, both the nature of the agent possessing it and Nature as a whole. The nature of the individual agent is just the constitutional structure and behaviourisms that universal Nature has deemed it best for it to possess. Nature as a whole is the rational system uniting all parts of the universe and guiding it towards the good. Particular objects have value, then, only in the case that they help those possessing in their endeavour to become one with these two sorts of nature.

So far, Stoic value theory closely resembles Spinoza's. The value of goods is a product of their utility to the agents whose goods they are. The specific use-value in question is the utility they might have for helping agents actualize their potential natures. It may be the case – in fact, it *is* the case – that some goods are unconditionally valuable for agents, given their natures. This would be true of virtue for humans, as there is no circumstance in which virtue will not have value for a human. To say that, however, is not to say that those goods are absolutely valuable, for there may be other agents in relation to whom the goods in question are not valuable and even do not exist. Like Spinoza, the Stoics should be seen as sanctioning the distinction between conditional versus absolute value.

Yet there is a further consideration. Some texts hint at it:

[Chrysippus argued that] that which is the best thing in the whole world should be found in something which is perfect and complete. But nothing is more perfect than the world, and nothing better than virtue. Therefore virtue is intrinsic to the world.[66]

Most majestic of immortals, many-titled, ever omnipotent Zeus, prime mover of nature, who with your law steer all things, hail to you. For it is proper for any

---

[65] *De fin.* III.20 (L-S 59D2). I am indebted to Long's comments on this passage, in Long (1986), 189 ff.
[66] Cicero, *ND*, II.39 (L-S 54H).

mortal to address you: we are your offspring, and alone of all mortal creatures which are alive and tread the earth we bear a likeness to God.[67]

[I]t was for the sake of gods and men that the world and everything in it was made.[68]

Stoic thought is deeply religious. Their universe was created by God. Their universe is wholly providential. God remains immanent in the universe, guiding it towards the ends that he has ordained. The God who is responsible for the existence and activity of the universe is anthropomorphic – or rather, since humans are made in his image, they should be said to be theomorphic. God is reason, the exact same reason that defines our essence. It is God's actions and nature which guarantees that the goods I have been discussing have value. It is because God gave the horse its nature, and hay its nature, that hay is valuable for the horse. Likewise for humans and nature. God forms the basis for value. As Phillip Mitsis puts it, 'For Stoics, rational providence guarantees the moral economy of the world.'[69]

Now, there are two facts about God that I want to assemble into an argument. The first is that the Stoics assign value to him. Not only is God the basis of the value of all other things but also God is valuable in his own right.[70] Second, God's existence is necessary and demonstrable.[71] From these premises, the conclusion which follows is that there exists something of value which is unconditionally good – namely, God. It is in this sense that Stoic value theory is absolutist. Unlike Spinoza, who postulated that all value is relative, the Stoics posited one category of absolute value, placing God in that category.

And yet: those goods that Spinoza conceived as non-circumstantially relatively valuable are, for all intents and purposes, absolutely valuable. The goods which the Stoics see us as personally possessing – the virtues – are only relatively valuable. So the differences between Spinoza and the Stoics are undeniable. Less certain is whether they matter.

4.5   The factualness of values

In Section 4.4.1, I argued that Spinoza classifies the true good (which is knowledge of God[72]) as a non-circumstantially relative good. Insofar as our natures are constituted by our minds, it follows that knowledge of

---

[67] Cleanthes, *Hymn to Zeus* (L-S 54I).   [68] Cicero, *ND*, II.133 (L-S 54N).
[69] Mitsis (2006).   [70] See, e.g., Cicero, *ND* II.39.
[71] See, e.g., the texts assembled in L-S 54.
[72] Again, I am only considering the good for us as mental beings. I am not talking about the good for us as extensional or physical beings. I am deferring discussion of this to the next chapter.

God is good for us. Because knowledge of God is always good for us, it follows that there is no possible circumstance or situation in which such knowledge is other than good.

Now I want to introduce another Spinozistic commitment: necessitarianism. Of course, necessitarianism *per se* is open to a wide variety of interpretations. Moreover, Spinoza's version of the theory has been the subject of increasing interest and debate. Given all of that, I cannot hope to provide a full account of Spinozistic necessitarianism here.[73] At a minimum, though, we can say that it is a theory making the following three claims: (1) that all things are fully determined by their antecedents plus the laws of nature (God);[74] (2) those things form a determining series;[75] and (3) the determining series itself is fully determined.[76]

Let us now bring together Spinoza's necessitarianism with his views about value. I have argued that some goods are morally valuable because of the way we are. So they remain relatively valuable. However, the way we are is the only possible way that we could be. Since those moral goods hinge on us and we must be exactly as we are, those moral goods are ineliminable parts of the world. To use parlance from the twentieth century, the world cannot be described without including normative terms.

Now, it may be unclear what a fact is. According to one source, there are three 'popular views about the nature of facts':
1. A fact is just a true truth-bearer.
2. A fact is just an obtaining state of affairs.
3. A fact is just a *sui generis* type of entity in which objects exemplify properties or stand in relations.[77]

Take (1): this asserts that 'a fact is a thought that is true'.[78] If so, then since the thought that knowledge of God has moral value for us is true, it is also a fact. If we conceive of a fact along the lines of (2), then because it obtains that knowledge of God has moral value for us, this is also a fact. Finally, if a fact is as defined by (3), then a fact is that which exemplifies properties. For example, if I say that 'the snowball is white', the only thing which makes my assertion true is the fact that the snowball possesses the quality whiteness. So if knowledge of God has moral value for us, this is

---

[73] I present my interpretation in Miller (2001). For a less opinionated guide to the issues, see Newlands (2013).
[74] See IP29.
[75] I have in mind the often-used phrases *ordo rerum* or *ordo et connexio idearum*. See, e.g., IIP7Sch (at G II, 90: 23–7).
[76] See IP33.   [77] See Mulligan and Correia (2013).
[78] Frege quoted in Mulligan and Correia (2013).

only because of the fact that knowledge of God possesses the quality of moral value.

Now, because the notion of a fact is so difficult, I acknowledge the incompleteness of my discussion here. However, I think it is safe to say, at least provisionally, that if a fact is any one of these things, then Spinoza believed that there are moral facts.

The same is true for the Stoics, though for very different reasons. Stoics were also determinists and possibly necessitarians.[79] For example, Cicero tells us that Chrysippus took all future events to be fully causally determined by the present.[80] Given their determinism, Stoics held that all features of the world are ineliminable features of the world. So far, this resembles Spinoza.

The difference lies in the source of the particular feature before us: viz., moral values. Whereas Spinoza leveraged moral values into the world on the basis of some members of the world, Stoics think that there are and must be moral values in the world *as part of the world itself*. Cicero credits Chrysippus with a battery of arguments to this effect:

For nor is there anything else besides the world which has nothing missing, and which is equipped from every point of view, perfect, and complete in all its measures and parts ... But the world, since it embraces everything and there is nothing that is not included in it, is perfect from every point of view. How then can it lack that which is best? But nothing is better than intellect and reason. Therefore the world cannot lack these ... Likewise, he argued that which is the best thing in the whole world should be found in something which is perfect and complete. But nothing is more perfect than the world, and nothing better than virtue. Therefore virtue is intrinsic to the world.[81]

It is impossible to give a description of the world without using normative terms. So there must be moral facts true of the world. The reason for this is that the world itself embeds those moral truths. As one scholar has written, 'the universe pulses with rationality, directionality, normativity. How things ought to be is given by the natural universe itself.'[82]

So both Spinoza and the Stoics agree that there are moral facts. So they agree that we *can* learn what we ought to do by studying what is the case. So they would disagree with Hume's famous claim that prescriptive

---

[79] Again, there are problems of interpretation. That they were charged with being necessitarians is incontestable; see, e.g., Cicero, *De fato* 12. Chrysippus led the response to this charge, developing a sophisticated modal theory especially designed to defeat Diodorus' Master Argument. See, e.g., Epictetus, *Discourses* 2.19.1–5 (L-S 38A). The fullest treatment of these issues remains Bobzien (1998), ch. 3.

[80] *De fato*, 20–1 (L-S 38G). For illuminating commentary, see Leibniz's *Theodicy* (Leibniz (1985), 229–32).

[81] *ND* II.37–9 (L-S 54H (part)).   [82] Shields (2012), 186.

propositions are 'entirely different' from descriptive ones.[83] At the same time, a vast gulf separates Spinoza and the Stoics. Whereas Spinoza thinks moral facts exist because of human nature,[84] the Stoics think they exist in or because of Nature's nature.[85]

4.6   Conclusion: what counts as good

The analysis given here of Spinoza and the Stoics' views on value has been almost entirely second-order: much has been said about the form of their theories but little about their contents. For example, we know that Spinoza took the highest good to be knowledge of God, and in what sense this knowledge is good, but we know hardly anything about what knowledge of God actually consists of. This is too big an issue to cover completely in the space available but to provide more of the flavour of the two parties' theories, a few comments should be made concerning the things they thought valuable. I shall focus on what each party took the most valuable of all goods to be.

In the case of Spinoza, it is, of course, knowledge of God. Rather than offer more analysis,[86] allow me to use an evocative quotation instead. Because I have been using the *Ethics* almost exclusively, I will draw on the *Theological–Political Treatise* this time:

Since our intellect forms the better part of us, it is evident that, if we wish to seek what is definitely to our advantage, we should endeavour above all to perfect it as far as we can, for in its perfection must consist our supreme good [*summum nostrum bonum*]. Now since all our knowledge, and the certainty which banishes every possible doubt, depend solely on the knowledge of God – because, firstly, without God nothing can be or be conceived, and secondly, everything can be called into doubt as long as we have no clear and distinct idea of God – it follows

---

[83] *A Treatise of Human Nature*, III.1. For more on exactly how the Stoics would disagree with Hume, see Shields (2012), 185. For more on Spinoza, see Curley (1973), 366–7.

[84] As Curley says, 'Spinoza is engaged in a project of commending a particular way of life to his fellow men. And the question we want to ask is how he would defend the claim that that way of life is an ideal ... [The answer] invokes Spinoza's conception of human nature. The kind of life set before us as an ideal is prescribed by reason because it is the life each of us, insofar as he acts according to his own nature ... necessarily seeks' (Curley (1973), 365, 366).

[85] As Inwood says of the Stoics, 'They do not aim to deduce ethical facts from psychological ones, nor vice versa. Both are deduced from their concept of nature. Nature is a complex and extraordinarily rich concept in Stoic psychology and ethics, and its richness permits the Stoics to align claims of fact and claims of value in a way that avoids the now traditional dichotomy between the two. The problem of the "is" and the "ought" does not arise in the Stoic version of naturalism' (Inwood (1985), 199).

[86] Among others, these commentaries on knowledge of God are especially helpful: Yovel (1989), 156 ff.; Wilson (1996), 126–31; LeBuffe (2010), ch. 11.

that our supreme good and perfection depends solely on the knowledge of God. Again, since nothing can be or be conceived without God, it is clear that everything in Nature involves and expresses the conception of God in proportion to its essence and perfection; and therefore we acquire a greater and more perfect knowledge of God as we gain more knowledge of natural phenomena. To put it another way, since the knowledge of an effect through its cause is nothing other than the knowledge of a property of that cause, the greater our knowledge of natural phenomena, the more perfect is our knowledge of God's essence, which is the cause of all things. So the whole of our knowledge, that is, our supreme good, not merely depends on the knowledge of God but consists entirely therein [*non tantum a Dei cognitione dependet, sed in eadem omnino consistit*].[87]

Spinoza thinks that our goal ought to be the perfection of the best part of ourselves, which is our intellect. We perfect our intellect by adding to our store of knowledge. Of all the knowledge we could possess, knowledge of God is the best kind. Knowledge of God is knowledge of Nature. Not any kind of knowledge of Nature, but knowledge of the laws and rules by which Nature operates and through which the behaviour of all natural phenomena are governed. Initially, we strive to know Nature rationally – that is, we strive to know mutable and temporal phenomena in relation to natural laws. As our understanding deepens, however, we pass to intuitive knowledge of Nature. When this happens, we know directly the essences of natural events and objects.[88] Such knowledge is possible because the human mind has 'adequate knowledge' of God's essence.[89] When we attain intuitive knowledge of God, we have attained our greatest good.

Here is a portrait of the Stoics:

Everything depends on its own good. Productivity and the flavour of the wine commend a vine, speed commends a stag ... In each thing, that for which it is born and by which it is judged ought to be its best.

What is best in a human being? Reason. By this humans surpass the animals and follow the gods. Therefore perfected reason is our proper good ...

[In a person] it is quite irrelevant how much land he tills, how much money he has invested, how many clients greet him, how expensive a couch he reclines on, how translucent a cup he drinks from; what matters is how good he is. But he is good if his reason is fully deployed, straight, and adapted to the inclinations of his nature.

This is termed virtue, that is, the honourable and the sole good of a human being. For since only reason completes a human being, only reason makes him perfectly happy. But this is the only good thing and the only thing by which he is made happy. We also say that those things which originate in virtue or are caused by it are good, i.e., all of its products. But it alone is good precisely because there is no good without it.

---

[87] *TTP* ch. 4 (at G III, 59–60).   [88] IIP40Sch2.   [89] IIP47.

If every good is in the mind, then whatever strengthens, exalts, or expands it is good. But virtue makes the mind stronger, loftier, and fuller. For other things which stimulate our desires also degrade the mind and make it weak; when they seem to raise it up, they are inflaming it and tricking it with their profound emptiness. Therefore the only good thing is that which makes the mind better.[90]

Like Spinoza, the Stoics follow Aristotle in thinking that our good can be found by reflecting on our function. Our function is what is unique to us. That which is unique to us is our reason. So our good lies in our reason, which we ought to seek to perfect. To perfect our reason we must strengthen our minds. To strengthen our minds we must increase our wisdom.[91] Wisdom is 'the human mind's good brought to perfection'.[92] Once we have achieved wisdom, we are perfect. When we are perfect, we are virtuous. When we are fully virtuous, we have completed ourselves. When we have completed ourselves, we are fully happy. This is the only route to happiness; it is through living the life of virtue. Virtue is the only good because it is the sole means to completing our lives.

---

[90] Seneca, *Ep.* 76.8–9, 15–17 (trans. Inwood).
[91] Seneca mentions wisdom a little earlier in this letter (see *Ep.* 76.5–6).
[92] Seneca, *Ep.* 89.4 (L-S 26G).

5 Happiness

> I pass on finally to that part of the *Ethics* which concerns the method or way leading to freedom. In this part, then, I shall be dealing with the power of reason, pointing out the degree of control reason has over the emotions, and then what is freedom of mind, or blessedness, from which we shall see how much to be preferred is the life of the wise to the life of the ignorant man.[1]

> They [the Stoics] say that being happy is the end, for the sake of which everything is done, but which is not itself done for the sake of anything. This consists of living in accordance with virtue, in living in agreement, or, what is the same, in living in accordance with nature.[2]

Cicero begins one of his most philosophical works, *De finibus*, with an apologia. He writes,

> [N]o one who has habitually and carefully read my philosophical works will judge that any is more worth reading than this one. For nothing in life is more worth investigating than philosophy in general, and the question raised in this work in particular: what is the end, what is the ultimate and final goal, to which all our deliberations on living well and acting rightly should be directed?[3]

Though Cicero is careful to speak about just his own philosophical priorities in these lines, he plainly thinks they are shared by the philosophers whose views he is about to canvass. If we ask whether there is a single most pressing question in all of Greek and Hellenistic philosophy, the answer will be affirmative. And if we ask what that question would be, Cicero is emphatic: what is happiness?

To say that ancients took happiness to be of paramount philosophical importance is not to say that they agreed on its nature. In a familiar passage from the *Nicomachean Ethics*, Aristotle allows that 'pretty well most people' took happiness to be 'the topmost of all achievable goods'. At the same time, he quickly adds, 'they are in dispute about

---

[1] VPref (trans. Shirley).   [2] Stobaeus *Ecl.* II.77.16 ff (L-S 63A1).
[3] Cicero, *De fin.* I.11 (trans. Woolf in Cicero (2001)).

what happiness actually is'.[4] Cicero reports that this dispute endured long after Aristotle, with 'violent disagreement on these matters among the most learned philosophers' persisting to his own day.[5] Indeed, the main task that Cicero sets himself in *De finibus* is to rehearse the arguments for and against the conceptions of happiness held by Epicureans, Stoics and Sceptics. It emerges through the course of his treatment that the structure and progress of moral philosophy in the Hellenistic era was delimited by ceaseless debates over happiness. Disagreement was not incidental to discourse about happiness; rather, it was constant and necessary.

Prima facie, there seem to be great similarities between ancient philosophy as I have just depicted it and early modern philosophy. The examples of Descartes and Spinoza may assure us that for many or perhaps most early moderns, the ultimate aim of philosophical inquiry was to present and defend particular conceptions of happiness.

Take this evocative image from the 'Preface' to Descartes' *Principles of Philosophy*:

[P]hilosophy as a whole is like a tree whose roots are metaphysics, whose trunk is physics, and whose branches, which issue from this trunk, are all the other sciences. These reduce themselves to three principal ones, viz. medicine, mechanics and morals – I mean the highest and most perfect moral science which, presupposing a complete knowledge of the other sciences, is the last degree of wisdom.

But just as it is not from the roots or the trunk of the trees that one culls the fruit, but only from the extremities of their branches, so the main use of philosophy is dependent on those parts that we cannot learn until the end.[6]

Like the ancients, Descartes took happiness to be of paramount importance: just a few lines earlier he said, 'we ought above all other things to endeavour to live well'.[7] Moreover, Descartes evidently has views regarding the nature of happiness. He cannot yet supply them, however, as they take for granted his views on their metaphysical and physical foundations, for which he will argue in this book. It is true that Descartes never did propound a full-fledged theory of happiness – the closest he came was in his correspondence with Elizabeth – but perhaps if he had lived longer, he would have gotten around to it.

Coming to Spinoza, consider again the opening to the *Treatise on the Emendation of the Intellect*, which I quoted in Chapter 4:

[4] *NE* I.4 1095a16–21 (trans. Rowe in Aristotle (2002)).
[5] *De fin.* I.11 (trans. Woolf in Cicero (2001)).
[6] A-T IXB: 14–15 (trans. Haldane and Ross in Descartes (1931)).
[7] A-T IXB: 13 (trans. Haldane and Ross in Descartes (1931)).

After experience had taught me that all the things which regularly occur in ordinary life are empty and futile, and I saw that all the things which were the cause or object of my fear had nothing of good or bad in themselves, except insofar as [my] mind was moved by them, I resolved at last to try to find out whether there was anything which would be the true good [*verum bonum*], capable of communicating itself, and which alone would affect the mind, all others being rejected – whether there was something which, once found and acquired, would continuously give me the greatest joy [*summa laetitia*], to eternity.[8]

The *TdIE* is motivated by Spinoza's desire to attain the greatest joy and the 'greatest happiness' (*summa felicitas*). Given the epistemic character-ization of these two objectives provided slightly later – they consist in knowledge 'of the union that mind has with the whole of Nature'[9] – it proves necessary to deal with some thorny epistemological matters before one can achieve them. So the great bulk of the *TdIE* is devoted to bringing 'the intellect back to the right path'.[10] Because the philosophical issues with which it grapples are overwhelmingly epistemological, it is easy to lose sight of the *TdIE*'s origins in the quest for happiness. Yet they seem to provide the ultimate justification for the entire enterprise of the incom-plete treatise – and perhaps the origins would have been revisited if Spinoza had managed to complete this work.

Now, it may be that the eudaimonic orientation of ancient philosophy has strong echoes in the work of the early moderns. A closer examination, however, finds the relationship to be much more complicated than just suggested. I will set aside the case of other early moderns, such as Hobbes or Locke, whose views on happiness are even less obviously eudaimonistic than Descartes' or Spinoza's.[11] If we start with Descartes, we can find reason for doubting the extent of his fidelity to the ancients in what I have already written. Notice how I had to allow that apart from in his corre-spondence, Descartes never got around to expounding a theory of happi-ness. If happiness were so important to him, one might wonder how this could have happened. Excuses like premature death or the distractions of other projects appear to be just that – excuses. Ancient philosophers also died relatively young, just as they were involved with many philosophical ventures. Yet this did not stop them from making happiness the centre-piece of their philosophical investigations. Maybe Descartes was not being fully honest with his readers – or himself – when he avowed the significance of happiness.

[8] *TdIE* §1.   [9] *TdIE* §13.   [10] *TdIE* §17.
[11] For discussion of Hobbes' views on happiness, see Kitanov (2011). For Locke, see Stuart (2013), ch. 10.

As for Spinoza, his case is more complicated. It is true that he never propounded a theory of happiness in the *TdIE*; there are just intimations that we might draw together to form a full-fledged theory. On the other hand, the *Ethics* culminates in an account of human freedom which many commentators take to be his equivalent to a proper account of flourishing or happiness.[12] But is what he says there at all comparable to what his ancient and especially his Stoic predecessors had written?

There is much more to be said about all of this but to make progress, the discussion needs to be tightened. For the remainder of this chapter, I shall eschew the bigger question of whether ancient and early modern philosophy were both geared towards happiness in favour of the smaller question of how Spinoza's views on happiness compare to those of the Stoics.[13] To commence my investigation, I shall look at the actual words used by ancient philosophers and Spinoza when they wrote about happiness.[14] This will reveal some intriguing similarities and differences that I shall then probe further by trying to determine the extent of the similarity of the form and content of Spinoza's concept of happiness to that of the Stoics. My perhaps unsurprising conclusion will be that the form and content of each party's concept of happiness is similar but not identical to the other's. The interest of this conclusion, I hope, will be augmented by the means employed to establish it. My final section is on the notion of living life in accordance with nature, a notion central to both Stoic and Spinozistic ethics.

5.1   The language of happiness

5.1.1 Normally, when Greeks talked about happiness,[15] whether they lived in early times (such as Solon), during the height of Athens

---

[12] I shall note many of these commentators in what follows. For now, I will just mention Kisner (2011) and LeBuffe (2010), as well as some of the papers in Kisner and Youpa (2014).

[13] Happiness in early modern philosophy is finally starting to receive the attention it deserves. In the previous note, I mentioned studies of Hobbes, Locke, and Spinoza. A more global account is given by Rutherford (2012). I will refer to other studies below.

[14] I start with the language of happiness because the specific words used in philosophical discussions of happiness are extremely important in determining the outcome of those discussions. If we are clearer on what terms the Stoics and Spinoza were using in their treatment of what I am calling 'happiness', we will have an easier time comparing their respective accounts.

[15] Because the Stoics used many of the terms that I am about to mention in basically the same ways as their ancient peers, it would be arbitrary to isolate them from everybody else. I shall canvass ancient philosophical literature widely to find the best examples of how the words are used. Even though I shall often speak of Aristotle or Epicurus, the point that I am making normally also holds for the Stoics. Where it does not, I shall say as much.

(Socrates), or later in antiquity (Epictetus), they were talking about *eudaimonia*.[16] This word is a compound, consisting of the adjectival prefix *eu* (meaning 'well' or 'having an abundance') plus the noun *daimon* (the power controlling the destiny of an individual). For someone to be *eudaimon* was for all of the key ingredients or factors in that person's life to be optimal. Because *eudaimonia* has this sense, some modern translators do not use 'happiness' when rendering the Greek into English. Instead, they prefer 'flourishing', 'well-being', 'success', etc. For my part, I think we need not be too bothered by the problem of translating *eudaimonia* as 'happiness' so long as we are careful to keep the Greek meaning before us. As Gregory Vlastos has argued, there 'is ample reason for sticking to the traditional translation [i.e., happiness], provided only we bear in mind that in its pre-theoretical uses *eudaimonia* puts a heavier loading on the objective factor in "happiness" than does the English word'.[17]

Above I said that *eudaimonia* is 'normally' the word for happiness. Not always. For example, Aristotle and Epicurus both use the adjective *makarios* in their writings on happiness.[18] *Makarios* has the sense of being blessed – it is often used in reference to the gods, who are blessed and who have the power to bless. Take this passage from the *Letter to Menoeceus*:

> We must reckon that some desires are natural and others empty, and of the natural some are necessary, others natural only; and of the necessary some are necessary for happiness [*pros eudaimonian*] ... [S]teady observance of these things makes it possible to refer choice and avoidance to the health of the body and the soul's freedom from disturbance, since this is the end belonging to the blessed life [*tou makarios*].[19]

The reference for *eudaimonia* seems to be mental tranquillity alone while that of *makarios*, mental tranquillity plus freedom from physical pain. The difference in nuance between being *makarios* versus being *eudaimon* has led some commentators to suggest that an important difference marks the two states: being *eudaimon* is being happy while being *makarios* is being blessed.[20] Some commentators, however, have rejected this suggestion. As A. A. Long puts it, all *eudaimonia* 'is a blessed (*makarios*) condition,

---

[16] See, respectively, DL I.50, DL I.37, and Epictetus' *Discourses* II.23.44.
[17] Vlastos (1991), 203.
[18] For Aristotle, see *NE* I.8 1098a19, I.10 1100b35, and IX.9 1169b5. See also *Eudemian Ethics* 1215a7–11 (where Aristotle cautions against calling a human life *makarios*) and 1215b13–14 (where he says a human life can only approximate a truly *makarios* life). For Epicurus, see Usener (1977), s.v.
[19] *Letter to Menoeceus* 127–8 (L-S 21B1).   [20] See, e.g., Ross (1923), 192.

and as such, quasi-divine or "godlike"'.[21] Thus, another option available to ancient philosophers when discussing the happy person may be *makarios*.

A third is the phrase *eu zen* – living well. This is found in Aristotle, who writes in the *Eudemian Ethics* that 'both acting well and living well are the same thing as being happy'.[22] He says much the same thing in the *NE*: 'happiness has virtually been defined as a sort of living well and doing well'.[23] It may be that *eu zen* and *eudaimonia* are not true synonyms in Aristotle, as some have argued.[24] It is also true that some philosophers during the Hellenistic era shied away from *eu zen*. Hence Epicurus sometimes spoke of 'living pleasantly' (*hedeos zen*), not of 'living well'.[25] However, questions about the similarity between *eu zen* and *eudaimonia* are eliminated in Stoicism. In that school, philosophers used *eudaimonia* and *eu zen* interchangeably when speaking of that end for the sake of which everything is (or should be) done.[26]

Leaving Greek for Latin, classical philosophers working in that language commonly used either of two alternatives: *beatus/beata* and *felicitas/felix*. Thus, when Seneca and Cicero write about the happy life, they speak of the *beata vita*.[27] Likewise, when Seneca discusses the happy man, he calls him *beatus*.[28] As for *felicitas*, this is what Seneca uses in his declaration that, 'when right and perfect', reason 'makes the full sum of human happiness [*felicitatem hominis*]'.[29] It also appears the quintessential Stoic idea that 'true happiness [*vera felicitas*] is placed in virtue alone'.[30] Seneca writes, 'Happy [*o felicem*] is the man who can make others better, not merely when he is in their company, but even when he is in their thoughts!'[31] In another letter he says, 'if you would be happy [*felix*], entreat the gods that none of their fond desires for you may be brought to pass'.[32] And elsewhere, 'no one could say that [rocks and beasts of the field] are blissful [*felicia*], when they have no comprehension of bliss [*felicitatis intellectus*]'.[33]

---

[21] Long (2011), 95. See also Nussbaum (1986), 330–4. Both Long and Nussbaum are talking about Aristotle. For an argument against taking Epicurus to distinguish being *makarios* from being *eudaimon*, see Caizzi (1994), 325–6.

[22] II.1 1219b1 (trans. Woods in Aristotle (1985)).

[23] I.8 1098b22 (trans. Rowe in Aristotle (2002)).

[24] See, e.g., Broadie in Aristotle (2002), 286.   [25] See, e.g., *K.D.* 5.

[26] See, e.g., DL VII.88.

[27] See, e.g., Seneca's eponymous *De vita beata*. For Cicero, see *TD* V.40, *De off.* I.13, etc.

[28] See, e.g., *Ep.* 92.3, *De vita beata* 5.2, etc. For Cicero, see *De fin.* I.5, *De legibus* I.32, etc.

[29] *Ep.* 76.10 (L-S 63D2).

[30] Seneca, *De vita beata* 16.1 (trans. Basore in Seneca (1932)).

[31] *Ep.* 11.9 (trans. Gummere in Seneca (1925)).

[32] *Ep.* 31.3 (trans. Gummere in Seneca (1925)).

[33] *De vita beata* 5.1 (trans. Basore in Seneca (1932)).

In addition to knowing which words were used to speak of what happiness is, it is also instructive to take note of words describing what happiness is not. Since Stoics took happiness to be a life lived according to nature, all that we need to be happy is to live as nature intended us. Since nature intended us to be fully rational beings, it follows that reason is necessary for happiness. When we are rational, we are virtuous. So reason/virtue is the sole constituent of happiness. This is why Seneca could write, 'not even that joy [*gaudium*] that arises from virtue, though a good, is part of the absolute good'.[34]

Cicero draws attention to another notion which Stoics exclude from happiness. He writes, 'When the mind is moved quietly and consistently, consistent with reason, this is termed joy [*gaudium*], but when it exults with a hollow sort of uplift, that is called "wild or excessive gladness" [*laetitia gestiens*].'[35] According to Cicero, there are two kinds of joy – *gaudium* and *laetitia*. The former is the kind of joy which is only inwardly expressed while the latter denotes that joy which is externally displayed. Of course, Stoics would have argued that neither belongs to happiness *per se*.

Let us leave the ancients for Spinoza. In his numerous writings on happiness or closely associated states, we find all of the Latin words just mentioned (and then some). So towards the end of *TTP* IV he writes,

> Thus Solomon, too, takes the view that the happiness [*felicitas*] and peace [*tranquillitas*] of the man who cultivates his natural understanding depends mainly not on the sway of fortune (that is, on God's external help) but on his own internal virtue (or God's internal help), because he owes his self-preservation mainly to his own vigilance, conduct and wise counsel.[36]

Later in the same work he says, '[Philosophers] place true happiness [*veram felicitatem*] solely in virtue and peace of mind [*tranquillitate animi*].'[37] *Felicitas* also appears in the *Ethics*. He writes in IIP49Sch, '[his] doctrine, apart from giving us complete tranquillity of mind [*animum omnimode quietum*], has the further advantage of teaching us wherein lies our greatest happiness or blessedness [*nostra summa felicitas, sive beatitudo*], namely in the knowledge of God alone'. In IVP18Sch, he argues that 'happiness [*felicitatem*] consists in a man's being able to preserve his own being'. In the Appendix to that part he says, 'the highest happiness or blessedness for mankind [*summa hominis felicitas, seu beatitudo*] consists in' perfecting the intellect or reason.[38]

Looking for paradigmatic uses of *beatus/beata*, IVP18 holds that 'No one can desire to be happy, to do well and to live well [*beatum esse, et bene*

---

[34] *De vita beata* 15.2 (trans. Basore in Seneca (1932)).
[35] *TD* IV.13 (trans. Graver (2007)).   [36] *TTP* IV (G III, 68: 4–8).
[37] *TTP* VI (G III, 88: 5).   [38] IVAppIV.

agree, et bene vivere] without at the same time desiring to be, to do, and to live; that is, actually to exist.' Spinoza adds in the demonstration to IVP18, 'the desire (Definition of Emotions 1) to live happily, to do well and so on [*Cupiditas (per 1. Aff. Defin.) beate, seu bene vivendi, agendi, etc.*] is the very essence of man'. In IVP54Sch he argues that those who cannot follow the dictates of reason ought to be humble and repentant, as people 'who are subject to these emotions can be far more readily induced than others to live by the guidance of reason in the end, that is, to become free men and enjoy the life of the blessed [*ut liberi sint, et beatorum vita fruantur*]'.[39] In the marvellous *Ep.* 78, Spinoza chooses to respond to the notion that 'if men sin from the necessity of their nature, they are therefore excusable'. Spinoza replies to this,

You do not wish to explain what conclusion you wish to draw from this. Is it that God cannot be angry with them, or it is that they are worth of blessedness [*beatitudine*]? If the former, I entirely agree that God is not angry ... But I deny that on that account all men ought to be blessed [*omnes beati esse debeant*]; for men may be excusable, but nevertheless be without blessedness [*beatitudine*] and afflicted in many ways. A horse is excusable for being a horse, and not a man; nevertheless, he must be a horse, and not a man.[40]

Some may have noticed the creep of words in the last paragraph. While Spinoza does talk about *beatus/beata*, he also employs another word starting with *beat: beatitudo/beatitudinis*. He opens Part II of the *Ethics* by explaining that he will not deduce all the implications of Part I but 'only those things that can lead us ... to the knowledge of the human mind and its utmost blessedness [*summae beatitudinis*]'.[41] Earlier I quoted IVApp4. Where Spinoza speaks of the 'highest happiness or blessedness' that humans can possess in the first sentence of that paragraph, he drops all mention of 'happiness' (*felicitas*) for the remainder. Instead, he speaks of 'blessedness' (*beatitudo*) alone.

In fact, we can find more uses of *beatitudo/beatitudinis* than of *felicitas/felicitatis* or *beatus/beata*. Sometimes *beatitudo* appears by itself, as when Spinoza declares in VP33Sch that 'blessedness [*beatitudo*] must surely consist in this, that the mind is endowed with perfection itself'.[42] Likewise for VP42: 'Blessedness [*beatitudo*] is not the reward of virtue, but virtue itself.' Often, however, *beatitudo* will be coupled with other concepts. Let me cite three examples. In VPref, Spinoza writes that this part will be about 'freedom of mind, or blessedness [*Mentis Libertas seu beatitudo*]'. Second, he pairs blessedness with our highest good, as when he writes in

---

[39] Trans. Shirley.   [40] G IV, 327a (trans. Shirley).   [41] IIPref (trans. Shirley).
[42] Trans. Shirley.

TTP IV that knowledge and love of God is 'the sum of our supreme good
and blessedness [*summum bonum, nostraque beatitudo*]'.[43] Finally, Spinoza
says that the Corollary to VP36 plainly reveals 'in what our salvation or
blessedness or freedom [*nostra salus, seu beatitudo, seu Libertas*] consists,
namely, in the constant and eternal love towards God'.[44]

One other brief point. The quotation from VP36Sch just given includes
the equation between *beatitudo* and *salus* – salvation. *Salus* also appears in
the penultimate sentence of the *Ethics*, where Spinoza writes, 'if salvation
[*salus*]were ready to hand and could be discovered without great toil, how
could it be that it is almost universally neglected?' Spinoza also speaks of
salvation in the *TTP*. Thus he says in Chapter VII, 'true salvation and
blessedness [*vera salus et beatitudo*] consists in true peace of mind [*vera
animi acquiescentia*]'.[45] In another context, he writes, 'it is not reason but
revelation that can teach us that it is enough for blessedness or salvation
[*salutem seu beatitudinem*] for us to accept the divine decrees as laws or
commandments, and that there is no need to conceive them as eternal
truths'.[46] I only note this now; I will comment on it shortly.[47]

5.1.2 Now, there are obvious explanations for why Spinoza should have
used new words not found in ancient philosophy and this leads me to the
next topic for discussion. What are the philosophical implications of the
foregoing linguistic considerations?

Start with the most recent point. Surely a key to Spinoza's use of
beatitudo and *salus* is that he writes in the wake of Christianity. By contrast, since the classical Stoics and other ancient philosophers flourished
before the rise of the Church, there is no surprise that they should not use
these terms. It is tempting to infer that since Spinoza is using Christian
terms, the ideas that he associates with those terms are also imbued with
Christian themes. Likewise, since the ancient Stoics did not use *beatitudo*
or *salus*, their views on happiness must differ to that extent from
Spinoza's. Before making this inference, however, it is necessary to ask
whether or not Spinoza uses *beatitudo* or *salus* conventionally. If he did
not, then the appearance of *beatitudo* or *salus* in his writings may not be so
telling after all.

---

[43] G III, 60: 16.   [44] VP36Sch.   [45] G III, 111: 26.   [46] *TTP* XV, note 31.
[47] Spinoza uses *salus* elsewhere in the *TTP*. For example, he speaks of the laws of nature as
the *populi salus* – the 'safeguard of the people' in Shirley's translation (*TTP* VII (G III,
218: 10). Elsewhere, he says that 'in a sovereign state ... the welfare of the whole people
[*salus totius populi*], not the ruler, is the supreme law' (*TTP* XVI (G III, 194: 31). These
passages provide additional support for the argument, which I am about to mount, that
Spinoza's notion of *salus* is not inflected with Christian dogma. I will not examine these
texts, however, as they are not closely connected to happiness.

Let us return to the texts. Take Section 4 of the Appendix to Part IV: 'In life, therefore, it is especially useful to perfect, as far as we can, our intellect, or reason. In this one thing consists man's highest happiness, or blessedness [*summa hominis felicitas, seu beatitudo*]. Indeed, blessedness is nothing but that satisfaction of mind that stems from the intuitive knowledge of God.' Here Spinoza treats *felicitas* and *beatitudo* as synonyms.[48] Moreover, *beatitudo* is treated as a 'satisfaction of mind'. Its (causal?) origins may be divine; it arises from intuitive knowledge of God. In itself, however, it is not this knowledge. Rather, it is the state of having a mind that is satisfied.

This differs in a subtle but key respect from what we can find in Christian treatments of *beatitudo*. Take Aquinas, for example. Like Spinoza, he treats *felicitas* and *beatitudo* as synonyms: 'Now, the ultimate end of man, and of every intellectual substance, is called felicity or happiness [*felicitas sive beatitudo*], because this is what every intellectual substance desires as an ultimate end, and for its own sake alone. Therefore, the ultimate happiness and felicity [*beatitude et felicitas*] of every intellectual substance is to know God.'[49] Though there are echoes of Spinoza in Aquinas, there is also one crucial difference. Where Spinoza says that *beatitudo* is a unique kind of satisfaction, Aquinas does not. Instead, he provides a purely epistemic characterization of *beatitudo*: it lies entirely in knowledge of God.

This rests a great deal of weight on one text, IVAppIV, especially since other characterizations of *beatitudo* are somewhat different than IVAppIV's. To repeat two prominent examples cited a few paragraphs ago, Spinoza speaks of 'knowledge of the human mind and its utmost blessedness' in IIPref and states in VP33Sch that blessedness 'must surely consist in this, that the mind is endowed with perfection itself'. In texts such as these, Spinoza does not incorporate any kind of feeling into blessedness. Rather, blessedness is purely perfection alone.

Indeed, the parallels between Spinozistic *beatitudo* and Aquinas' may seem to deepen when we draw on another Spinozistic text quoted previously. In IIP49Sch Spinoza writes that 'our greatest happiness or blessedness [*nostra summa felicitas, sive beatitudo*]' consists in 'the knowledge of God alone'. This could be lifted almost verbatim out of Aquinas, who wrote, e.g., 'the happiness of any intellectual substance is to know God'.[50] Moreover, Spinoza thinks here that this knowledge will always rise to a feeling which he calls 'complete tranquillity of mind'. Similarly,

[48] Cf. IVP49Sch (at G II, 135: 32), where they are also synonymous.
[49] *Summa contra gentiles*, III.25.14, trans. Aertsen (1993).
[50] *Summa contra gentiles*, III.25, trans. Aertsen (1993).

Aquinas argued that a feeling of delight (*delectatio*) was always concomitant upon *beatitudo*; indeed, he argues that this feeling of delight had a
necessary connection to happiness.[51] So the upshot is that (1) both
philosophers conceive of blessedness in purely intellectual terms and
that (2) both took some kind of feeling to be necessarily connected to
blessedness, though as a consequent to it and not a constituent of it.
    More will be said on how Spinoza relates between happiness and the
feeling associated with it below (see Section 5.5.2). For right now, I have a
narrower objective, which is determining whether Spinoza's conception
of *beatitudo* is so Christianized as to render any of his statements about
beatitudo decidedly different from statements made by the Stoics about
beatitudo. I do not think it does, despite the foregoing parallels between
Spinoza and Aquinas. There are three reasons for this, one of which is that
sometimes Spinoza implicates a feeling into blessedness itself, something
Aquinas consistently shuns. Because we have already considered this, I
will move immediately on to the other two.
    The second concerns the attainability of blessedness. Though he con-
ceives of blessedness as knowledge of God, because his God is not
transcendent, Spinoza does not think this impossible. Quite the contrary:
his whole enterprise in the *Ethics* and in other works is to show how
philosophy can lead us to blessedness. Aquinas is diametrically opposed.
Happiness is knowledge of God. However, human beings' ability to know
is limited to what the senses can perceive. Because the essence of God is
not perceptible, we cannot know his essence. For vision of his essence, we
must await the after life. So true or full blessedness is not possible in this
life; it can only happen in the next.[52]
    Third, where Aquinas says that blessedness is the reward of virtue,
Spinoza totally disagrees. Blessedness is not the reward of virtue, argues
Spinoza; it is virtue itself. 'Hence we clearly understand how far astray
from the true estimation of virtue are those who, failing to understand that
virtue itself and the service of God are happiness itself and utmost freedom, expect God to bestow on them the highest rewards in return for
their virtue and meritorious actions.'[53] I have no basis for thinking that
Aquinas is in Spinoza's sights here; he could be criticizing any number of
Christians.[54] The point is that the position which Spinoza vehemently

---

[51] See, e.g., *Summa Theologicae* II.1.4.1.
[52] For discussion of Aquinas on these issues, see Aertsen (1993), 30–3.
[53] IIP49Sch. See also, e.g., VP42.
[54] For example, William of Ockham argues that virtue is something we choose both for its
own sake and for the sake of something else (namely happiness), while happiness is
something we choose only for its own sake. It follows as a consequence that virtue and

rejects is conventional for Christians, for which reason we need not be too troubled by the linguistic continuity between them.[55] What about *salus*? Let me just discuss the passages from the *Ethics*. In VP36Sch, *salus* is equivalent to *beatitudo*. He also treats them as equivalents in the two passages from the *TTP* that I have cited. Since his conception of *beatitudo* is not redolent of Christian dogma, it follows that *salus* will not be, either. Admittedly, the other instance where Spinoza mentions *salus* – in the penultimate sentence of the *Ethics* (VP42Sch) – he does not connect it with *beatitudo*. In itself, however, I do not see how the *salus* of VP42Sch would be unrecognizably Christian to ancient Stoics or even objectionable in any way to them. Like Spinoza, they also took happiness to be the ultimate achievement, reached by very few or maybe none. Indeed, insofar as being *eudaimon* is being *makarios*, then it is as great an achievement as Spinoza seems to regard *salus*.

Rather than seeing Spinoza as borrowing traditional Christian vernacular because he seeks to place himself in the Christian traditions which originated the vernacular, I think it is better to see him here borrowing the vernacular only to change it, to co-opt it for his own ends.[56] At a minimum, his usage of *beatitudo* and *salus* does not by itself distinguish his conception of happiness from that of the Stoics. If his conception of happiness is different, it will have to be for other reasons.

5.1.3 Indeed, so far from taking the language of happiness to indicate a divide between the Stoics' ways of thinking about happiness and Spinoza's, I think they show broad overlap. For both parties, the words for happiness apply to the overall course of an agent's life. For the Stoics, this is obviously true in the case of *eu zen* but it is equally true of the other words. If someone is *eudaimon*, then the power controlling her destiny is said to be favourable. The person who is *makarios* is called blessed because his life has such an abundance of goodness. The same scope holds for Spinoza's various expressions. *Beatitudo seu salus*, he says in one place, is the 'constant and eternal love towards God'.[57] This is not something which comes and goes; it is without end. Likewise for *beatus*, about which he says, e.g., that no one can desire 'to live well' without actually

happiness must be distinct. See his commentary on the *Sentences* of Peter Lombard, Question 2, Answer 2d (p. 356 of McGrade et al. (2001)).

[55] For a different discussion of Aquinas' relation to Spinoza, see Carriero (forthcoming). I shall return to the place of virtue in happiness below (see Section 5.6.1).

[56] Another relevant case is Spinoza's use of natural law language in a way that is reminiscent of the natural law tradition but differs greatly from it. See Curley (1991), 97.

[57] VP36Sch.

existing.[58] Thus both the Stoics and Spinoza take happiness to be a state that one is in; it is not a transient, fleeting experience.

There is a second way in which the language of happiness reveals significant continuities. For both the Stoics and Spinoza, the nature of happiness is the same for all agents who are able to be happy. What makes one person happy, they hold, is the same that will make another person happy. There is a set of fixed conditions for happiness such that any agent who would be happy must satisfy those conditions. I shall soon expound on those conditions. For now, what matters is that both the Stoics and Spinoza stipulate the necessity of their satisfaction for the person who seeks happiness. That is, they would deny the notion that 'whether a person is happy ... is determined not by any objective conditions of her life but by her own (positive or negative) attitudes towards it'.[59]

5.2   The form and content of happiness

In the previous section, I commenced my comparison of Spinoza's and the Stoics' conceptions of happiness by looking at the actual words they used. In this section, I want to change tactics. Instead of looking closely at the texts, I will construct an analytical framework for interpreting them. I shall try to motivate this framework in the next section. For now, my goal is just to explain it. To get started, I need to rehearse some familiar ideas from logic.

In logic, the form of an argument is its syntax. This syntax concerns the relationships that exist among the sentences (or, if you prefer, propositions) of the argument. It is *not* about the truth-values or meaning of those sentences. Truth-values and meaning belong to the domain of semantics. The semantics of an argument is its content. Since form and content are distinct, it is possible for one argument form to be instantiated with multiple different contents. Given the nesting of the crucial properties of validity and soundness (the soundness of an argument depends on its validity but not vice versa), an argument's form is a more basic determinant of its logical properties than its contents.[60] Because I borrow, quite deliberately, the vernacular of form and content from their logical home, the concept of form and content as I apply them to happiness shares these same features.

---

[58] IVP18.   [59] Sumner (2002), 24.
[60] There are many other reasons for the importance of logical form, some of which further explain why an argument's logical form is more important than its contents. To cite two examples, logical form determines the specification of the truth-conditions of the argument, and it shows which aspects of the argument's meaning follow from the logical role of certain terms.

Mutatis mutandis, it will come as no surprise that modifications must be made to form and content as they are removed from logic and applied to happiness. Three changes in particular should be noted. First, while logical form concerns the relationships that exist among sentences/propositions, what I shall call eudaimonic[61] form specifies the structural conditions that any putative theory of happiness must satisfy before it will be recognized as a legitimate contender. They are the shared assumptions of all those who theorized philosophically about happiness; if someone does not share those assumptions, one is not approaching happiness in the same manner as those who do. Second, while logical form is orthogonal to the conceptual content of an argument, eudaimonic form is not entirely content-free: eudaimonic form does entail some conceptual commitments among those who subscribe to it. Since these commitments are universally held by all those who subscribe to that form, however, they can be taken as part of the form of the theory, not its individuating contents. Third and finally, because eudaimonic form is not entirely content-free, eudaimonic form sets limits on what contents are possible. For this reason, eudaimonic form is arguably more important than eudaimonic content.

With these refinements to eudaimonic form and content in mind, let me directly explain my understanding of it. As I shall understand it, the form of a theory of happiness is its abstract and content-free[62] elements. These elements serve the crucial function of limiting the set of possible accounts which could be given of happiness. Yet they do not restrict the set so severely as to make it single. Given that the eudaimonic form of two theories x and y can remain fixed even as the contents of those theories vary from x to y, it follows that x and y will differ on the level of content.

5.3   Eudaimonic form and content in Stoicism

While the distinction between eudaimonic form and eudaimonic content has intrinsic value, I have a more mercenary interest in it. Here comes the motivation that I promised to give at the beginning of the previous section. When we try to compare the view of two philosophers or two

---

[61] The word is perhaps unfortunate, in that it resembles so closely *eudaimonia*, the ethics of ancient philosophers. The problem is that there are many possible types of eudaimonic form, only one of which is that of the ancients. In contrast to the ancients' eudaimonic form, there is also a eudaimonic form for contemporary subjectivist accounts of happiness. So long as we are aware that eudaimonic form is not the same as the form of happiness held by the ancients, we should avoid the problem.

[62] Content-free to the extent noted in the previous paragraph.

groups of philosophers on happiness, we can quickly become enmeshed in detail or, even worse, fail to relate them properly. The most familiar example of this failing would be when one compares a subjective conception of happiness with an objective conception without realizing the difference between the two.[63] I believe that my distinction between eudaimonic form and content makes it very difficult to commit such mistakes, for it fixes precisely just what should be considered and how those concepts matter. I also think the distinction captures some important features of philosophical treatments of happiness, such as that two philosophers can argue about the content of happiness even as they think it has the same basic form.

While there are other benefits of the form/content distinction, I do not want to delay any longer my application of this distinction to the prime topic of this chapter, which is comparing Spinoza's conception of happiness to that of the Stoics. So I shall commence this comparison, beginning with the Stoics. In this section, I shall present some texts from Stoics of both the ancient and early modern worlds. My goal will be to offer a nearly complete *précis* of their conception of happiness – both its form and its content.

Let me start with eudaimonic form. The Stoics held that happiness is our highest good and perfection.[64] Because happiness is the highest state of human existence, anyone who is happy lacks nothing.[65] It follows from this that happiness is self-sufficient and complete.[66] When someone is happy, her or his life is said to be in a certain state. As described by Zeno, 'happiness is a good flow of life'.[67] All rational agents are capable of happiness, which they can attain by satisfying the one (and only one) condition for happiness: virtue.[68] This condition holds for everyone who could possibly be happy, which allows it to be described as the single set of necessary and sufficient conditions for happiness. Finally, the Stoics divide ethics into a sophisticated set of specialized subtopics.[69] There is a practical aim behind these divisions. By distilling a complex subject into its individual parts, learning will be facilitated. This points to the overarching goal of Stoic moral philosophy: to help train 'the would-be honourable and good man'.[70]

---

[63] Roughly speaking, subjective happiness takes happiness to be a state of mind while objective happiness sees happiness as consisting in a life that is going well for the person whose life it is. For more, see Kahneman (1999).
[64] See, e.g., Stobaeus *Ecl.* II.77.16 ff.   [65] See, e.g., Seneca *Ep.* 76.10.
[66] See, e.g., Cicero *TD* V.71–2.   [67] Stobaeus *Ecl.* II.77.21.   [68] See, e.g., DL VII.89.
[69] See, e.g., DL VII.84.   [70] Epictetus, *Discourses* III.2.1.

Table 5.1 *The form of happiness in Stoicism*[71]

	1. Highest good (*summum bonum*?	2. Ultimate end (*finis ultimus*)?	3. Goal of ethics?	4. Feeling?	5. State of being?	6. Nec & Suff?
STOICS	Yes	Yes	Yes	No	Yes	Yes

Table 5.1 displays much, though not all, of the form of happiness in Stoic ethics.[72] As such, it displays what might be called the syntax of happiness, as construed by Stoics. These are the shared assumptions of Stoics; theorizing about happiness began from this starting point. Because they are assumed parts of the discourse about happiness, they do not deserve special attention (Stoics did not argue about them – they argued about the content of happiness, such as displayed in Table 5.2, below). At the same time, they are not content-free; as I said above, eudaimonic form as a concept differs from logical form in that it does entail some conceptual commitments. Given the conceptual commitments that the form of happiness carries, important restrictions on theorizing about happiness arise. For example, the eudaimonic form displayed in Table 5.1 is incompatible with a subjectivist account of happiness, which takes happiness to be an episodic and transient feeling, variable from individual to individual, into which the individual has special epistemic insight. Because of the limits placed on what could count as an account of happiness, the eudaimonic form of Table 5.1 ought to attract our attention first, as we compare Stoic accounts of happiness to accounts of those who lived and thought outside its parameters.

[71] The six columns are asking six different questions: (1) Does the philosophical school (which is Stoicism, in the present case) take happiness to be the highest good (*summum bonum*)? (2) Does it take happiness to be the ultimate end (*finis ultimis*)? (3) Is presenting and defending a conception of happiness the primary goal of philosophical ethics for that school? (4) Does it take happiness to be a feeling, which the agent experiences briefly before it passes away? (5) Does it take happiness to be a state of being which perdures through time? (6) Does the school hold that there are a set of necessary and sufficient conditions for happiness that all agents must satisfy before they can be considered happy?

[72] It is the same as the form of happiness held by almost all ancient philosophers. I have argued for this in Miller (2010). Indeed, it is also the form of happiness held by philosophers of the late middle ages. For example, after going through the views of Stoics, Epicureans, and Aristotelians on the nature of happiness, Leonardo Bruni (writing in 1425) concluded, 'All of them seem to say the same things, or nearly so, at least about the highest good' (Bruni (1987), 273). The commonalities which Bruni noticed concerned what I am calling the form of happiness. See, e.g., Cicero *TD* V.36.

Turning to eudaimonic content in Stoicism, I want to start with an important and sometimes overlooked point: there was actually vigorous argument among Stoics themselves regarding some of the contents of happiness. Take something I shall call the V Thesis: that virtue was both necessary and sufficient for happiness. All Stoics accepted this thesis.[73] They disagreed, however, on its implications. Most Stoics allowed that even though virtue is necessary and sufficient for happiness, some external goods could play a part in the happy life. Health or wealth may not be morally good but they are typically appropriate or suitable for us and so they are to be preferred to their opposites. *Ceteris paribus*, most Stoics would accord such external goods that sort of position in the happy life.[74] However, Aristo held otherwise, arguing that if the V thesis were true, then nothing else matters for happiness, including all external goods, no matter how welcome they might appear from some perspective.[75]

Now, I do not wish to exaggerate the arguments among Stoics about the contents of happiness. As I shall soon say, Stoics by and large agreed. Still, I wanted to note the foregoing disagreement, as it shows how Stoics could disagree on something (an aspect of the contents of happiness) while agreeing on something else (the basic shape or form of happiness). This is true not just for Stoicism but also for other major philosophical schools.

Be that as it may, let me highlight some of the other contents of happiness according to Stoics. It is not true that a single virtue suffices for happiness. This is untrue because it supposes an impossibility: namely, that someone could possess a single virtue (e.g., justice) without simultaneously having them all.[76] Since the true good of happiness is not increased by time, they further maintained that a long life is not necessary for happiness.[77] A final important issue concerns the place of pleasure in happiness. On this matter, Stoics were unequivocal: pleasure was a passion; like all other passions, it is an excessive rational impulse; as such, it has no place in the healthy rational life which constitutes happiness.[78] Granted, there is a healthy version of pleasure which may attend

---

[73] See, e.g., Cicero *TD* V.36.

[74] To be clear, Stoics did not think we need external goods in order to be happy. On this matter, they disagreed with Aristotle. The point I am presently making is that most Stoics allowed those external goods which are in accordance with nature to have selective value and hence to be part of the happy life.

[75] For more on Aristo and his relation to Stoicism, see Chapter 4, Sections 4.1–4.2. I shall return to this issue in Section 5.6.2 below.

[76] See, e.g., Plutarch *Stoic Rep.* 1046e and Stobaeus II.63.6 ff.

[77] See, e.g., Plutarch *De comm. not.* 1061 ff.   [78] See, e.g., Stobaeus *Ecl.* II.88 ff.

Table 5.2 *The content of happiness in Stoicism*[79]

	1. Single virtue?	2. Virtues?	3. Longevity?	4. Pleasure?	5. External goods?
STOICS	N & ~S	N & S	~(N v S)	~(N v S)	~(N v S)

N = necessary; S = sufficient; IN = instrumentally necessary

happiness.[80] However, even it is only a by-product of the happy life and not a constituent of it (see Table 5.2).[81]

5.4   Cartesian innovations

My goal is of course to compare Spinoza's views on happiness to the Stoics. I shall aim to fill in the empty cells in Tables 5.3 and 5.4, below. Because Descartes is a crucial intermediary between Spinoza and the Stoics, I need to consider some of his innovations before coming directly to Spinoza.

In the letters to Elizabeth from the summer and autumn of 1645, Descartes carefully separated happiness, virtue, and the *summum bonum*. The distinction between happiness and virtue is conveyed in the letter of 18 August 1645: 'happiness consists solely in contentment of mind ... But in order to achieve a contentment which is solid, we need to pursue virtue – that is to say, to maintain a firm and constant will to bring about everything we judge to be the best.'[82] According to Descartes, happiness *strictly speaking* is a feeling – the feeling of contentment. For this reason, Descartes tells Elizabeth, Seneca in particular but all ancient philosophers in general were mistaken in saying that *virtue* had a part in happiness. Rather, virtue forms the essential condition for happiness: it is if and only if we conform to the dictates of reason or are virtuous that we will feel contented with ourselves, for it is only when we have so acted that we can be assured that we have done the best we can.[83]

---

[79] The five columns are posing five different questions: (1) Does the philosophical school being considered (in our case, the Stoics) take a single virtue to be necessary and sufficient for happiness? (2) Does it take the virtues to be necessary and sufficient for happiness? (3) Is longevity necessary and sufficient for happiness? (4) Does the school accord pleasure a necessary or sufficient place in happiness? (5) Does it hold that external goods are needed for happiness?

[80] See, e.g., DL VII.116.

[81] See, e.g., DL VII.101. For discussion, see Graver (2007), 157–8.

[82] A-T IV: 280 (CSMK: 262).   [83] For more on this, see Svensson (2011).

Table 5.3 *The form of happiness in Descartes and Spinoza*

	1. Highest good (*summum bonum*)?	2. Ultimate end (*finis ultimus*)?	3. Goal of ethics?	4. Feeling?	5. State of being?	6. Nec & Suff?
DESCARTES	No	Yes/no	Yes (???)	Yes	???	Yes
SPINOZA						

Table 5.4 *The content of happiness in Descartes and Spinoza*

	1. Single virtue?	2. Virtues?	3. Longevity?	4. Pleasure?	5. External goods?
DESCARTES	IN & ~ S	IN & ~S	~(N v S)	N & S	~(N v S)
SPINOZA					

N = necessary; S = sufficient; IN = instrumentally necessary

But what about the *summum bonum*? Descartes' views on it are expressed in the letter of 6 October 1645: 'I make a distinction between the supreme good – which consists in the exercise of virtue ... – and the satisfaction of mind which results from that acquisition.'[84] The 'satisfaction of mind' of which Descartes speaks here is the 'contentment' that he described in the earlier letter. Since happiness is contentment, happiness is also the feeling of satisfaction. It is also and pointedly *not* the *summum bonum*; that lies in virtue or the firm and constant resolution to follow reason. As Descartes says, the supreme good 'consists only in virtue, because this is the only good, among all those we can possess, which depends entirely on our free will'.[85] In contrast to the ancients, then, Descartes expressly denies that happiness is our greatest good. To the contrary, our greatest good is virtue and it is only fortunate that happiness follows from virtue. (Note that the *finis ultimus* can be either of these, 'for the supreme good is undoubtedly the thing we ought to set ourselves as the end of all our actions, and the resulting contentment of mind is also rightly called our end, since it is the attraction that makes us seek the supreme good'.[86])

[84] A-T IV: 305 (CSMK: 268).
[85] Descartes to Elizabeth, 18 August 1645 (A-T IV: 275 (CSMK: 261)). [86] Ibid.

Rutherford nicely summarizes the importance of Descartes' innovations for the history of happiness:

> The position Descartes outlines for Elisabeth breaks decisively with a key assumption of ancient eudaimonism ... For both Stoics and Epicureans, the aim of ethical inquiry is to articulate the concept of happiness (*eudaimonia*), which is identified as our supreme good and final end ... By disengaging the notion of happiness from that of the supreme good, Descartes lays the foundations of a theory that is distinct from both these ancient views. The difference can be expressed in terms of a distinction between the intension and extension of the word 'happiness'. Stoics and Epicureans operate with the same concept of happiness: it is the supreme good, and final end, of action. By contrast, Descartes begins with a different understanding of happiness. For him, 'happiness' means a kind of pleasure.[87]

In Tables 5.3 and 5.4, these developments are graphically expressed.[88]

5.5   Spinoza's eudaimonic form

So Descartes gives one way in which happiness can be pulled apart from the *summum bonum*. It is not part of Descartes' eudaimonic form to identify happiness as the supreme good. Does Spinoza follow Descartes' lead? In the next two sections, I shall attempt to answer that question by proceeding systematically through some of the cells on Tables 5.3 and 5.4. I shall start in this section with Table 5.3.

5.5.1   *The status of happiness in philosophical ethics*

Let me start with the status of happiness in Spinoza's philosophy. Spinoza explicitly acknowledges the orientation towards happiness (or something like happiness) of some of his works, such as *TdIE* §1, quoted in the introduction to this chapter. I have already discussed it, so I will turn instead to the *Ethics*.

Now, it would be a mistake to underestimate the intrinsic interest for a man of Spinoza's predilections of the subjects treated in Parts I–IV of that work. The nature of substance, the nature of the mind, the theory of ideas, human psychology, the limits and possibility of freedom – the richness and importance of these issues would have induced Spinoza to investigate them even if he saw no connection between them and happiness. Yet the fact remains that he did perceive such a connection. Part V is called 'On

---

[87] Rutherford (2004), 182.

[88] For the sake of completeness, I have added Descartes' views on issues beyond those that I have just discussed. I hold that a close reading of Descartes' correspondence with Elizabeth supports all my attributions.

the Power of the Intellect, or [*sive*] on Human Freedom'. Since he equates freedom with blessedness in the second sentence of VPref, it seems that Part V is about blessedness. As with the *TdIE*, there are excursions through terrain which seem only distantly related to blessedness or happiness. But Spinoza reinforces the eudaimonic tenor by returning to blessedness in the very last proposition, VP42.

On the other hand, a sceptical reply to the foregoing is to point out that it serves only to identify the similarity of Spinoza's overall philosophical methodology to that of the Stoics: both parties thought it necessary to study logic/method and metaphysics/nature before proceeding to ethics. Yet that is immaterial to the locus of ethical questions *per se*. Julia Annas says that eudaimonistic ethical theory such as the Stoics' 'holds that ethical questions are centered on the question of what happiness is and how best to achieve it'.[89] If the locus of Stoic ethics is happiness, the question to be asked is whether the same is true of Spinozistic ethics.

Before answering that question, I should isolate two distinct if related features of the Stoic view. One is that the 'entry point'[90] for Stoic ethics is one's life as a whole. This is in contrast to a prominent strand of contemporary ethics, which has concentrated on duty and obligation.[91] To do ethics in the eudaimonistic tradition is to ask what it is for a human to live well. And here we come to the second feature. The answer to the question of what it is for a human to live well is that living well is being happy. So understood, happiness is very robust: it involves or incorporates all the really important aspects of one's life. Now, because they had different views on what aspects of one's life are really important – Stoics thought that our rationality alone mattered while Aristotelians had a more expansive view – eudaimonists differed on the requirements for living well. But while they differed on the specifics, they agreed in taking

---

[89] Annas (1999a), 37.
[90] These are Annas' words (see Annas (1993), 27). Though she is speaking of ancient ethics generally, her claim holds of Stoic ethics in particular.
[91] This point of course has been made many times. I particularly like how Stuart Hampshire captures the difference: 'Aristotle is almost entirely concerned to analyse the problems of the moral *agent*, while most contemporary moral philosophers seem to be primarily concerned to analyse the problems of the moral *judge* or critic. Aristotle describes and analyses the processes of thought, or types of argument, which lead up to the *choice* of one course of action, or way of life, in preference to another, while most contemporary philosophers describe the arguments . . . which lead up to the acceptance or rejection of a moral *judgment about actions* . . . [Given its orientation], much of contemporary moral philosophy is concerned with a relatively trivial side-issue' in comparison to Aristotle (Hampshire (1949), 466, 469 (his emphasis)). Hampshire talks about Aristotle in particular but I take his point to cover all major ancient schools.

happiness to be flourishing in a full sense, for they agreed that one is happy if and only if all the important parts of one's life are thriving.[92]

Taking the foregoing to explain the meaning of the claim that Stoic ethics centres on happiness, let us return to Spinoza. For him, the primary ethical problem is not duty or obligation; it is how we ought to live our lives, given our extreme frailties and the enormous power of nature. Evidence of this orientation abounds. Part IV of the *Ethics* is called 'On Human Bondage'; within this part, there are numerous propositions addressing the conduct of life. Part V deals with the converse; it explains how our lives can be blessed, despite our weaknesses. So the final two parts of the *Ethics*, described in the broadest of terms, concern the question of how we can live well. In addition, Spinoza answers that question by arguing that we live well when we flourish. As he writes in IVP18Sch, 'happiness [*felicitatem*] consists in man's being able to preserve his being'.[93] A few propositions later, he is even more obviously on target, when he says that 'to live blessedly' is the same as to live 'well' and to act 'well'.[94] Since, like the Stoics, Spinoza thinks that ethics begins (and ends) by reflecting on the question of what it is for one's life as a whole to flourish, and since he thinks that one flourishes when one is happy, I think it safe to conclude that the eudaimonic form of Spinoza's concept of happiness shares a key property with that of the Stoics: namely, its overarching objective is the articulation and defence of a conception of happiness. So turning to Table 5.3, the form of happiness, I think we should put a 'Yes' in the cell across from Spinoza and under column 3.

5.5.2   Feeling

The question here is whether happiness is a feeling or not. As I have argued, Descartes took it to be. He wrote to Elizabeth, 'I make a distinction between the supreme good – which consists in the exercise of virtue … – and the satisfaction of mind which results from that acquisition.'[95] For Descartes, happiness *strictly speaking* is the feeling of contentment that the mind enjoys when it knows it has done its best.

---

[92] Irwin clearly identifies the requirements for true happiness, as construed by common sense in ancient Greece: '(1) wealth; (2) health, beauty, and other bodily advantages; (3) good birth and honour in one's own city; (4) temperance, justice, and bravery; (5) wisdom; and (6) good fortune' (Irwin (1995), 33). Irwin is good on showing how these common-sense views of happiness generate tensions 'between the different apparent aspects of happiness', and how ancient philosophers dealt with these tensions.
[93] G II, 222: 27–8.   [94] IVP21Dem.
[95] Letter of 6 October 1645 (A-T IV: 305; CSMK III: 268).

So what of Spinoza? There is some indication of his waffling on the matter. On the one hand, he will say that happiness or blessedness 'is nothing but that satisfaction of mind that stems from the intuitive knowledge of God'.[96] In a similar spirit he writes in the *TTP*, '[Philosophers] place true happiness [*veram felicitatem*] solely in virtue and peace of mind [*tranquillitate animi*].'[97] In both these cases, happiness is held to be the satisfaction that the mind enjoys because it has obtained some end (which the former quotation identifies as intuitive knowledge of God).

On the other hand, Spinoza writes that 'blessedness [*beatitudo*] must surely consist in this, that the mind is endowed with perfection itself' or that 'happiness [*felicitatem*] consists in a man's being able to preserve his own being'.[98] Here and elsewhere happiness is not made to be the reward of virtue, a blissful state that the happy person enters as a result of his happiness. Rather, happiness just is virtue or perfection.

Spinoza also distinguishes two conditions in the *Ethics*: *becoming* perfect and *being* perfect. Attendant upon these two conditions are two related emotions. According to Spinoza, joy (*laetitia*) is 'that passion by which the Mind passes to a greater perfection'.[99] If one were to be perfect, one could not experience normal joy.[100] Instead, one experiences a special kind of positive emotion, which Spinoza calls 'intellectual love of God'.[101]

Now, this intellectual love of God that one would experience if one were perfect and hence happy is not part of our perfection and happiness. It is, however, necessarily connected to it. The thought here is quite similar to one found in Aquinas. He argued that because delight (*delectatio*) was 'concomitant' upon happiness, it had a necessary connection to happiness.[102] Yet he and other medieval philosophers denied delight, or any feeling, a part in the essence of happiness *per se*. It is also highly reminiscent of something we have found in Stoicism. In Section 5.1 above, I quoted Seneca's remark that 'not even that joy that arises from virtue, though a good, is part of the absolute good'.[103] Seneca and other Stoics thought there was a feeling associated with happiness, as a consequence of it. In Seneca's case, he called that feeling *gaudium*.

So the evidence is conflicting. On balance, I do not think that Spinoza took happiness to be a feeling, as Descartes did. Though he may use the terms inconsistently, I think his considered view is like Aquinas' and Seneca's: happiness *per se* is our perfection; when we achieve happiness,

---

[96] IVAppIV.   [97] *TTP* VI (G III, 88: 5–6).   [98] VP33Sch and IVP18Sch, respectively.
[99] IIIP11Sch (G II, 149: 2–3).
[100] As Spinoza says, 'If a man were born with the perfection to which he passes, he would possess it without an affect of Joy.'
[101] VP32Cor.   [102] *Summa Theologiae* II.1.4.1.
[103] *De vita beata* 15.2 (trans. Basore in Seneca (1932)).

we enjoy a unique feeling that is caused by our happiness but that feeling is not part of our happiness. In sum, then, I think we should put a 'No (?)' in the cell on Table 5.3 across from Spinoza and under column 4.

5.5.3 Highest good

Let's look first at the *TdIE*. Halfway through the protrepticus, Spinoza provides a simple argument. We are weak beings who suffer many limitations, and we know it. Yet we can conceive 'a human nature much stronger and more enduring' than our own. At the same time, we believe that 'nothing prevents [our] acquiring such a nature'. So we go for it. This perfected human nature, which consists in 'the knowledge of the union that the mind has with the whole of Nature', is our *summum bonum*.[104]

Given that early moderns were starting to separate the concept of the *summum bonum* from that of happiness – I have already shown how this happens in Descartes' case – it would be a mistake to draw any immediate inferences about *happiness* specifically from his views on the *summum bonum*. It is possible that our *summum bonum* should be a certain kind of knowledge while our happiness should be something else. Interestingly, however, as if he wants to clarify any possible ambiguity, Spinoza proceeds to mention happiness in the very next paragraph: 'This, then, is the end I aim at: to acquire such a nature, and to strive that many acquire it with me. That is, it is part of my happiness [*felicitate*] to take pains that many others may understand as I understand.'[105] Spinoza's happiness involves the acquisition of a 'stronger and more enduring' nature which can be acquired only by understanding how he is or exists as part of nature. Since this is also his *summum bonum*, it seems that happiness and *summum bonum* go together. As he writes in the *TTP*, 'our supreme good and blessedness [*summum bonum, nostraque beatitudo*]' consist in one and the same thing: knowledge and love of God.[106]

Turning to the *Ethics*, I shall first reconstruct an argument that I find there, before offering some accompanying comments.

1. Happiness consists in our being able to preserve our being (IVP18Sch (at G II 222: 27–8)).
2. According to his *conatus* doctrine, our being is defined in terms of power (IIIP6, P7).
3. *Qua* thinking beings, our power is knowledge (see IVP36Sch, VPref (at G II 280: 22), etc.).

---

[104] All quotations are from *TdIE* §13. [105] *TdIE* §14. [106] *TTP* IV (G III, 60: 16).

4. So *qua* thinking beings, our being is best preserved by knowledge and more specifically, a certain kind of knowledge – viz., intuitive knowledge of God (VP25).
5. So *qua* thinking beings, our happiness consists in knowledge and especially in intuitive knowledge of God.
6. IVP28 says that 'Knowledge of God is the Mind's greatest good; its greatest virtue is to know God.'
7. Since happiness is knowledge (and knowledge of God), and our greatest good is knowledge (and knowledge of God), it follows that happiness and *summum bonum* are equivalent.

Two comments, one about a crucial step in the argument and the second concerning its conclusion.

The argument assumes that the knowledge in which our happiness consists is identical to the knowledge which is our greatest good. If the relationship between the two bodies of knowledge should be anything less than identical, the degree of confidence that should be placed in the affinity of the relationship between happiness and our greatest good would be commensurately weakened. Now, while conceding vagueness in Spinoza's manner of expression – he often does not use technical terms with the precision and consistency that we might like – I think it unlikely that he intended to convey any difference in the two bodies of knowledge. Yet it is possible that he did and so I ought to flag the possibility as we assess the argument.

Regarding the conclusion, I said that happiness and *summum bonum* are equivalent. This is not the same as saying they are *identical*. They are not. Instead, a sequence of thought is required to connect them. This sequence is shown in the argument itself. It starts with the idea that we are happy when we are able to preserve our being. To preserve our being, we have to acquire and maintain certain goods, such as knowledge. The best of these goods is our highest good, our *summum bonum*. So when we are truly happy, we are also in possession of our *summum bonum*.[107] Since, as I have shown, the sequence of thought required to connect them

---

[107] Spinoza takes happiness and *summum bonum* to be equivalent in the same way that happiness and virtue are taken to be equivalent by the ancient Stoics. They demonstrate the equivalence between happiness and virtue by a series of steps: happiness is possession of the good; the genuine good must benefit its possessor in all circumstances; virtue alone does this; so one is happy only in the case that one is virtuous. Alternatively: happiness is living in agreement with nature; to live in agreement with nature is to be rational; to be rational is to be virtuous; so, happiness is virtuousness. Each step in these series is argued for; moreover, the gap between the first and the last steps is regarded by Stoics themselves as serious and in need of filling. So, although happiness is equivalent to virtuousness, they are not identical. For more on how Stoics divided the parts of ethics, see DL VII.84 and Epictetus, *Discourses* III.2.1–5.

involves several steps, they are best taken as standing in a relationship of equivalence and no stronger.

So the eudaimonic form of Spinoza's concept of happiness shares an important property with that of the Stoics: the form of happiness includes, inter alia, the idea of the *summum bonum*. On Table 5.3, then, we should write 'Yes' in the appropriate cell.

5.6   Spinoza's eudaimonic content

I have prescribed a method for comparing Spinoza's eudaimonic form to that of the Stoics. So although I have not examined all of the categories on Table 5.3,[108] the way in which such an examination would proceed is plain. The evidence for what can be said about Spinoza's views on the categories of the table varies widely, which is not surprising. The table is an exegetical device I have created; there is no reason why he must speak to everything on it. If insufficient evidence exists for determining his views on a particular issue, then the cell must reflect that uncertainty. This method is applicable, of course, not just to Spinoza but also to other early modern philosophers. It is useful for determining the extent to which they conform to and deviate from Stoic ethics. Of course, it has its limitations, foremost among them being that it reveals only the similarity of form, not of content. To address this problem, I will shift from one to the other, by noting some (of many) affinities between what I have called the 'semantics' of Spinoza's conception of happiness and that of Stoics.

5.6.1   Virtue

The first semantical feature of Spinoza's conception of happiness I will discuss concerns the status of virtue in the happy life. I hold that Spinoza's view is Stoical. He writes, 'Acting absolutely from virtue is nothing else in us but acting, living, and preserving our being (these three signify the same thing) by the guidance of reason.'[109] We are virtuous when we preserve our being. Since the preservation of our being is also the foundation of our happiness, when and insofar as we are virtuous, we are happy. Now, it may be that Spinoza and the Stoics differ on what it means to be virtuous. At least, it is not part of my present point to insist that the concept of virtue is identical in both cases. Rather, I want to note the

---

[108] To be precise, the only column that I have not addressed is column 2, on whether happiness is our ultimate end. In Section 5.1.3, I addressed (albeit briefly) columns 5 and 6. In the section just ended, I addressed columns 3, 4, and 1.

[109] IVP24.

sameness of the status of virtue. For both parties, we are happy when, and only when, we are virtuous.

This seems to have been an important point to Spinoza, for it is central to the very last proposition of the *Ethics*, VP42: 'Blessedness [*beatitudo*] is not the reward of virtue, but virtue itself.' While I must grant that Spinoza uses the word '*beatitudo*' here and not 'felicitas', I noted above (Section 5.1.1) that he sometimes treats the words as synonyms. Moreover, it is possible that, as Kisner notes, Spinoza 'uses so many terms in recognition of the difficulty of translating "*eudaimonia*"'.[110] Finally, even if *beatitudo* differs somewhat from *felicitas*, they are at least cognate terms. Given the foregoing, I think we need not be too troubled by the appearance of *beatitudo* rather than *felicitas* in VP42.

Taking that to be so, turn to the proposition's central claim: blessedness just is virtue itself. If anything, this claim asserts an even stronger relationship between blessedness/happiness and virtue than that virtue is the necessary and sufficient condition for happiness. It holds that blessedness/happiness is *identical* to virtue.

If we want to complete the cell in Table 5.4 across from Spinoza and under virtue, then plainly we should have to say that virtue is both necessary and sufficient for happiness. There is a complication, however, as given by Table 5.4 itself. On the table, there are two columns about happiness. Column 1 asks whether a single virtue is necessary and/or sufficient for happiness, while column 2 asks about *virtues*, plural. I have not addressed this difference previously; now is the time.

I can illustrate it by referring to a couple of familiar passages in Plato. In *Republic* I, Socrates argues that one virtue alone is needed to live well and hence be happy: justice.[111] By contrast, we find in the *Protagoras* a dispute between Protagoras and Socrates about whether (as Protagoras holds) courage does not equal justice and other virtues, in which case the person who would be fully virtuous must partake of all them.[112] The issue of whether happiness required a single virtue or many virtues was very much alive in Spinoza's day and the era preceding him.[113] So what was Spinoza's view?

---

[110] Kisner (2011), 75 n. 5.   [111] See 353e–354a.

[112] As Protagoras says, 'many are courageous but unjust, and many again are just but not wise' (329e 5–6, trans. Lombardo and Bell in Protagoras (1997)).

[113] For example, Ficino has this to say: 'The same thing happens with moral virtues: once one of them is acquired you immediately possess all the others. For who will make a just distribution, if he is afraid of threats or a slave to lust? ... So the virtues are so closely tied together that they are all in one' (Ficino (2001), VIII.iii.10). Lipsius also weighs in on the subject, though it is less certain what his considered view might be. In his *Politica*, he 'divides' (his word) virtue into two subjects, which he calls 'belief' and 'worship'. They are irreducible and both required for happiness. See Lipsius (2004),

Let us return to his definition of virtue, IVD8: 'By virtue and power I understand the same thing, i.e. (by IIIP7), virtue, insofar as it is related to man, is the very essence, or [*seu*] nature, of man.' At bottom, Spinoza takes virtue to be just one thing: it is seeking our own advantage. As he later says in his so-called 'Dictates of Reason', 'the foundation of virtue is this very striving to preserve one's one being'.[114] Because our being is complicated – not only are we both minds and bodies but also our minds and bodies are made up of many parts – we will find it necessary to undertake different sorts of activities aimed at the preservation of the different parts of our being. For this reason, Spinoza will talk about different individual virtues: strength of mind (*fortitudo*) and the two kinds of *fortitudo*, tenacity and nobility;[115] freedom;[116] etc. He can also distinguish between private virtue and public virtue or 'the virtue of a state'.[117] This rich analysis of the virtues may be necessitated by the complex requirements under which we find ourselves as we seek to maintain our being. Since all such actions are really just different ways of seeking our advantage, however, it seems that there is ultimately just one virtue. So if we want to complete Table 5.4, I think we should say that across from Spinoza and under column 1, we should write 'necessary and sufficient'. Likewise for what we should write under column 2, though with the proviso that the individual virtues necessary and sufficient for happiness are reducible to the single virtue of pursuing what is to our greatest advantage.

5.6.2   External goods (1)

There is another proviso. Whether virtue is necessary and sufficient for happiness will depend on what we should say about Spinoza's views on the value of external goods. So let us turn next to that topic.

External goods are those things which are external to the agent and do not have disvalue.[118] Classic examples include health, wealth, noble birth, good reputation, friendship, etc. As we have seen, even the Stoics were divided on whether external goods were needed for happiness.[119] I shall now try to show that Spinoza's own views were also mixed.

I.2; for discussion, Brooke (2012), 26–7). Elsewhere, however, he holds there is only one virtue needed for happiness, a right attitude towards God (see Lipsius (1604), II.19).

[114] IVP18Sch.   [115] IIIP59Sch.   [116] *TP* II.7 (at G III, 279: 1).

[117] *TP* I.6. I want to acknowledge my indebtedness here to Michael Rosenthal's excellent discussion of virtue in Rosenthal (2001).

[118] For more on the value of external goods, see Chapter 4, Section 4.2.

[119] See Section 5.3 above.

The key to understanding whether any philosopher took external goods to be necessary for happiness lies in the notion of their being external *to the agent*. So when we consider a philosopher's views on the importance of external goods, we have to ask what he took the agent to be. In Spinoza's case, he took the agent to be conceivable as mental or physical beings.[120] Insofar as the agent is a mental being, Spinoza consistently holds that only one thing is needed for happiness: virtue. I have just gone through this, so I will not draw it out any further. In the cell on Table 5.4 across from Spinoza and under external goods, if we are taking the agent to be a mental being, then we should write 'neither necessary nor sufficient'.

While I will not dwell on the arguments for taking external goods to be neither necessary nor sufficient for happiness for us insofar as we are mental beings, I do want to correct a confusion. Take this passage:

It is the part of a wise man . . . to refresh and restore himself with pleasant food and drink, with scents, with the beauty of green plants, with decoration, music, sports, the theatre, and other things of this kind, which anyone can use without injury to another. For the human Body is composed of a great many parts of different natures, which constantly require new and varied nourishment, so that the whole Body may be equally capable of all the things which can follow from its nature, and hence, so that the Mind also may be equally capable of understanding many things.[121]

On the basis of this passage, some commentators think that Spinoza takes external goods to be necessary for happiness.[122] This is not right. It overlooks the difference between what is necessary and sufficient for happiness *per se* with the contribution that external goods may make to a happy life. Insofar as we are mental beings, we only need to be virtuous in order to be happy. At the same time, we can pursue external goods which may help us be virtuous.

The ancient Stoics can shed light on Spinoza's position. They faced a difficulty similar to the one that I am attributing to him now. On the one hand, ancient Stoics took the moral good to be the only true good. On the other hand, ancient Stoics (apart from the heterodox, such as Aristo) also allowed for things that are in accordance with nature, such as health and

---

[120] Indeed, Spinoza explicitly notes the necessity of attending to the difference of the agent conceived as a mind or as a body when considering what is good for that person (see IVAppXXX).

[121] IVP45Cor2Sch.

[122] For example, Kisner writes, 'There is a difference between Spinoza's and the Stoics' views of virtue. The Stoics reject Aristotle's suggestion that our goods include external things that promote commodious living, whereas Spinoza admits that anything promoting our power contributes to our virtue, including such external things' (Kisner (2011), 81). See also DeBrabander (2007), 36.

wealth, to have value as well. Stoics allowed for external goods which are in accordance with our natures to have value because they furthered our goal of living in accordance with nature. So those goods might be thought to have a part in our end, which is living a life according to nature.[123]

There are two obvious solutions to this difficulty. One would be to follow the Peripatics and allow that our end *does* include getting some of these goods. The other would be to follow Aristo and hold that our end does *not* include these goods, that we should be completely indifferent to them.[124] Orthodox Stoics resisted both, arguing instead that while our end is just living a virtuous and rational life, we can still be benefitted by some external goods. Indeed, Zeno is supposed to have said life would be impossible if we adopted Aristo's total indifference towards indifferents.[125] Cicero tells us how the Stoics tried to strike the balance: 'the final good [*summum bonum*] is a life in which one applies knowledge of those things that happen by nature, selecting those in accordance with nature and rejecting those contrary to nature, that is – a life in agreement and consistent with nature'.[126]

For Stoics as for Spinoza, external goods are not *per se* desirable; they are only desirable as means to the one end which is desirable in itself, happiness. Our physical health and the company of friends are external goods which, if given a choice, we always ought to pursue.[127] If we do not obtain them, then since they are external to us, whether we should get them is not really up to us. It is still possible to be virtuous and hence happy without them, which shows that they are neither necessary nor sufficient for happiness.

5.6.3   External goods (2)

Let me move now to consider Spinoza's views on the status of external goods for the agent conceived as a physical being. The passage from IVP45Cor2Sch quoted above shows that because of their contributions to the body, the wise man does (and therefore all of us should) attach value to external goods such as nourishing food, stimulating exercise and more. So it seems that insofar as we are conceived as bodies, then external goods are necessary but not sufficient for our happiness. The two

---

[123] For discussion and references, see Chapter 4, Section 4.2.

[124] See, e.g., Cicero *De fin.* IV.78 (L-S 64L).

[125] 'What does Zeno say? That Aristo's doctrine is a monstrosity; no life can be lived by such a rule' (Cicero, *De fin.* IV.70, trans. Woolf in Cicero (2001)).

[126] *De fin.* III.31 (L-S 64A).

[127] For the Stoics, see, e.g., DL VII.109. For Spinoza, IVP35Cor2Sch (at G II, 234: 8–10).

complications that I am about to note notwithstanding, I think this is what we should write in the appropriate cell on Table 5.4 (though with a question mark by it).

The complications, however, are of critical importance. The first is that it seems *all* goods for us *qua* extended beings must be external. Food, drink, exercise, health – these are all goods for the body. Whether we are fortunate enough to have them is not entirely due to us; the circumstances in which we find ourselves are also germane. This is true not only of those goods which I have just listed; it is also true of all conceivable goods for the body. Even if we imagine that there should be a perfect pill which would provide all the nourishment required for our body, one which would keep our body in the best state it can be in, whether we will be allowed to obtain and consume that pill depends on our circumstances. So it seems that if something is a good for us *qua* extended beings, then it is *eo ipso* an external good.

The second complication follows from the first. If it is the case that all goods for the body are external goods, then since external goods are not true goods, it seems that there is not a true (i.e., moral) good for the body. Here we enter uncomfortable terrain. On the one hand, parallelism would seem to commit Spinoza to the requirement that there must be a true good for the body, since there is one for the mind.[128] Spinoza himself strives to uphold this commitment in places such as VP39: 'He who has a Body capable of a great many things has a Mind whose greatest part is eternal.' If the mind which has succeeded in making its greatest part eternal is the mind which has achieved the true good,[129] then the body which parallels that mind must also have achieved its true good. On the other hand, I have just argued there is and can be no true good for the body. So it seems that either Spinoza incorrectly maintains that the good of the body is always paralleled by the good of the mind,[130] or else that he incorrectly maintains that the mind and the body are always parallel to each other.[131]

There is a solution to this impasse, one which will look decidedly Stoic. Officially, Spinoza wants to subject us – all of us, our bodies and our minds – to the overwhelming causal forces of Nature. He says as much in

---

[128] This is the view of Kisner (2010), ch. 4, section 2.

[129] This is the implication of VP33 plus VP25.

[130] This is the view of Bidney (1962): '*There is no necessary connection between physical and mental virtue as Spinoza at times strives so hard to maintain*' (293 (his emphasis)).

[131] This was charged by Bennett, among others (see his treatment of parallelism in Bennett (1984) at, e.g., 134–5, 184–7). For a more recent and sympathetic account, see Melamed (2013a), ch. 5.

many oft-cited places.[132] I do not question that this is his actual view. What I want to ask is whether it is the view he should have espoused.[133]

If we were totally subjected to the forces of Nature, there should be no part of us protected from Nature. All states of our bodies would be fully causally determined, as would all states of our minds. If that were the case, then there would be no point whatsoever in drawing a distinction between what is inside us and outside us, at least in respect of what is within our control. If we were fully subjected to the forces of Nature, nothing would be within our control. The distinction between what is inside and what is outside would be immaterial. There would be no 'inside' and 'outside', for Nature reaches everywhere.

Yet the fact is Spinoza often invokes this distinction and he does so in service of explaining why we should not be concerned when things turn out contrary to our expectations or desires. Consider this part of IVAppXXXII: 'But human power is very limited and infinitely surpassed by the power of external causes. So we do not have an absolute power to adapt things outside us to our use [*atque adeo potestatem absolutam non habemus, res, quae extra nos sunt, ad nostrum usum aptandi*].' If Nature's reach were complete, then of course we would not have the power to adapt things outside us to our use. Moreover, if Nature's reach were complete, then we would not have the power to adapt things *inside* us to our use. If Nature's reach were complete, everything that happened anywhere would be the result of Nature's determinations.

IVAppXXXII is not the only place where Spinoza talks about 'things outside us' in the *Ethics*.[134] Evidently, Spinoza was committed to the distinction between things being inside us and outside us. He does not explicitly take the distinction in this direction but I think it is tied to a second distinction, between the realm where we have some autonomy (the internal realm) and that realm where we do not (the external). If this is correct, then Spinoza has – perhaps inadvertently – crafted a remarkably Stoic set of views. In Section 4.2, I noted Epictetus' distinction between things that are up to us (*eph' hēmin*) and those which are not (*ouk eph' hēmin*). Since Epictetus took the human agent to be defined by his rationality, everything which is up to us must fall within the domain of the rational. Within that domain, the agent reigns supreme; he is free of

[132] See, e.g., IIIPref (at G II, 138: 12 ff), IVA1, IVP50Sch (at G II, 247: 18), VPref (at G II, 277: 17).
[133] To be clear, I am not advocating a Straussian interpretation here, where he intentionally says one thing so as to obscure his true different meaning. Instead, I am about to argue that Spinoza was himself confused about what his position should be.
[134] Other important passages include IIP31, IIID2, IVP18Sch (at G II, 222: 34 to 223: 3), and IVAppII.

the causal forces that determine all else. To quote the familiar opening lines from the *Enchiridion*, 'Our opinions are up to us, and our impulses, desires, aversions – in short, whatever is our own doing.'[135]

Bringing this back to the impasse noted above, suppose it is correct that Spinoza holds a distinction between things that are up to us and things that are not. Suppose furthermore that he thinks things up to us are up to us only insofar as we are rational creatures. If so, it seems that the agent which has control over things is defined by his reason. Such an agent can have his own true good; it is the good identified in Chapter 4, namely knowledge of God. There will be no physical correlate to this mental agent. So it is true that (as Bidney alleged) the good of the mind is not always matched by a good for the body. So the good of the body can be an external good, as I said earlier in this section.

5.7   Conclusion: life according to nature

There is more to be said about the foregoing. I could also address more of the categories on Table 5.4, as I have only spoken directly to columns 1, 2, and 5. However, I need to draw the discussion to a close. To conclude the chapter, I want to bring the focus squarely on how it is that we can be happy, according to Spinoza and the Stoics. For both parties, true happiness is only to be found by living a life in accordance with nature.

Let me begin with an observation. When Spinoza speaks about the highest moral achievement or state we can be in, he uses a bewildering array of words: freedom,[136] happiness,[137] blessedness,[138] perfection,[139] peace of mind,[140] supreme good,[141] rationality,[142] knowledge or understanding.[143] Just the same occurs in Stoicism. Granted, a degree of fixity occurs in the way Stoics always stipulate that the end is happiness. Enormous variation arises, however, in the many ways that they define happiness: happiness is virtue;[144] it is *ataxaria* or tranquillity;[145] it is freedom from harmful emotions;[146] it is rationality;[147] etc. Behind this

[135] *Enchiridion* I.1 (trans. White in Epictetus (1983)).   [136] See, above all, *Ethics* Part V.
[137] See, e.g., *TdIE* §2, IIP49Sch (at G II, 135: 38), IVAppIV, and Letter 43 (at G IV, 220a).
[138] See, e.g., *TTP* IV (at G III, 60), *TTP* V (at G III: 69), VP42, and Letter 78.
[139] See, e.g., *TTP* IV (at G III, 59), IVApp4, VP33Sch, and VP40.
[140] See, e.g., *Short Treatise* II.XXVI, IIP49Sch (at G II, 135), IVP52, VP27, and *TTP* VI (at G III, 88).
[141] See, e.g., *TdIE* §13, IVP36 and its scholium, VP20Dem.
[142] See, e.g., IVP35 and its first corollary, IVAppIV, and *TP* II.7–8 (at G III, 278).
[143] See, e.g., IVApp5 and VPref (at G II, 280).   [144] See, e.g., DL VII.89.
[145] See, e.g., Seneca *Ep.* 92.3.   [146] See, e.g., Cicero *TD* V.81–2.
[147] See, e.g., Seneca *Ep.* 76.9–10.

seemingly disparate array, however, both Spinoza and the Stoics did hold that there is one primary moral goal. It is life according to nature.[148]

Here is not the place to examine thoroughly their conceptions of life in accordance with nature (LAN, for short). Instead, I will just go into one issue, which is why they thought LAN was important. Let us call this the 'why question'.

Stoics might offer different answers to the why question. One is suggested in these often-quoted lines:

[Zeno and Chrysippus] affirmed that everything is fated, with the following model. When a dog is tied to a cart, if it wants to follow it is pulled and follows, making its spontaneous act coincide with necessity, but if it does not want to follow it will be compelled in any case. So it is with men too: even if they do not want to, they will be compelled in any case to follow what is destined.[149]

This simile seems designed to make a point not about the metaphysics of determinism but rather our response to it. Given that all states and events are fully determined, we have to follow the fated order of things, no matter what we want. In light of that, it is in our best interest to seek to conform to that order, for we will suffer less if we do not resist our destiny.

There is much that Spinoza might like in this. It is an egoistic justification of LAN: we should seek to live in accordance with nature because it is the best way for us to preserve our own well-being. However, for two reasons, we cannot stop here. First, the authenticity of the simile has been challenged.[150] Second and more importantly, the simile does not contain the deeper Stoic answer to the why question. To find that, we have to look elsewhere.

For the Stoics, the answer to the why question emerges in the following way.[151] It begins with self-discovery, with the realization of the 'regularity' and 'harmony' of events in one's own life. Then one comes to attach value to this order and to seek to extend it further. As one reflects on the order of one's own life and how important that order is,

---

[148] For Spinoza, see, e.g., *TdIE* §13 and 40, *Ethics* IVP18Sch, IVP24Dem, etc. For commentary, see Miller (2014). For the Stoics, see, e.g., Stobaeus II.77.28 ff. For commentary, see Striker (1983), 222.

[149] Hippolytus, *Refutation of All Heresies*, I.21.

[150] See Bobzien (1998), 354 ff. Bobzien challenges the authenticity in two different ways. First, she argues that the simile was not in fact advanced by Zeno and Chrysippus but rather by members of the Roman Stoa. Second and quite apart from the authorship, Bobzien says (355), the simile contradicts some of Chrysippus' chief innovations, such as his so-called 'idle argument', which seeks to prove even if everything is fated, action is not pointless.

[151] I am relying principally here on Cicero *De fin.* III.17, 20–2, 33.

one begins to look for the source of that order. One comes to believe that this order could have not happened on its own but required the direction of another being. The only being capable of producing such order, one eventually concludes, is nature itself. Since nature bestowed this order and harmony on one's life, it must also have those same properties. For nature to have those properties, it must be rational as well. Since nature's rationality must far exceed one's individual rationality, it will be better for one to seek to conform to the rationality evident in nature itself. The upshot of this process is twofold: first, one learns what one should desire, which is to live a life in accordance with nature; second, one learns the profoundly providential and teleological structure of nature. As one commentator says, 'The Stoic conception of the end does not arise as a natural continuation of one's concern for self-preservation, but rather as a result of one's reflection upon the way nature has arranged human behaviour in the context of an admirable cosmic order.'[152]

Now, Spinoza would admire some of this Stoic answer to the why question. He would allow that reflection and study of the natural order reveals how human beings fit into that order. He might also allow that humans have an end (in some sense of that word) similar to the end posited by the Stoics. In both cases, the end is to live naturally. However, he would do more than merely balk at the teleological and anthropomorphic innuendo. It may be that the natural order provides for human flourishing. It most definitely may not be that this is because nature wanted to nourish us. Nature does not act for an end and it certainly does not act for the end of our well-being. If the key to our well-being lies in living naturally, this is a mere by-product of nature's actions, not the pre-conceived intention.

For a better answer to the why question, let me draw upon a long passage from one of Spinoza's last letters:

I see at last what it was that you urged me not to publish. However, since this is the principal basis of all the contents of the treatise which I had intended to issue, I should here like to explain briefly in what way I maintain the fatalistic necessity of all things and actions.

In no way do I subject God to fate, but I conceive that all things follow with inevitable necessity from God's nature in the same way that everyone conceives that it follows from God's nature that God understands himself. Surely no one denies that this follows necessarily from God's nature, and yet no one conceives that God is forced by some fate to understand himself; it is conceived that God understands himself altogether freely, though necessarily.

---

[152] Striker (1983), 230.

Next, this inevitable necessity of things does not do away with either divine or human laws. For moral precepts, whether or not they receive from God himself the form of command or law, are nonetheless divine and salutary, and whether the good that follows from virtue and the divine love is bestowed on us by God as judge, or whether it emanates from the necessity of the divine nature, it will not on that account be more or less desirable, just as on the other hand the evils that follow from wicked deeds and passions are not less to be feared because they necessarily follow from them. And finally, whether we do what we do necessarily or contingently, we are still led by hope and fear.

Furthermore, men are without excuse before God for no other reason than that they are in God's hands as clay in the hands of the potter, who from the same lump makes vessels, some to honour and some to dishonour. If you would give just a little attention to these few points, I doubt not that you will find it easy to reply to all the objections that are usually raised against this view . . .[153]

Notice the closing assertion: if the reader reflects on the 'few points' just made, then he will find answers to 'all the objections' raised against Spinoza's deterministic metaphysics and the ethical system based on that metaphysics. According to Spinoza, then, these paragraphs contain crucial information.

What is that information? Here, I take it, are the key claims:

1. 'In no way do I subject God to fate';
2. '[A]ll things follow with inevitable necessity from God's nature';
3. 'Next, this inevitable necessity of things does not do away with either divine or human laws. For moral precepts, whether or not they receive from God himself the form of command or law, are nonetheless divine and salutary';
4. 'Furthermore, men are without excuse before God for no other reason than that they are in God's hands as clay in the hands of the potter'.

These propositions can be used to explain why it is good to live in agreement with nature. How so?

Suppose (as (2) maintains) that universal causal determinism obtains. Then (as (4) says) humans are fully determined creatures. Because we are fully determined creatures, we have to live in agreement with the life mapped out for us by nature. To say that we have to, however, is not the end of the story. Despite the truth of universal causal determinism, morality (what Spinoza calls 'moral precepts' (3)) still obtains. To say that morality still obtains is to say that humans are still bound by moral obligations. A key moral obligation is to live virtuously. Living virtuously is living in agreement with our nature. Given the compatibility of moral codes with universal causal determinism, then, we ought to want

---

[153] *Ep.* 75. These are the first four paragraphs (in translation) of the letter.

to live in agreement with nature, for therein lies our surest path to flourishing. To put the matter more colloquially: Spinoza thinks that we have to live in agreement with nature, in any case. We will be better off once we appreciate this truth and seek to organize our lives in accordance with it.

Conclusion: Spinoza and the Stoics?

At the beginning of his agenda-setting monograph on Spinoza, Edwin Curley quoted these lines from Robert Frost: 'We dance round in a ring and suppose,/ But the Secret sits in the middle and knows.'[1] Curley does not say what Secret he had in mind. I suppose it was Spinoza's system itself. If so, it is indeed a Secret.

In this volume, I have been dancing round another Secret, this one involving Spinoza and the Stoics. I have probed the extent of their similarity on a range of issues. Now I am about to approach the Secret directly, which is how Spinoza became so Stoical. I will venture an answer but I confess that it still remains a Secret from me and something of a Mystery to me.

Let me start with a crucial declaration: Spinoza was not a Stoic.[2] This is true in various respects. Doctrinally, he differed from them on points large and small. Even setting aside the large examples of teleology and divine providence,[3] many other disagreements emerged in the chapters above. Unlike the Stoics, he denied that there was anything purely passive in Nature.[4] His epistemology is strongly internalist while theirs is strongly externalist.[5] He thought our essences were defined by our *conatus*, our striving to preserve our being, while Stoics thought we aspire to something more.[6] He was a value dualist whereas the Stoics were value monists.[7] His parallelism put pressures on his conception of happiness which are simply not found in Stoicism.[8]

---

[1] See Curley (1969), v.
[2] So I disagree with the very title of James (1993). In James' defence, as I noted in my Introduction (see Section 3), James' study needs to be placed in its context, a time when the affinities between Spinoza and the Stoics were largely overlooked. It is understandable that she should take such a strong position, if only as a response to the state of scholarship when she wrote.
[3] The issues of teleology and divine providence came up several times in the body of my work; see, e.g., Chapter 1, Section 1.4, and Chapter 3, Section 3.2.4.
[4] See Chapter 1, Section 1.2.3.   [5] See Chapter 2, Section 2.1.
[6] See Chapter 3, Section 3.3.   [7] See Chapter 4, Section 4.3.1.
[8] See Chapter 5, Section 5.6.3.

All of those are examples of what I think of as doctrinal differences between Spinoza and the Stoics. They differ, however, in more than just doctrinal ways. Additionally, Stoicism was a powerful movement (or 'school', to use the more common term) lasting centuries. There are various explanations for this success, not the least of which is that it allowed for a high degree of dissent.[9] For example, while most Stoics had a monistic conception of the soul, Posidonius reverted to a divided soul.[10] Or, as we saw in Chapter 4, while most Stoics divided values into three categories (good, bad, and indifferent), Aristo argued for a twofold division (good and bad).[11] Much more recently, Lawrence Becker has argued that one can even be a Stoic without accepting cosmic teleology and divine providence.[12] Stoicism thrives partly because it admits such a range of interpretations and variations.

The contrast between the rich and varied history of Stoicism to Spinoza could not be starker. It may be that he had historical influence[13] and perhaps someday there will even be a recognizable school of Spinozists.[14] But when we consider Spinoza as he was, we encounter a philosopher who formed his system alone or, at most, with the relatively minor help of some friends and correspondents. There were no immediate or even mediate heirs to take over and refine his amazing achievement. Without taking anything away from what he accomplished, one has to admit that his system has problems.[15] If he had formed a school with successor heads, in the way that ancient Stoicism worked, these

---

[9] In this respect, Stoicism has traditionally been said to differ from Epicureanism, which was thought to hew dogmatically to the views laid out by Epicurus and other early founders of the school. Whether this is an accurate portrayal of Epicureanism is another matter. For a stout defender of the traditional interpretation, see especially Sedley (1989). For a revisionist take, see the collection in Fish and Sanders (2011).

[10] See, e.g., Galen, *PHP* IV.7.24 ff. (L-S 65P).

[11] See Chapter 4, Section 4.2. For a qualification, see n. 15 of that chapter.

[12] See Becker (1998), ch. 3. See also Section 1.4.2 of Chapter 1 in this volume.

[13] The extent of Spinoza's influence on philosophy and related fields is a subject of controversy. In the article on Spinoza in his *Dictionary*, Bayle famously alleged that 'It is not true that his followers have been very numerous' (trans. Popkin in Bayle (1965)). In recent years, the opposite view has tended to predominate. For example, Förster and Melamed assert that 'there can be little doubt that without Spinoza, German idealism would have been just as impossible as it would have been without Kant' (see Förster and Melamed (2012), 1).

[14] For the distinction between Spinoza and Spinozism, see the preface to Hampshire (2005). I also briefly explain what I take the difference to be in my Introduction, note 15.

[15] We have encountered some of these in this volume, such as the 'problem of the attributes' in Chapter 1, Section 1.2.2, and Bidney's allegations dealt with in the Appendix to Chapter 3. To be clear, I am not asserting that those problems are insoluble. My point is rather that if Spinoza did have immediate heirs, in the way that Zeno did with Cleanthes and Chrysippus, the problems might have been addressed more fully and quickly.

problems might have been sorted out. As the saying goes, two heads are better than one.[16]

So Spinoza is not a Stoic. At the same time, there is no doubt that he contrived a system with striking similarities to Stoicism. Anyone who has read through to these pages will know about the extent of those similarities, so I will not repeat myself here.[17] Instead, I will pose this question: all the substantial differences notwithstanding, how is it that Spinoza could be so Stoical? The question is especially pressing for me, since I am inclined to think that the Stoics' actual influence on Spinoza was not great.[18] How is it that Spinoza, working largely independently of the Stoics, formulated a worldview that is so Stoical?

There is no single answer to this question. As I noted in my Introduction,[19] Wilhelm Dilthey thought there were three possible views to take on the nature of the world, and that Stoicism and Spinozism were two different iterations of one of these three types. It is beyond me to argue for such a sweeping perspective on the history of philosophy. Instead, I will offer a different account.[20]

One can either think of the world as constituting a single unified and active entity or not. If one does, then one can either think of that entity as operating in strictly deterministic terms or not. If one thinks of it as determined, one can also think of the world as ultimately rational and

---

[16] We are at an interesting point in the history of Spinozism, for some contemporary Spinoza scholars are undertaking to rectify the problems with Spinoza's system. A prime example of this is Michael Della Rocca's work on the principle of sufficient reason (PSR) in Spinoza (see, e.g., Della Rocca (2003b), (2010), (2012)). It seems to me that Della Rocca is taking the PSR well beyond what Spinoza himself explicitly licensed. Yet he is taking the PSR in directions indicated by Spinoza. So he can be said to complete what Spinoza set out to do.

[17] Some readers might want my conclusion to summarize the results of my investigation. Because I do not have the room to explore both the question of the next sentence (which is so important) and offer such a summary, I will have to omit it here. Instead, I will refer those who are interested back to the body of my book, especially the conclusions of each chapter, for indication of what has been shown.

[18] For more on this matter, see Section 3 of the Introduction.

[19] See the opening and Section 5.4.

[20] A. A. Long says something similar to what I am about to say: 'If one posits strict determinism, the dependence of everything on a single, intelligent causal principle, the physical extension of that principle everywhere, the self-preservative drive of all creatures, the ideal conformity of human nature to rationality and understanding, the incompatibility of happiness with servitude to passions and dependence on worldly contingencies; and if one also believes, as Spinoza and the Stoics did, that a mind perfectly in tune with nature has a logical structure that coheres with the causal sequence of events – if one believes all these things and follows up their implications, the rational constraints on ethics will lead one to a ground shared by Spinoza and the Stoics: a denial of free will, ... an acceptance of the way things are, and an interest in cultivating the understanding as the only basis for achieving virtue, autonomy, and emotional satisfaction' (Long (2003), 15).

intelligible or not. If one thinks this, one can think of the world as fundamentally self-preserving or not. If one thinks that the world bears all those properties, then one may think of members of the world (especially human beings) as sharing the same features of the world or not. If one does, then one thinks that members of the world are also determined, rational, intelligible, and self-preserving beings. If one thinks this of members of the world, then one can think that their flourishing lies in identifying fully with their natures and Nature as a whole or not.

Of course, Stoics and Spinoza did think of the world and ourselves in roughly those terms. They advanced deep and powerful arguments in favour of their views. For all the differences between them, it is this way of looking at the world and the arguments for it that lie at the basis of their congruence. Of this, I am sure. But even as I am sure of this, I am also unsure whether it is enough to explain the Secret. If there is a Secret remaining about the similarity between Spinoza and the Stoics, I suppose it must concern how it is that one comes to accept those views about the world and ourselves together with the underlying arguments in the first place.

Bibliography

Adams, Robert Merrihew (1994). *Leibniz: Determinist, Theist, Idealist* (Oxford: Oxford University Press).

Aertsen, Jan A. (1993). 'Aquinas's philosophy in its historical setting', in Norman Kretzmann and Eleonore Stump, eds., *The Cambridge Companion to Aquinas* (Cambridge: Cambridge University Press): 12–37.

Alanen, Lilli (2003). *Descartes's Concept of Mind* (Cambridge, MA: Harvard University Press).

—— (2011). 'Spinoza on the human mind', *Midwest Studies in Philosophy*, 35: 4–25.

Algra, Keimpe (2003). 'Stoic Theology', in Inwood (2003): 153–79.

Algra, Keimpe, Jonathan Barnes, Jaap Mansfeld, and Malcolm Schofield (eds.) (1999). *The Cambridge History of Hellenistic Philosophy* (Cambridge: Cambridge University Press).

Allison, Henry (1987). *Benedict de Spinoza: An Introduction* (New Haven: Yale University Press).

Aloni, Nimrod (2008). 'Spinoza as educator: from eudaimonistic ethics to an empowering and liberating pedagogy', *Educational Philosophy and Theory*, 40: 531–44.

Alston, William P. (1980). 'Internalism and externalism in epistemology', *Midwest Studies in Philosophy*, 5. Reprinted in Kornblith (2001a): 179–221.

Alter, J. M. M. (ed.) (1965). *Catalogus van de biblioteek der Vereniging 'het Spinozahuis' te Rijnsburg* (Leiden: E. J. Brill).

Annas, Julia (1990). 'Stoic epistemology', in Stephen Everson, ed., *Epistemology: Cambridge Companions to Ancient Epistemology* (Cambridge: Cambridge University Press): 184–203.

—— (1992). *Hellenistic Philosophy of Mind* (Berkeley and Los Angeles: University of California Press).

—— (1993). *The Morality of Happiness* (New York: Oxford University Press).

—— (1999a). *Platonic Ethics, Old and New* (Ithaca: Cornell University Press).

(1999b). 'Aristotle on virtue and happiness', in Nancy Sherman, ed., *Aristotle's Ethics: Critical Essays* (Lanham, Maryland: Rowman & Littlefield Press): 35–55.

(2007). 'Ethics in Stoic philosophy', *Phronesis*, 52: 58–87.

Ansaldi, Saverio (2001). 'Amour, perfection et puissance: un modèle de la nature humaine? en marge de la cinquième partie de l'éthique (Spinoza et G. Bruno)', *Archives De Philosophie*, 64: 741–57.

Aristotle (1984). *The Complete Works of Aristotle*, ed. Jonathan Barnes (Princeton: Princeton University Press).

(1985). *Aristotle's Eudemian Ethics: Books I, II, and VIII*, trans. Michael Woods (Durham, NC: Duke University Press).

(2002). *Aristotle: Nicomachean Ethics*, trans. Christopher Rowe, introduction and commentary by Sarah Broadie (Oxford: Oxford University Press).

Barbone, Steven (2002). 'What counts as an individual for Spinoza?', in Koistinen and Biro (2002): 89–112.

Barbour, Reid (1998). *English Epicures and Stoics: Ancient Legacies in Early Stuart Culture* (Amherst, MA: University of Massachusetts Press).

Barker, Peter, and Bernard R. Goldstein (1984). 'Is seventeenth century physics indebted to the Stoics?', *Centaurus*, 27: 148–64.

Barnes, Jonathan (1988). 'Bits and pieces', in Barnes and Mignucci (1988): 225–93.

Barnes, Jonathan, and Mario Mignucci (eds.) (1988). *Matter and Metaphysics* (Naples: Bibliopolis).

Barney, Rachel (2003). 'A puzzle in Stoic ethics', *Oxford Studies in Ancient Philosophy*, vol. XXIV: 303–40.

Bayle, Pierre (1740). *Dictionnaire historique et critique* (Amsterdam: Chez P. Brunel).

(1965). *Pierre Bayle: Historical and Critical Dictionary – Selections*, trans. Richard H. Popkin (New York: Library of Liberal Arts).

Becker, Lawrence C. (1998). *A New Stoicism* (Princeton: Princeton University Press).

Bennett, Jonathan (1983). 'Teleology and Spinoza's conatus', *Midwest Studies in Philosophy*, 8: 143–60.

(1984). *A Study of Spinoza's Ethics* (Indianapolis, IN: Hackett Publishing).

(2001). *Learning from Six Philosophers* (Oxford: Clarendon Press).

Betegh, Gábor (2003). 'Cosmological ethics in the *Timaeus* and early Stoicism', *Oxford Studies in Ancient Philosophy*, 24: 273–302.

Bidney, David (1962). *The Psychology and Ethics of Spinoza: A Study in the History and Logic of Ideas*, 2nd edn (New York: Russell & Russell).

Blecher, Ian (2006). 'The Stoic method of happiness', *Apeiron: A Journal for Ancient Philosophy and Science*, 39: 157–76.

Blom, Hans W., and Laurens C. Winkel (eds.) (2004). *Grotius and the Stoa* (Assen: Royal van Gorcum Press).

Bobzien, Susanne (1998). *Determinism and Freedom in Stoic Philosophy* (Oxford: Clarendon Press).

BonJour, Laurence (1998). *In Defense of Pure Reason* (Cambridge: Cambridge University Press).

Boeri, Marcelo D. (2001). 'The Stoics on bodies and incorporeals', *Review of Metaphysics*, 54: 723–52.

——— (2004). 'Socrates, Aristotle, and the Stoics on the apparent and real good', *Proceedings of the Boston Area Colloquium in Ancient Philosophy*, 20: 109–41.

Boudouris, K. J. (ed.) (1994). *Hellenistic Philosophy*, vol. II (Athens: International Center for Greek Philosophy and Culture, 1994).

Brandt, Reinhard (2003). 'Selbstbewusstsein und Selbstsorge–Zur Tradition der oikeiosis in der Neuzeit', *Archiv fuer Geschichte der Philosophie*, 85: 179–97.

Brennan, Tad (2003). 'Stoic moral psychology', in Inwood (2003): 257–94.

——— (2005). *The Stoic Life: Emotions, Duties, and Fate* (Oxford: Oxford University Press).

Bridoux, André (1966). *Le Stoïcisme et son influence* (Paris: J. Vrin).

Brink, C. O. (1955). 'Οἰκείωσις and Οἰκεότης: Theophrastus and Zeno on nature and moral theory', *Phronesis*, 1: 123–45.

Broad, C. D. (1959). *Five Types of Ethical Theory* (Paterson, NJ: Littlefield, Adams & Co.).

Brooke, Christopher (2012). *Philosophic Pride: Stoicism and Political Thought from Lipsius to Rousseau* (Princeton: Princeton University Press).

Bruni, Leonardo (1987). *The Humanism of Leonardo Bruni*, ed. and trans. Gordon Griffiths, James Hankins and David Thompson (Binghamton, NY: SUNY Press).

Brunschwig, Jacques (1986). 'The cradle argument', in Schofield and Striker (1986): 113–44.

——— (1988). 'La théorie stoïcienne du genre suprême et l'ontologie platonicienne', in Barnes and Mignucci (1988): 19–127.

——— (1990). 'Sur une façon stoïcienne de ne pas être', *Revue de théologie et de philosophie*, 122: 389–403.

——— (1999). 'Introduction: the beginnings of Hellenistic epistemology', in Algra et al. (1999): 229–59.

——— (2003). 'Stoic metaphysics', in Inwood (2003): 206–32.

Brunschwig, Jacques, and Martha C. Nussbaum (eds.) (1993). *Passions and Perceptions: Studies in Hellenistic Philosophy of Mind* (Cambridge: Cambridge University Press).

Buddeus, Johann Franz (1701). *Spinozismo ante Spinozam* (Halle: Henckel).

Burge, Tyler (1986). 'Cartesian error and the objectivity of perception', in Philip Pettit and John McDowell, eds., *Subject, Thought and Context* (Oxford: Clarendon Press): 120–40.

Buys, Ruben (2010). 'Between actor and spectator: Arnout Geulincx and the Stoics', *British Journal for the History of Philosophy*, 18: 741–61.

Byers, Sarah Catherin (2013). *Perception, Sensibility, and Moral Motivation in Augustine: A Stoic- Platonic Synthesis* (Cambridge: Cambridge University Press).

Caizzi, Fernanda Decleva (1994). 'The porch and the garden: early Hellenistic images of the philosophical life', in Anthony Bulloch, Erich S. Gruen, A. A. Long and Andrew Stewart, eds., *Images and Ideologies: Self-Definition in the Hellenistic World* (Berkeley and Los Angeles: University of California Press): 303–29.

Carnap, Rudolf (1998). 'The value of laws: explanation and prediction', excerpted from Rudolf Carnap, *Philosophical Foundations of Physics;* reprinted in Martin Curd and J. A. Cover, eds., *Philosophy of Science: The Central Issues* (New York: W. W. Norton and Co.): 678–84.

Carriero, John P. (1991). 'Spinoza's views on necessity in historical perspective', *Philosophical Topics*, 19: 47–96.

(2002). 'Monism in Spinoza', in John Biro and Olli Koistinen, eds., *Spinoza: Metaphysical Themes* (Oxford: Oxford University Press): 38–59.

(2005). 'Spinoza on final causality', *Oxford Studies in Early Modern Philosophy*, vol. II: 105–47.

(2011). 'Conatus and perfection in Spinoza', *Midwest Studies in Philosophy*, 35: 69–92.

(forthcoming). 'The highest good and perfection in Spinoza', in Michael Della Rocca, ed., *The Handbook to Spinoza* (Oxford: Oxford University Press).

Cicero (1931). *Cicero: De Finibus Bonorum et Malorum*, trans. H. Rackham (Cambridge, MA: Harvard University Press).

(2001). *Cicero: On Moral Ends*, ed. Julia Annas, trans. Raphael Woolf (Cambridge: Cambridge University Press).

Colerus, Johannes (1706). *The Life of Benedict de Spinosa, Done out of French* (London: printed by D. L. and sold by Benj. Bragg).

Collingwood, R. G. (1993). *The Idea of History*, revised edition, ed. Jan van der Dussen (Oxford: Oxford University Press).

Cooper, J. M. (2005). 'The emotional life of the wise', *Southern Journal of Philosophy*, 43: 176–218.

(2009). 'Chrysippus on physical elements', in Salles (2009a): 93–117.

Curley, Edwin (1969). *Spinoza's Metaphysics: An Essay in Interpretation* (Cambridge, MA: Harvard University Press).

(1973). 'Spinoza's moral philosophy', in Grene (1973): 354–76.

(1986). 'Analysis in the *Meditations*: the quest for clear and distinct ideas', in Amélie Oksenberg Rorty, ed., *Essays on Descartes' Meditations*, (Berkeley and Los Angeles: University of California Press): 153–76.

(1988). *Behind the Geometrical Method* (Princeton: Princeton University Press).

(1990). 'Bennett on Spinoza on teleology', in Edwin M. Curley and P. F. Moreau, eds., *Spinoza: Issues and Directions* (Leiden: E. J. Brill): 39–52.

(1991). 'The state of nature and its law in Hobbes and Spinoza', *Philosophical Topics*, 19: 97–117.

D'Angers, Julien Eymard (1976). *Recherches sur le Stoïcisme aux XVIe et XVIIe siècles* (New York: Georg Olms Verlag).

Davidson, Donald (1999). 'Spinoza's causal theory of the affects', in Yovel (1999a): 95–111.

DeBrabander, Firmin (2007). *Spinoza and the Stoics: Power, Politics and the Passions* (London: Continuum International Publishing).

De Dijn, Herman (1996). *Spinoza: The Way to Wisdom* (West Lafayette, Indiana: Purdue University Press).

Della Rocca, Michael (1996a). 'Spinoza's metaphysical psychology', in Garrett (1996a): 192–266.

(1996b). *Representation and the Mind–Body Problem in Spinoza* (Oxford: Oxford University Press).

(2003a). 'The power of an idea: Spinoza's critique of pure will', *Noûs*, 37: 200–31.

(2003b). 'A rationalist manifesto: Spinoza and the principle of sufficient reason', *Philosophical Topics*, 31: 75–93.

(2008). *Spinoza* (London and New York: Routledge).

(2010). 'PSR', *Philosopher's Imprint*, 10: 1–13.

(2012). 'Violations of the principle of sufficient reason in Leibniz and Spinoza', in Fabrice Correia and Benjamin Schnieder, eds., *Grounding and Explanation* (Cambridge: Cambridge University Press): 139–65.

Den Uyl, Douglas J. (1983). *Power, State and Freedom: An interpretation of Spinoza's Political Philosophy* (Assen, the Netherlands: Van Gorcum).

Descartes, René (1931). *The Philosophical Works of Descartes*, vols. I–II, trans Elizabeth S. Haldane and G. R. T. Ross (Cambridge: Cambridge University Press).

(1964–74). *Oeuvres*, vols. I–X, ed. Charles Adam and Paul Tannery (Paris: J. Vrin/CNRS).

(1984–91). *The Philosophical Writings of Descartes*, vols. I–II, ed. and trans. J. Cottingham, R. Stoothoff, D. Murdoch; vol. III, ed. and trans. J. Cottingham, R. Stoothoff, D. Murdoch and A. Kenny (Cambridge: Cambridge University Press).

Dilthey, Wilhelm (1924). *Die geistige Welt: Einleitung in die Philosophie des Lebens. Erste Hälfte*, ed. G. Misch (Göttingen, Germany: Vandenhoek & Ruprecht).

(1957). *Dilthey's Philosophy of Existence*, trans. William Kluback and Martin Weinbaum (New York: Bookman Associates).

Diogenes Laertius (1972). *Diogenes Laertius: Lives of Eminent Philosophers*, vols. I–II, trans. R. D. Hicks (Cambridge, MA: Harvard University Press).

Donini, Pierluigi (1999). 'Stoic ethics', in Algra et al. (1999): 675–738.

Eisenberg, Paul D. (1971). 'How to understand *De Intellectus Emendatione*', *The Journal of the History of Philosophy*, 9: 171–91.

(1977). 'Is Spinoza an ethic naturalist?', in Siegfried Hessing, ed., *Speculum Spinozanum, 1677–1977* (London: Routledge & Kegan Paul): 145–64.

Emilsson, Eyjólfur Kjalar (1996). 'Cognition and its object', in Lloyd Gerson, ed., *The Cambridge Companion to Plotinus* (Cambridge: Cambridge University Press): 217–49.

Engberg-Pedersen, Troels (1990). *The Stoic Theory of Oikeiosis* (Aarhus, Denmark: Aarhus University Press).

Engstrom, Stephen, and Jennifer Whiting (eds.) (1996). *Aristotle, Kant, and the Stoics: Rethinking Happiness and Duty* (Cambridge: Cambridge University Press).

Epictetus (1928). *Epictetus: The Discourses, Books II–IV*, trans. W. A. Oldfather (Cambridge, MA: Harvard University Press).

(1983). *Handbook of Epictetus*, trans. Nicholas White (Indianapolis, IN: Hackett Publishing).

Ettinghausen, Henry (1972). *Francisco de Quevedo and the Neostoic Movement* (Oxford: Oxford University Press).

Everson, Stephen (ed.) (1991). *Companions to Ancient Thought II: Psychology* (Cambridge: Cambridge University Press).

Feuer, Lewis Samuel (1958). *Spinoza and the Rise of Liberalism* (Boston: Beacon Hill Press).

Ficino, Marsilio (2001). *Platonic Theology*, trans. Michael J. B. Allen, ed. James Hankins, vols. I–VI (Cambridge, MA: Harvard University Press).

Fish, Jeffrey, and Kirk R. Sanders (eds.) (2011). *Epicurus and the Epicurean Tradition* (Cambridge: Cambridge University Press).

Forman, D. (2008). 'Free will and the freedom of the sage in Leibniz and the Stoics', *History of Philosophy Quarterly*, 25: 203–19.

Förster, Eckart, and Yitzhak Y. Melamed (2012). 'Introduction', in Eckart Förster and Yitzhak Y. Melamed, eds., *Spinoza and German Idealism* (Cambridge: Cambridge University Press): 1–6.

Frankena, William K. (1975). 'Spinoza's "new morality": notes on Book IV', in Mandelbaum and Freeman (1975): 85–100.

Franks, Paul (2005). *All or Nothing: Systematicity, Transcendental Arguments, and Skepticism in German Idealism* (Cambridge, MA: Harvard University Press).

Frede, Michael (1983). 'Stoics and skeptics on clear and distinct impressions', in Myles Burnyeat, ed., *The Skeptical Tradition* (Berkeley: University of California Press): 65–93.

(1986). 'The affections of the soul', in Schofield and Striker (1986): 93–112.

(1994). 'The Stoic conception of reason', in Boudouris (1994): 50–63.

(1999). 'The Stoic conception of the good', in Katerina Ierodiakonou, ed., *Topics in Stoic Philosophy* (Oxford: Oxford University Press): 71–94.

(2011). *A Free Will: Origins of the Notion in Ancient Thought*, ed. A. A. Long (Berkeley: University of California Press).

Furley, David (1999). 'Cosmology', in Algra et al. (1999): 412–51.

Gabbey, Alan (1996). 'Spinoza's natural science and methodology', in Garrett, D. (1996a): 142–91.

Garber, Daniel (1992). 'Descartes' physics', in John Cottingham, ed., *The Cambridge Companion to Descartes* (Cambridge: Cambridge University Press): 286–334.

Garrett, Aaron (2003). *Meaning in Spinoza's Method* (Cambridge: Cambridge University Press).

Garrett, Don (1990). '"The free man always acts honestly": freedom and the good in Spinoza's *Ethics*', in E. Curley and P.-F. Moreau, eds., *Spinoza: Issues and Directions* (New York: E. J. Brill): 221–38.

(ed.) (1996a). *The Cambridge Companion to Spinoza* (Cambridge: Cambridge University Press).

(1996b). 'Spinoza's ethical theory', in Garrett (1996a): 267–314.

(2002). 'Spinoza's conatus argument', in Koistinen and Biro (2002): 127–58.

(2008). 'Representation and consciousness in Spinoza's naturalistic theory of the imagination', in Charlie Huenemann, ed., *Interpreting Spinoza* (Cambridge: Cambridge University Press): 4–25.

Garver, Eugene (2006). 'Spinoza and the discovery of morality', *History of Philosophy Quarterly*, 23: 357–74.

Gill, Christopher (2003). 'The School in the Roman imperial period', in Inwood (2003): 33–58.

Goff, Philip (ed.) (2012). *Spinoza on Monism* (New York: Palgrave Macmillan).

Goldman, Alvin (1980). 'The internalist conception of justification', *Midwest Studies in Philosophy*, 5. Reprinted in Kornblith (2001a).

Goodman, Lenn E. (2009). 'An idea is not something mute like a picture on a pad', *Review of Metaphysics*, 62: 591–631.

Gourinat, Jean-Baptiste (2009). 'The Stoics on matter and prime matter: "corporealism" and the imprint of Plato's Timaeus', in Salles (2009a): 46–70.

Graeser, Andreas (1991). 'Stoische Philosophie bei Spinoza', *Revue Internationale de Philosophie*, 45: 336–46.

Graver, Margaret R. (ed. and trans.) (2002). *Cicero on the Emotions: Tusculan Disputations 3 and 4* (Chicago: University of Chicago Press).

(2007). *Stoicism and Emotion* (Chicago: University of Chicago Press).

Grene, Marjorie (ed.) (1973). *Spinoza: A Collection of Critical Essays* (Garden City, NY: Anchor Books).

Grotius, Hugo (1925). *De iure belli ac pacis*, Latin text with an English translation by Francis W. Kelsey (Oxford: Clarendon Press).

Guéroult, Martial (1968–74). *Spinoza*, vols. I–II (Paris: Aubier-Montaigne).

Guigon, Ghislain (2012). 'Spinoza on composition and priority', in Goff (2012): 183–205.

Gullan-Whur, Margaret (2000). *Within Reason: A Life of Spinoza* (New York: Thomas Dunne Books).

Hacking, Ian (1973). 'Leibniz and Descartes: proof and eternal truth', *Proceedings of the British Academy*, 59. Reprinted in Ian Hacking, *Historical Ontology* (Cambridge, MA: Harvard University Press, 2002): 175–88.

(1999). *The Social Construction of What?* (Cambridge, MA: Harvard University Press).

Hahm, D. E. (1977). *The Origins of Stoic Cosmology* (Columbus: Ohio State University Press).

Hallett, H. F. (1957). *Benedict de Spinoza* (London: The Athalone Press).

Hampshire, Stuart (1949). 'Fallacies in moral philosophy', *Mind*, 58: 466–82.

Hankinson, R. J. (2003). 'Stoic epistemology', in Inwood (2003): 59–84.

Hegel, G. W. F. (1896). *Lectures on the History of Philosophy*, vols. I–III, ed. and trans. E. S. Haldane and Frances H. Simson (London: Kegan Paul).

Heller, Bernard (1932). *Stoic Elements in the Philosophy of Spinoza*, unpublished doctoral dissertation (Ann Arbor: University of Michigan).

Hoffman, Paul (2011). 'Final causation in Spinoza', *Logical Analysis and History of Philosophy*, 14: 40–50.

Horgan, Terry, and Matjaž Potrč (2012). 'Existence monism trumps priority monism', in Goff (2012): 51–76.

Huenemann, Charlie (2014). *Spinoza's Radical Theology* (Durham, UK: Acumen Publishing).

Hurka, Thomas (2006). 'Value theory', in David Copp, ed., *The Oxford Handbook of Ethical Theory* (Oxford: Oxford University Press): 357–79.

Ierodiakonou, Katerina (ed.) (1999). *Topics in Stoic Philosophy* (Oxford: Oxford University Press).

Inwood, Brad (1985). *Ethics and Human Action in Early Stoicism* (Oxford: Oxford University Press).

(1999). 'Stoic ethics', in Algra et al. (1999): 675–738.

(ed.) (2003). *The Cambridge Companion to Stoicism* (Cambridge: Cambridge University Press).

(2009). 'Why physics?', in Salles (2009a): 201–23.

(2012). 'How unified is Stoicism, anyway?', in Rachana Kamtekar, ed., *Virtue and Happiness: Essays in Honour of Julia Annas* (Oxford: Oxford University Press): 223–44.

Inwood, Brad, and L. P. Gerson (eds. and trans.) (1997). *Hellenistic Philosophy*, 2nd edn (Indianapolis, IN: Hackett Publishing).

Irvine, William B. (2009). *A Guide to the Good Life: The Ancient Art of Stoic Joy* (Oxford: Oxford University Press).

Irwin, T. E. (1995). *Plato's Ethics* (Oxford: Oxford University Press).

(2007–9). *The Development of Ethics: A Historical and Critical Study*, vols. 1–3 (Oxford: Oxford University Press).

Jacobsen, Eric Paul (2005). *From Cosmology to Ecology: The Monist World-View in Germany from 1770–1930* (Berlin: Peter Lang).

James, Susan (1993). 'Spinoza the Stoic', in T. Sorrell, ed., *The Rise of Modern Philosophy* (Oxford: Oxford University Press): 289–316.

James, William (1978). 'The knowing of things together', reprinted in his *Essays in Philosophy*, F. H. Burkhardt and I. K Skrupskelis, eds. (Cambridge, MA: Harvard University Press): 372–80.

(1981). *Pragmatism* (Indianapolis, IN: Hackett Publishing).

Jarrett, Charles (1976a). 'Spinoza's ontological argument', *Canadian Journal of Philosophy*, 6: 685–92.

(1976b). 'A note on Spinoza's ontology', *Philosophical Studies*, 29: 415–18.

(1978). 'The logical structure of Spinoza's *Ethics*, Part I', *Synthese*, 37: 15–65.

(2002). 'Spinoza on the relativity of good and evil', in Koistinen and Biro (2002): 159–81.

Joachim, Harold H. (1940). *Spinoza's Tractatus de Intellectus Emendatione: A Commentary* (Oxford: Clarendon Press).

Kahneman, Daniel (1999). 'Objective happiness', in D. Kahneman, E. Diener and N. Schwarz, eds., *Well-Being: The Foundations of Hedonic Psychology* (New York: Russell Sage Foundation): 3–25.

Kant, Immanuel (1965). *Immanuel Kant's Critique of Pure Reason*, trans. Norman Kemp-Smith (New York: St Martin's Press).

Kenny, Anthony (1998). 'Descartes on the will', reprinted in John Cottingham, ed., *Descartes* (Oxford: Oxford University Press): 132–59.

Kidd, I. G. (1971). 'Stoic intermediates and the end for man', in Long (1971a): 150–72.

Kisner, Matthew J. (2011). *Spinoza on Human Freedom: Reason, Autonomy and the Good Life* (Cambridge: Cambridge University Press).

Kisner, Matthew J., and Andrew Youpa (eds.) (2014). *Essays on Spinoza's Ethical Theory* (Oxford: Oxford University Press).

Kitanov, Severin V. (2011). 'Happiness in a mechanistic universe: Thomas Hobbes on the nature and attainability of happiness', *Hobbes Studies*, 24: 117–36.

Koistinen, Olli, and John Biro (eds.) (2002). *Spinoza: Metaphysical Themes* (Oxford: Oxford University Press).

Kornblith, Hilary (ed.) (2001a). *Epistemology: Internalism and Externalism* (Malden, MA: Blackwell Publishers).

(2001b). 'A brief historical introduction', in Kornblith (2001a): 1–9.

Korsgaard, Christine M. (1996). *The Sources of Normativity* (Cambridge: Cambridge University Press).

Kraye, Jill (1988). 'Moral philosophy', in Charles B. Schmitt and Quentin Skinner, eds., *The Cambridge History of Renaissance Philosophy* (Cambridge: Cambridge University Press): 303–86.

(ed.) (1997). *Cambridge Translations of Renaissance Philosophical Texts*, vol. I *Moral Philosophy* (Cambridge: Cambridge University Press).

Kristeller, Paul Oskar (1984). 'Stoic and Neoplatonic sources of Spinoza's *Ethics*', *History of European Ideas*, 5: 1–15.

Kulstad, Mark (2008). 'Newton, Spinoza, Stoics and others: a battle line in Leibniz's wars of (natural) religion', *The Leibniz Review*, 18: 81–121.

Laerke, Mogens (2011). 'Spinoza's cosmological argument in the *Ethics*', *Journal of the History of Philosophy*, 49: 439–62.

(2012). 'Spinoza's monism? What monism?', in Goff (2012): 244–61.

Lagrée, Jacqueline (2004). *Spinoza et le débat religieux* (Presses Universitaires de Rennes).

(2010). *Le néostoïcisme* (Paris: J. Vrin).

Lapidge, Michael (1973). '*Archai* and *stoicheia*: a problem in Stoic cosmology', *Phronesis*, 18: 140–78.

(1978). 'Stoic cosmology', in Rist (1978): 161–85.

LeBuffe, Michael (2004). 'Why Spinoza tells people to try to preserve their being', *Archiv Fuer Geschichte Der Philosophie*, 86: 119–45.

(2010). *From Bondage to Freedom: Spinoza on Human Excellence* (Oxford: Oxford University Press).

Leibniz, Gottfried Wilhelm (1969). *Gottfried Wilhelm Leibniz: Philosophical Papers and Letters*, 2nd edn, trans. and ed. Leroy E. Loemker (Dordrecht: D. Reidel Publishing Co.).

(1985). *Theodicy*, ed. Austin Farrer, trans. E. M. Huggard (Chicago and La Salle, Illinois: Open Court Publishing).

(1989). *G. W. Leibniz: Philosophical Essays*, ed. and trans. Roger Ariew and Daniel Garber (Indianapolis, IN: Hackett Publishing).

Lennon, Thomas M. (2005). 'The rationalist conception of substance', in Alan Nelson, ed., *A Companion to Rationalism* (Malden, MA: Blackwell Publishing): 12–30.

Lesses, Glenn (1998). 'Content, cause, and Stoic impressions', *Phronesis*, 43: 1–25.

Lin, Martin (2004). 'Spinoza's metaphysics of desire: the demonstration of IIIP6', *Archiv Fuer Geschichte Der Philosophie*, 86: 21–55.

(2006). 'Teleology and human action in Spinoza', *Philosophical Review*, 115: 317–54.

Lipsius, Justus (1604). *Manuductio ad Stoicam Philosophiam* (Antwerp: J. Moretus).

(2004). *Politica: Six Books of Politics or Political Instruction*, ed. and trans. Jan Waszink (Assen, the Netherlands: Royal Van Gorcum Press).

(2006). *On constancy*, trans. John Stradling, ed. John Sellars (Exeter, UK: Bristol Phoenix Press).

Liu, Irene (2008). 'Nature and knowledge in Stoicism: on the ordinariness of the Stoic sage', *Apeiron: A Journal for Ancient Philosophy and Science*, 41: 247–76.

Lloyd, Genevieve (1994). *Part of Nature: Self-Knowledge in Spinoza's Ethics* (Ithaca: Cornell University Press).

(2008). *Providence Lost* (Cambridge, MA: Harvard University Press).

Long, A. A. (ed.) (1971a). *Problems in Stoicism* (London: Athlone Press).

(1971b). 'Language and thought in Stoicism', in Long (1971a): 75–113.

(1983). 'Greek ethics after Macintyre and the Stoic community of reason', *Ancient Philosophy*, 3. Reprinted in Long (1996): 184–97.

(1986). *Hellenistic Philosophy*, 2nd edn (Berkeley and Los Angeles: University of California Press).

(1989). 'Stoic Eudaimonism', *Proceedings of the Boston Area Colloquium in Ancient Philosophy*, 4. Reprinted in Long (1996): 77–101.

(1991). 'Representation and the self in Stoicism', in Everson (1991). Reprinted in Long (1996): 246–85.

(1996). *Stoic Studies* (Cambridge: Cambridge University Press).

(2002). *Epictetus* (Oxford: Clarendon Press).

(2003). 'Stoicism in the philosophical tradition: Spinoza, Lipsius, Butler', in Miller and Inwood (2003): 7–29.

(2011). 'Aristotle on *eudaimonia, nous,* and divinity', in Jon Miller, ed., *Aristotle's Nicomachean Ethics: A Critical Guide* (Cambridge: Cambridge University Press): 92–113.

Long, A. A., and D. N. Sedley (eds. and trans.) (1987). *The Hellenistic Philosophers*, vols. I–II (Cambridge: Cambridge University Press).

Manning, Richard (2002). 'Spinoza, thoughtful teleology, and the causal significance of content', in Koistinen and Biro (2002): 182–209.

MacIntyre, Alasdair (1998). *A Short History of Ethics*, 2nd edn (Notre Dame, Indiana: Notre Dame University Press).

Mandelbaum, Maurice, and Eugene Freeman (eds.) (1975). *Spinoza: Essays in Interpretation* (LaSalle, Illinois: Open Court Publishing).

Mark, Thomas (1978). 'Truth and adequacy in Spinozistic ideas', in Shahan and Biro (1978): 11–34.

Marshall, Eugene (2013). *The Spiritual Automaton: Spinoza's Science of the Mind* (Oxford: Oxford University Press).

Marshall, John (1998). *Descartes's Moral Theory* (Ithaca: Cornell University Press).

Mason, Richard (1986). 'Spinoza on modality', *The Philosophical Quarterly*, 35: 313–42.

(1997). *The God of Spinoza* (Cambridge: Cambridge University Press).

Matheron, Alexandre (1994). 'Le moment stoïcien de l'Éthique de Spinoza', in Moreau (1994): 147–61.

Matson, Wallace (1994). 'Spinoza on beliefs', in Yirmiyahu Yovel, ed., *Spinoza on Knowledge and the Human Mind* (Leiden: E. J. Brill): 67–81.

McDonough, Jeffrey K. (2011). 'The heyday of teleology and early modern Philosophy', *Midwest Studies in Philosophy*, 35: 179–204.

McGrade, Arthur Stephen, John Kilcullen, and Matthew Kempshall (eds. and trans.) (2001). *The Cambridge Translations of Medieval Philosophical Texts*, vol. II (Cambridge: Cambridge University Press).

McRae, Robert (1965). ' "Idea" as a philosophical term in the seventeenth century', *Journal of the History of Ideas*, 26: 175–90.

Méchoulan, Henry (1994). 'Quevedo stoïcien?', in Moreau (1994): 81–94.

Meinwald, Constance (2005). 'Ignorance and opinion in stoic epistemology', *Phronesis*, 50: 215–31.

Melamed, Yitzhak Y. (2013a). *Spinoza's Metaphysics: Substance and Thought* (Oxford: Oxford University Press).

(2013b). 'Spinoza's metaphysics of thought: parallelisms and the multifaceted structure of ideas', *Philosophy and Phenomenological Research*, 86: 636–83.

Menn, Stephen (1995). 'Physics as a virtue', *Proceedings of the Boston Area Colloquium in Ancient Philosophy*, 11: 1–34.

(1998). *Descartes and Augustine* (Cambridge: Cambridge University Press).

Mercer, Christia (2001). *Leibniz's Metaphysics: Its Origins and Development* (Cambridge: Cambridge University Press).

Meyer, Susan Sauvé (2008). *Ancient Ethics: A Critical Introduction* (New York: Routledge).

Miller, Jon (2001). 'Spinoza's possibilities', *The Review of Metaphysics*, 54: 779–814.

(2003). 'Spinoza and the concept of a law of nature', *History of Philosophy Quarterly*, 20: 257–76.

(2005). 'Stoics and Spinoza on suicide', in Gábor Boros, ed., *Der Einfluss des Hellenismus auf die Philosophie der Frühen Neuzeit* (Wiesbaden: Harrasowitz Verlag): 107–35.

(2009). 'Grotius and Stobaeus', in Hans Blom, ed., *Property, Piracy and Punishment: Hugo Grotius on war and booty in De iure praedae* (Leiden: E. J. Brill): 104–26.

(2010). 'A distinction regarding happiness in ancient philosophy', *Social Research: An International Quarterly of the Social Sciences*, 77: 595–624.

(2014). 'Spinoza on the life according to nature', in Kisner and Youpa (2014): 102–23.

Miller, Jon, and Brad Inwood (eds.) (2003). *Hellenistic and Early Modern Philosophy* (Cambridge: Cambridge University Press).

Miraeus, Aubertus (1629). *Iusti Lipsi Sapientiae et Litterarum Antistitis Fama Postuma*, editio tertia (Antwerp: J. Moretus).

Mitsis, Phillip (2003). 'Locke's offices', in Miller and Inwood (2003): 45–61.

(2006). Review of Nancy Sherman's *Stoic Warriors*, published in *Studies in the History of Ethics*, February 2006.

(2013). 'Epicurus: freedom, death, and hedonism', in Roger Crisp, ed., *The Oxford Handbook of the History of Ethics* (Oxford: Oxford University Press): 73–87.

Moreau, Pierre-François (ed.) (1994). *Le Stoïcisme aux XVIe et XVIIe siècles* (Caen: Presses Universitaires de Caen).

Morford, M. (1991). *Stoics and Neostoics: Rubens and the Circle of Lipsius* (Princeton: Princeton Univerity Press).

Morrison, James C. (1994). 'Spinoza on the self, personal identity, and immortality', in Graeme Hunter, ed., *Spinoza: The Enduring Questions* (Toronto: University of Toronto Press): 31–47.

Mulligan, Kevin, and Fabrice Correia (2013). 'Facts', in Edward N. Zalta, ed., *The Stanford Encyclopedia of Philosophy* (Spring 2013 Edition): http://plato.stanford.edu/entries/facts/ (last checked 4.12.14).

Nadler, Steven (1999). *Spinoza: A Life* (Cambridge: Cambridge University Press).

(2001a). *Spinoza's Heresy: Immortality and the Jewish Mind* (Oxford: Oxford University Press).

(2001b). 'Spinoza in the garden of good and evil', in Elmar Kremer and Michael Latzer, eds., *The Problem of Evil in Early Modern Philosophy* (Toronto: University of Toronto Press): 66–80.

(2006). *Spinoza's Ethics: An Introduction* (Cambridge: Cambridge University Press).

Newlands, Samuel (2010). 'Another kind of Spinozistic monism', *Noûs*, 44: 469–502.

(2013). 'Spinoza's modal metaphysics', in Edward N. Zalta, ed., *The Stanford Encyclopedia of Philosophy* (Winter 2013 Edition): http://plato.stanford.edu/entries/spinoza-modal/ (last checked 4.12.14).

Nuchelmans, Gabriel (1980). *Late-Scholastic and Humanist Theories of the Proposition* (Amsterdam: North-Holland Press).

Nussbaum, Martha (1986). *The Fragility of Goodness* (Cambridge: Cambridge University Press).

(1994). *The Therapy of Desire: Theory and Practice in Hellenistic Ethics* (Princeton: Princeton University Press).

(2000). *Sex and Social Justice* (Oxford: Oxford University Press).

(2001). *Upheavals of Thought: The Intelligence of the Emotions* (Cambridge: Cambridge University Press).

Papy, Jan (2011). 'Lipsius' Stoic physics and the Neostoic reading of the world', in Hiro Hirai and Jan Papy, eds., *Justus Lipsius and Natural Philosophy* (Brussels: Royal Academy of Belgium): 9–18.

Parmenides (1994). *Philosophy Before Socrates*, trans. Richard D. McKirahan, Jr (Indianapolis, IN: Hackett Publishing).

Parkinson, G. H. R. (1954). *Spinoza's Theory of Knowledge* (Oxford: Clarendon Press).

Pembroke, S. G. (1971). 'Oikeiosis', in Long (1971a): 114–49.

Pereboom, Derk (1994). 'Stoic psychotherapy in Descartes and Spinoza', *Faith and Philosophy*, 11: 592–625.

Perin, Casey (2005). 'Stoic epistemology and the limits of externalism', *Ancient Philosophy*, 25: 383–401.

Plutarch (1976). *Plutarch: Moralia, Parts I–II*, trans. Harold Cherniss (Cambridge, MA: Harvard University Press).

Protagoras (1997). *Plato: Complete Works*, ed. John M. Cooper, trans. Stanley Lombardo and Karen Bell (Indianapolis, IN: Hackett Publishing).

Putnam, Hilary (1981). *Reason, Truth and History* (New York: Cambridge University Press).

Quevedo, Francisco de (1997). 'Defense of Epicurus against commonly held opinions', in Kraye (1997): 211–22.

Ramelli, Ilaria (1973). *Hierocles the Stoic: Elements of ethics, fragments and excerpts*, trans. David Konstan (Atlanta: Society of Biblical Literature).

Reed, Baron (2002). 'The Stoic account of the cognitive impression', *Oxford Studies in Ancient Philosophy*, 23: 147–80.

Renz, Ursula (2009). 'Spinozas erkenntnistheorie: Eine naturalisierte epistemologie?', *Deutsche Zeitschrift Für Philosophie*, 57: 419–432.

Reynolds, L. D. (1983). 'Introduction', in L. D. Reynolds, ed., *Texts and Transmission: A Survey of the Latin Classics* (Oxford: Clarendon Press): 1–48.

Reynolds, L. D., and N. G. Wilson (1991). *Scribes and Scholars: A Guide to the Transmission of Greek and Latin Literature*, 3rd edn (Oxford: Clarendon Press).

Rice, Lee (1975). 'Spinoza on individuation', in Mandelbaum and Freeman (1975): 195–214.

Rist, John (ed.) (1978). *The Stoics* (Berkeley and Los Angeles: University of California Press).

Rorty, Amélie Oksenberg (1996). 'The two faces of Stoicism: Rousseau and Freud', *Journal of the History of Philosophy*, 34: 1–22.

Rorty, Richard (1979). *Philosophy and the Mirror of Nature* (Princeton: Princeton University Press).

Rosenthal, Michael A. (2001). 'Tolerance as a virtue in Spinoza's *Ethics*', *Journal of the History of Philosophy*, 39: 535–57.

Ross, G. M. (1974). 'Seneca's philosophical influence', in C. D. N. Costa, ed., *Seneca* (London and Boston: Routledge & Kegan Paul): 116–65.

Ross, W. D. (1923). *Aristotle* (London: Methuen & Co.).

Russell, D. C. (2004). 'Stoic value theory: indifferent things and conditional goods', *Southwest Philosophy Review: The Journal of the Southwestern Philosophical Society*, 20: 125–37.

Rutherford, Donald (1999). 'Salvation as a state of mind: the place of *acquiescentia* in Spinoza's *Ethics*', *British Journal for the History of Philosophy*, 7: 447–73.

(2004). 'On the happy life: Descartes vis-à-vis Seneca', in Strange and Zupko (2004): 177–97.

(2012). 'The end of ends? Aristotelian themes in early modern ethics', in Jon Miller, ed., *The Reception of Aristotle's Ethics* (Cambridge: Cambridge University Press): 194–221.

Salles, Ricardo (2001). 'Compatibilism: Stoic and modern', *Archiv Fuer Geschichte Der Philosophie*, 83: 1–23.

(ed.) (2009a). *God and Cosmos in Stoicism* (Oxford: Oxford University Press).

(2009b). 'Chrysippus on conflagration and the indestructibility of the cosmos', in Salles (2009a): 118–34.

Sambursky, S. (1959). *Physics of the Stoics* (New York: Macmillan).

Sandbach, F. H. (1971). 'Ennoia and prolepsis', in Long (1971a): 22–37.

Schaffer, Jonathan (2003). 'Is there a fundamental level?', *Noûs*, 37: 498–517.

(2010). 'Monism: the priority of the whole', *Philosophical Review*, 119. Reprinted in Goff (2012): 31–76.

(2014). 'Monism', in Edward N. Zalta, ed., *The Stanford Encyclopedia of Philosophy* (Winter 2014 Edition): http://plato.stanford.edu/entries/monism/ (last checked 4.12.14).

Schneewind, J. B. (1998). *The Invention of Autonomy* (Cambridge: Cambridge University Press).

(2003). 'Introduction', in Miller and Inwood (2003): 1–6.

Schofield, Malcolm (1980). 'Preconception, argument, and God', in Schofield et al. (1980): 283–308.

(1999). 'Social and political thought', in Algra et al. (1999): 739–70.

Schofield, Malcolm, Myles Burnyeat, and Jonathan Barnes (eds.) (1980). *Doubt and Dogmatism: Studies in Hellenistic Epistemology* (Oxford: Clarendon Press).

Schofield, Malcolm, and Gisela Striker (eds.) (1986). *The Norms of Nature* (Cambridge: Cambridge University Press).

Schroeder, Mark (2012). 'Value theory', in Edward N. Zalta, ed., *The Stanford Encyclopedia of Philosophy* (Summer 2012 Edition):http://plato.stanford.edu/entries/value-theory/ (last checked 4.12.14).

Scott, Dominic (1995). *Recollection and Experience: Plato's Theory of Learning and Its Successors* (Cambridge: Cambridge University Press).

Scott, William Robert (1900). *Francis Hutcheson: His Life, Teaching and Position in the History of Philosophy* (Cambridge: Cambridge University Press).

Sedley, David (1982). 'The Stoic criterion of identity', *Phronesis*, 27: 255–75.

(1985). 'The Stoic theory of universals', *The Southern Journal of Philosophy*, 23, supplement: 87–92.

(1989). 'Philosophical allegiance in the Greco-Roman World', in Miriam Griffin and Jonathan Barnes, eds., *Philosophia Togata* (Oxford: Clarendon Press): 97–119.

(1999). 'Hellenistic physics and metaphysics', in Algra et al. (1999): 355–411.

(2003). 'The School, from Zeno to Arius Didymus', in Inwood (2003): 7–34.

Seneca (1925). *Seneca: Epistulae Morales*, trans. Richard M. Gummere (Cambridge, MA: Harvard University Press).

(1932) *Moral Essays*, vol. II, trans. John W. Basore (Cambridge, MA: Harvard University Press).

(1995) *Seneca: Moral and Political Essays*, ed. and trans. John M. Cooper and J. F. Procopé (Cambridge: Cambridge University Press).

(2007). *Seneca: Selected Philosophical Letters*, trans. Brad Inwood (Oxford: Oxford University Press).

Shahan, R. W., and J. I. Biro (eds.) (1978). *Spinoza: New Perspectives* (Norman, OK: University of Oklahoma Press).

Shaver, Robert (1996). 'Grotius on Scepticism and self-interest', *Archiv für Geschichte der Philosophie*, 78: 27–47.

Shein, Noa (2009a). 'The false dichotomy between the objective and subjective interpretations of Spinoza's theory of attributes', *British Journal for the History of Philosophy*, 17: 505–32.

(2009b). 'Spinoza's theory of attributes', in Edward N. Zalta, ed., *The Stanford Encyclopedia of Philosophy* (Spring 2009 Edition): http://plato.stanford.edu/entries/spinoza-attributes/ (last checked 4.12.14).

Shields, Christopher (1994). 'The Stoic lekton', in Boudouris (1994): 137–48.

(2012). *Ancient Philosophy: A Contemporary Introduction*, 2nd edn (New York: Routledge).

Sider, Theodore (2001). *Four Dimensionalism* (Oxford: Oxford University Press).

Simplicius (2002). *Commentary on Epictetus' Handbook*, vols. I–II, ed. and trans. Charles Brittain and Tad Brennan (Ithaca: Cornell University Press).

Sorabji, Richard (1980). *Necessity, Cause and Blame* (London: Duckworth).

(1990). 'Perceptual content in the Stoics', *Phronesis*, 35: 301–14.

(2000). *Emotion and Peace of Mind: From Stoic Agitation to Christian Temptation* (Oxford: Oxford University Press).

Spinoza, Baruch/Benedict de (1925). *Spinoza Opera*, vols. I–V, ed. Carl Gebhardt (Heidelberg: Carl Winters).

(1985). *The Collected Works of Spinoza*, vol. I, ed. and trans. E. Curley (Princeton: Princeton University Press).

(2002). *Spinoza: The Complete Works*, trans. Samuel Shirley, ed. Michael L. Morgan (Indianapolis, IN: Hackett Publishing).

Steinberg, Justin (2013). 'Spinoza's political philosophy', in Edward N. Zalta, ed., *The Stanford Encyclopedia of Philosophy* (Winter 2013 Edition): http://plato.stanford.edu/entries/spinoza-political/ (last checked 4.12.14).

Strange, Steven K. (2004). 'The Stoics on the voluntariness of the passions', in Strange and Zupko (2004): 31–51.

Strange, Steven K., and Jack Zupko (eds.) (2004). *Stoicism: Traditions and Transformations* (Cambridge: Cambridge University Press).

Straumann, Benjamin (2003/2004). '*Appetitus societatis* and *oikeiosis*', *Grotiana* (n.s.), 24/25: 41–66.

Striker, Gisela (1974). 'Κριτήριον τῆς ἀληθείας', *Nachrichten der Akademie der Wissenschaften zu Göttingen*, I.Phil.-hist. Klasse, 2 (1974). Reprinted in Striker (1996): 48–110.

(1983). 'The role of oikeiosis in Stoic ethics', in *Oxford Studies in Ancient Philosophy I*. Reprinted in Striker (1996): 145–67.

(1986). 'Antipater, or the Art of Living', in Schofield and Striker (1986). Reprinted in Striker (1996): 185–204.

(1990). 'The problem of the criterion', in Stephen Everson, ed., *Epistemology: Companions to Ancient Thought 1* (Cambridge: Cambridge University Press). Reprinted in Striker (1996): 143–60.

(1991). 'Following nature: a study in Stoic ethics', in *Oxford Studies in Ancient Philosophy IX*. Reprinted in Striker (1996): 1–73.

(ed.) (1996). *Essays on Hellenistic Epistemology and Ethics* (New York: Cambridge University Press).

Stuart, Matthew (2013). *Locke's Metaphysics* (Oxford: Oxford University Press).

Sumner, L. W. (2002). 'Happiness now and then', in Lawrence J. Jost and Roger A. Shiner, eds., *Eudaimonia and Well-Being* (Kelowna, BC: Academic Printing and Publishing): 21–39.

Svensson, Frans (2011). 'Happiness, well-being, and their relation to virtue in Descartes' ethics', *Theoria*, 77: 238–60.

Tararkiewicz, Wladyslaw (1976). *Analysis of Happiness*, trans. Edward Rothert and Danuta Zielinskn (The Hague: Martinus Nijhoff).

Todd, Robert B. (1978). 'Monism and immanence: the foundations of Stoic physics', in Rist (1978): 137–60.

Tuck, Richard (1987). 'The "modern" theory of natural law', in Anthony Pagden, ed., *The Languages of Political Theory in Early-Modern Europe* (Cambridge: Cambridge University Press): 99–119.

Usener, Hermannus (1977). *Glossarium Epicureum*, ed. M. Gigante and W. Schmid (Rome: Edizioni dell'Ateneo e Bizzarri).

Verbeke, Gerard (1973). 'Le stoïcisme, une philosophie sans frontières', *Aufstieg und Niedergang der römischen Welt*, 1–4: 3–42.

Vico, Giambattista (1948). *The New Science*, 3rd edn (of 1744), trans. Thomas Goddard Bergin and Max Harold Fisch (Ithaca: Cornell University Press).

Viljanen, Valterri (2011). *Spinoza's Geometry of Power* (Cambridge: Cambridge University Press).

Vlastos, Gregory (1991). *Socrates, Ironist and Moral Philosopher* (Princeton: Princeton University Press).

Vogt, Katja Maria (2009). 'Sons of the earth: are the Stoics metaphysical brutes?', *Phronesis*, 54: 136–54.

von Arnim, H. (1964). *Stoicorum Veterum Fragmenta*, vols. I–IV (reprint, Stuttgart: Teubner Verlag).

Watson, Gerard (1994). 'The concept of "phantasia" from the late Hellenistic period to early Neoplatonism', *Aufstieg und Niedergang der römischen Welt*, II.36.7: 4765–4810.

White, Michael J. (2003). 'Stoic natural philosophy (physics and cosmology)', in Inwood (2003): 124–52.

Wilson, Catherine (2008). *Epicureanism at the Origins of Modernity* (Oxford: Oxford University Press).

Wilson, Margaret D. (1996). 'Spinoza's theory of knowledge', in Garrett (1996a): 89–141.

Wolfson, H. A. (1934). *The Philosophy of Spinoza*, vols. I and II (Cambridge, MA: Harvard University Press).

Youpa, Andrew (2007). 'Spinoza's theory of motivation', *Pacific Philosophical Quarterly*, 88: 375–90.

(2010). 'Spinoza's theories of value', *British Journal for the History of Philosophy*, 18: 209–29.

Yovel, Yirmiyahu (1989). *Spinoza and Other Heretics, 1: The Marrano of Reason* (Princeton: Princeton University Press).

(ed.) (1999a). *Desire and Affect: Spinoza as Psychologist* (New York: Little Room Press).

(1999b). 'Transcending mere survival: from Conatus to Conatus Intelligendi', in Yovel (1999a): 45–62.

Zanta, Léontine (1975). *La Renaissance du Stoïcisme au XVIe Siècle* (first published 1914; reprinted in Genève: Slatkine Reprints).

Index of names

Achilles
  Introduction to Aratus, 40
Adams, Robert Merrihew, 25
Aertsen, Jan A., 179, 180
Aetius, 4, 62, 126, 127
Alanen, Lilli, 67, 68, 153
Alexander of Aphrodisias, 89
  De fato, 3, 18, 45, 89, 90
  On Aristotle's Prior Analytics, 17
  On Aristotle's Topics, 17, 31
  On Mixture, 17, 48
Algra, Keimpe, 16
Allison, Henry, 140
Alston, William P., 70, 73
Alter, J. M. M., 9, 21, 106
Anaximenes, 24
Annas, Julia, 30, 66, 87, 88, 92, 129,
  134, 190
Antiochus, 91
Apuleius, 22
Aquinas, Thomas, 19, 179–81, 192
  *Commentary on Aristotle's Nicomachean
    Ethics*, 148
  Summa contra gentiles, 179
  Summa Theologicae, 180
Aristo, 145, 146, 148, 186, 198, 199, 208
Aristocles, 55
Aristotle, 19, 22, 24, 38, 61, 135, 138, 147,
  169, 173–5, 186, 190, 198
  Divisiones Aristoteleae, 147
  Eudemian Ethics, 174, 175
  Nicomachean Ethics, 147, 148, 170, 171,
    174, 175, 212, 222
Arrian, 20
Augustine, 19
  Contra academicos, 2
Aurelius, Marcus, 29, 106
  Meditations, 61

Bacon, Francis, 58
Barbeyrac, Jean, 106
Barbone, Steven, 125

Barbour, Reid, 10
Barker, Peter, 10
Barnes, Jonathan, 24
Bayle, Pierre, 1, 60, 208
  Dictionary, 1
Becker, Lawrence, 57–8, 59, 94,
  134, 208
Bennett, Jonathan Francis, 31, 35, 37, 38,
  73, 74, 78–9, 87, 88, 100, 103, 108,
  124, 141, 156, 200
Bentham, Jeremy, 58
Berkeley, George
  Third Dialogue, 62
Bidney, David, 2, 13, 117, 138–41, 143,
  145, 156–7, 200, 202, 208
  The Psychology and Ethics of Spinoza,
    156, 212
Blom, Hans W., 106
Bobzien, Susanne, 44, 65, 72, 88–91, 92,
  93, 96, 166, 203
Boethius, 90
Boethus, 53
Boxel, Hugo, 22
Brennan, Tad, 74–5, 80, 82, 85, 88, 89, 92,
  93, 102
Bridoux, André, 10
Brink, C. O., 101
Broad, C. D., 102
Broadie, Sarah, 175
Brooke, Christopher, 1, 10, 20, 197
Bruni, Leonardo, 185
Brunschwig, Jacques, 31, 61, 64, 103
Buddeus, Johann Franz, 1
Burge, Tyler, 74
Buys, Ruben, 10
Byers, Sarah Catherin, 102

Caizzi, Fernanda Decleva, 175
Calcidius, 12, 18, 29, 48
Carnap, Rudolf, 46
Carriero, John, 39, 48–50, 51,
  113, 181

Chrysippus, 10, 14, 29, 44, 46, 47, 53, 55, 59, 63, 84, 85, 90, 92, 94, 96–7, 104, 107, 113–14, 119, 123, 127, 128, 129, 163, 166, 203, 208
Peri Nomou, 46
Physical Propositions, 28
Cicero, Marcus Tullius, 11, 20, 21, 29, 31, 54, 55, 91, 102, 104, 106, 163, 166, 170, 171, 175, 176, 199
Academica, 17, 31, 91
De fato, 17, 18, 44, 89, 90, 129, 166
De natura deorum, 3, 15, 17–18, 44, 48, 50, 53–5, 56, 114, 163, 164, 166
On Duties, 11, 18, 175
On Ends, 18, 45, 55, 75, 102–4, 110, 121, 163, 170, 171, 175, 199, 203
Tusculan Disputations, 6, 18, 102, 175, 176, 184, 185, 186, 202
Cleanthes, 16, 29, 53, 54, 59, 113, 114, 119, 128, 129, 208
Hymn to Zeus, 15, 16, 55, 113, 164
Cleomedes, 18
De motu circulari corporum caelestium, 18, 20
Colerus, Johannes, 2
Cooper, J. M., 32
Correia, Fabrice, 165
Curley, Edwin M., 51, 69, 100, 107, 111, 124, 141, 156, 159, 167, 181, 207

D'Angers, Julien Eymard, 10
DeBrabander, Firmin, 7, 118, 140, 145, 198
Della Rocca, Michael, 33, 35, 68, 69, 71, 72, 100, 108, 209
Den Uyl, Douglas J., 119
Descartes, René, 3, 8–10, 16, 19, 20, 21, 25, 36, 49, 50, 58, 59, 62, 63, 68, 77, 79, 80, 87, 91, 108–9, 132, 133, 138, 148, 150, 171, 172, 187–9, 191, 192, 193
Comments on a Certain Broadsheet, 133
Meditations, 10, 77, 91, 133, 215
Passions of the Soul, 87
Principles of Philosophy, 16, 21, 25, 37, 49, 87, 108, 171
Dilthey, Wilhelm, 2, 14, 209
du Vair, Guillame, 21, 22

Eisenberg, Paul D., 138, 152
Emilsson, Eyjólfur Kjalar, 27
Empedocles, 22
Empiricus, Sextus, 18, 20, 21, 81
Against the Mathematicians, 3, 4, 17, 18, 25, 31, 40, 48, 54, 64, 75, 76, 144, 146, 150
Outlines of Pyrrhonism, 17, 45
Engberg-Pedersen, Troels, 103
Engstrom, Stephen, 93
Epictetus, 4, 9, 20, 21, 81, 82–5, 126, 149, 174, 201
Discourses, 4, 16, 18, 57, 61, 81, 82, 83, 91, 114, 126, 146, 166, 174, 184, 194
Enchiridion, 5, 18, 21, 82, 83, 84–5, 149, 150, 202
Epicurus, 93, 173, 174, 175, 208
Letter to Menoeceus, 174
Ettinghausen, Henry, 21
Eusebius, 129
Evangelical Preparation, 39, 53, 54, 55, 129

Feuer, Lewis Samuel, 118
Ficino, Marsilio, 196
Fish, Jeffrey, 208
Förster, Eckart, 25, 208
Frankena, William, 138, 151, 156
Franks, Paul, 25, 26
Frede, Michael, 64, 65, 66, 73, 88, 89, 90, 91, 92, 93, 127, 144, 149
Frege, Gottlob, 165
Furley, David, 47

Gabbey, Alan, 21, 125
Galen, 94, 127
On Bodily Mass, 29
On Incorporeal Qualities, 35
On the Opinions of Hippocrates and Plato, 4, 5, 17, 18, 66, 94, 127, 208
Garrett, Aaron, 44
Garrett, Don, 57, 108, 131, 151
Gellius, Aulus, 44, 65–6, 74, 131
Attic Nights, 17, 18, 44, 55, 65, 89, 131
Giles of Rome, 148
On the Instruction of Rulers and the Governance of Kings, 148
Goldman, Alvin, 70, 73
Goldstein, Bernard R., 10
Gourinat, Jean-Baptiste, 32
Graeser, Andreas, 2, 37
Graver, Margaret, 4, 5, 6, 66, 102, 132, 176, 187
Grotius, Hugo, 8, 9, 19, 20, 21, 105–7, 108, 109, 114, 118, 119
De iure belli ac pacis, 19, 105, 106, 218
Guigon, Ghislain, 52
Gullan-Whur, Margaret, 21

Hacking, Ian, 43
Haeckel, Ernst, 25
Hahm, David, 30, 38, 54
Hampshire, Stuart, 190, 208
Hankinson, R. J., 76
Hegel, Georg Wilhelm Friedrich, 1, 2, 19,
    37, 60
Heller, Bernard, 7
Hempel, Carl Gustav, 46
Hierocles, 63, 71, 103
Hippolytus
    Refutation of All Heresies, 203
Hobbes, Thomas, 10, 58, 59, 138, 155,
    172, 173
Hoffman, Paul, 39
Horgan, Terry, 26
Huenemann, Charlie, 16, 118
Hume, David, 58, 166
    A Treatise of Human Nature, 167
Hurka, Thomas, 145
Hutcheson, Francis, 52
    *Philosophiae Moralis Institutio
    Compendiaria*, 52

Inwood, Brad, 10, 30, 45, 75, 76, 80,
    83, 87, 95, 102, 104, 121–2, 145,
    167, 169
Irwin, T. E., 52, 116, 118, 155, 191

Jacobi, Friedrich Heinrich, 25
Jacobsen, Eric Paul, 25
James, Susan, 2, 8, 9, 207
James, William, 24, 26–7
Jarrett, Charles, 156, 157

Kahneman, Daniel, 184
Kant, Immanuel, 58, 93, 208
    Critique of Pure Reason, 26
Kenny, Anthony, 87
Kisner, Matthew, 154, 155, 173, 196,
    198, 200
Kitanov, Severin V., 172
Kornblith, Hilary, 70,
Korsgaard, Christine, 93
Kraye, Jill, 21
Kristeller, P. O., 8, 9
Kulstad, Mark, 10

Laertius, Diogenes, 4, 20, 42, 63, 64, 75,
    104, 128, 148
    Lives of Eminent Philosophers, 3, 4, 6, 16,
    17, 18, 20, 21, 24, 29, 30, 32, 38, 40,
    42, 46, 48, 54, 61, 62, 63, 64, 71, 75,

76, 81, 90, 100, 103–4, 111, 113, 114,
    119, 120, 127, 128, 129, 132, 146,
    147–9, 151, 174, 175, 184, 187, 194,
    199, 202, 214
Lapidge, Michael, 39
LeBuffe, Michael, 116, 154, 167, 173
Leibniz, Gottfried Wilhelm, 1, 19, 25, 60
    Theodicy, 44, 166
Lennon, Thomas M., 32, 33
Lesses, Glenn, 64
Lessing, Gotthold Ephraim, 25
Lin, Martin, 51
Lipsius, Justus, 20, 21, 196
    Manuductio ad Stoicam Philosophiam, 19
    Politica, 196
Lloyd, Genevieve, 2, 115, 142
Locke, John, 11, 58, 172, 173
Long, A. A., 2, 5, 6, 16, 30, 31, 33, 35, 37,
    45, 46, 47, 57, 61, 64, 66, 73, 81, 135,
    163, 174, 175, 209
Lucullus, 91

MacIntyre, Alasdair, 101
Marcian, 46
Mark, Thomas, 68, 74
Marshall, Eugene, 109
Matheron, Alexandre, 2, 6, 8, 9
Matson, Wallace, 74
McGrade, Arthur Stephen, 181
McRae, Robert, 61, 62
Méchoulan, Henry, 21
Melamed, Yitzhak, 10, 25, 42,
    200, 208
Menn, Stephen, 80, 91
Mercer, Christia, 25
Miller, Jon, 10, 19, 42, 110, 203
Miraeus, Aubertus, 20
Mitsis, Phillip, 11, 93, 164
Moreau, Pierre-François, 18
Morrison, James C., 124
Mulligan, Kevin, 165

Nadler, Steven, 71, 79, 156–7
Nemesius
    On the Nature of Man, 39
Nero, 123
Newlands, Samuel, 96, 165
Nuchelmans, Gabriel, 20
Nussbaum, Martha, 5, 175

Ockham, William of, 180
    commentary on the *Sentences* of Peter
    Lombard, 181

Olympiodorus, 128
  On Plato's Gorgias, 128
Origen, 85–7
  On Principles, 86

Panaetius, 53
Papy, Jan, 19, 20
Parmenides
  On Nature, 24
Pembroke, S. G., 101, 103, 104, 127
Pereboom, Derk, 5
Perin, Casey, 71
Philo, 63
  Allegories of the laws, 63
  On the Eternity of the World, 18, 53
Plantin, Christopher, 18
Plato, 2, 4, 22, 24, 31, 38, 61, 138, 147
  Laws, 147, 214
  Protagoras, 196
  Republic, 196
  Sophist, 31
  Timaeus, 24
Plotinus, 2, 25
  Enneads, 25, 27
Plutarch, 6, 20, 22, 46, 86, 120, 130
  On Common Opinions Against the Stoics,
    18, 75, 114, 120, 186
  On Moral Progress, 128
  On Moral Virtue, 4
  On Stoic Self-Contradictions, 6, 17, 18, 28,
    39, 46, 53, 54, 55, 86, 107, 114, 186
  On the Fortune of Alexander, 118
Porphyry
  On Abstinence, 54
Posidonius, 4, 208
Potrč, Matjaž, 26
Proclus, 25

Quevedo, Francisco de, 21
Quine, W. V. O., 27

Ramelli, Illaria, 119
Reed, Baron, 71
Reynolds, L. D., 17, 18
Rice, Lee, 124, 125
Rorty, Amélie Oksenberg, 2
Rorty, Richard, 61
Rosenthal, Michael, 197
Ross, W. D., 174
Russell, Bertrand, 27
Rutherford, Donald, 6, 23, 173, 189

Salles, Ricardo, 53
Sambursky, S., 135

Sandbach, F. H., 72
Sanders, Kirk R., 208
Schaffer, Jonathan, 26, 27, 28
Schneewind, J. B., 10, 11, 107
Schofield, Malcolm, 106
Schroeder, Mark, 145, 146
Scott, Dominic, 127
Scott, Robert William, 52
Sedley, David, 31, 34, 35, 47, 121,
    123, 208
Seneca, 6, 18, 20, 21, 30, 32, 66,
    74, 102, 121–3, 175, 176,
    187, 192
  De otio, 18, 118
  De vita beata, 18, 20, 175, 176, 192
  Letters, 4, 6, 18, 32, 103, 110, 121–3, 151,
    169, 175, 184, 202
  On Anger, 6, 18, 21, 66
  On Benefits, 18
Shaver, Robert, 106
Shein, Noa, 32, 33, 52
Shields, Christopher, 46, 64, 88, 151,
    166, 167
Sider, Theodore, 27
Simplicius, 9, 20, 21, 82, 85, 121
  Commentary, 83, 85, 212, 220, 228
  On Aristotle's Categories, 29, 121
  On Epictetus' Handbook, 85
Socrates, 22, 63, 174, 196
Solon, 173
Sorabji, Richard, 64, 66, 89
Spinoza, Baruch/Benedictus de
  Ethics. passim
  Short Treatise, 30, 37, 115, 145, 151,
    161, 202
  Tractatus de Intellectus Emendatione, 4, 9,
    22, 30, 77, 133–4, 135, 136, 144, 145,
    150, 156, 161, 171, 172, 173, 189,
    190, 193, 202, 203
  Tractatus Politicus, 9, 197, 202
  Tractatus Theologico-Politicus, 9, 16, 43,
    57, 111, 154, 167, 168, 176, 178, 181,
    192, 193, 202
Steinberg, Justin, 151
Stobaeus, 4–6, 8, 18, 19, 20, 21, 38, 44, 48,
    53, 75, 86, 128, 145, 148, 149, 184,
    186, 203
  Eclogues, 18, 75, 86, 88, 128, 148,
    150, 170
Strange, Steven, 10, 80, 92
Straumann, Benjamin, 106
Striker, Gisela, 76, 81, 103, 203, 204
Stuart, Matthew, 172
Sumner, L. W., 182
Svensson, Frans, 187

Tacitus, 21, 123
Todd, Robert B., 40
Tuck, Richard, 105, 106
Tyrius, Maximus, 22

Usener, Hermannus, 174

Vico, Giambattista
    New Science, 1
Viljanen, Valterri, 43, 101, 112
Vlastos, Gregory, 174

Watson, Gerard, 62
White, Michael, 45
Whiting, Jennifer, 93
Wilson, Catherine, 10, 19

Wilson, Margaret, 133, 140, 141, 167
Wilson, N. G., 18
Winkel, Laurens C., 106
Wolff, Christian
    Philosophica rationalis, sive logica, 25
    Psychologia rationalis, 25
Wolfson, Harry Austryn, 50, 101, 102, 103, 156

Youpa, Andrew, 110, 173
Yovel, Yirmiyahu, 143, 167

Zeno, 20, 24, 29, 40, 59, 128, 184, 199, 203, 208
Zeno of Tarsus, 53
Zupko, Jack, 10

General index

activity, 36, 37, 39, 58, 68, 114, 124, 139, 140, 164
adequate ideas. *See* ideas, adequate
aether, 22, 135
affects
  active, 6
archai, 32, 36
assent
  faculty of, 88, 91, 93,
  Stoic, 95, 96
attribute, 32, 33, 41, 43, 49, 52, 159, 208
  of extension, 32–6, 41–3, 68, 95, 189, 209
  of God, 37, 42, 111
  of thought, 32, 33–4, 35, 36, 41, 42, 86, 153

beliefs
  propositional content of, 67

causation, 5, 38, 39, 51, 90, 95
commanding faculty. *See hegemonikon*
compatibilism, 92
conatus, 100–43
cosmology, 44, 47, 53, 57, 58, 120, 217
cosmopolitanism, 106, 118
cosmos, 26, 29, 30, 53–5, 56, 118

determinism, 44, 57, 89, 117, 166, 203, 205, 209
dualism, 35, 36

emotions, 5, 66, 77, 129, 138, 139, 170, 177, 192, 202
  propositional content of, 5, 88
eph' hēmin, 9, 149, 201
Epicurean, 19, 47, 103, 134
epistemology, 7, 11, 12, 75, 85, 99, 207

essence
  actual, 36, 103, 108, 116
  eternal, 36
  of animals, 13
  of God, 28, 180
  of substance, 32, 41
eudaimonia, 173–5, 183, 189, 196, 222
eupatheiai, 6, 131
explanation
  causal, 39
externalism, 70–1, 73

false ideas. *See* ideas, false
fate, 1, 90, 133, 204, 205
fear, 6, 144, 172, 205
flourishing, 55, 150, 155, 173, 174, 191, 204, 206, 210
free will, 3, 93, 188, 209
freedom, 3, 89, 95, 170, 173, 174, 177, 180, 189, 197, 202

German idealism. *See* idealism, German
God
  as Nature, 3, 55
good feelings. *See eupatheiai*

happiness, 28, 170–206
  conception of, 13, 14, 173, 181, 183–4, 189, 191, 195, 207
hegemonikon, 29, 64, 121, 127, 129
hexis, 42, 128
hope, 6
horme, 87, 101–3, 137

idealism, 1–2
  German, 25, 208
ideas
  adequate, 72, 78–80, 98, 139
  false, 78, 98
  propositional content of, 68, 79, 98
immanence, 1, 3, 25, 44, 55, 164

impressions
  cataleptic, 65, 71, 74–7, 80, 81–4, 91, 92
  hormetic, 74–7, 80, 81–4, 86, 87, 91, 92,
    94, 97
  impulsive, 88, 90, 94, 149
  propositional content of, 89
indifferents, 148–50, 199
  preferred, 128, 151
individuals
  identity, 120–6
intellect, 31, 32, 33, 40, 41, 87, 91, 112,
    139, 140, 172, 176
internalism, 68, 70, 73

knowledge
  intuitive, 140, 168, 179, 192, 194
  of God, 13, 132, 154–5, 161, 164–8, 176,
    178–80, 192, 194, 202

law
  natural, 46, 181
laws
  of nature, 16, 43, 44, 46, 96–7, 132, 133,
    165, 178
lekta, 64, 88
logic, 17, 18, 20, 30, 45, 57, 85, 113, 114,
    128, 182, 183, 190
  Aristotelian, 20
  Stoic, 17, 20
logos, 127
love
  of God, 16, 178, 192, 193

metaphysics, 2, 7, 11, 12, 17, 28, 38, 44,
    57, 94, 95, 112, 120, 140, 171, 190,
    203, 205
method
  geometrical, 44, 45, 47
  nomological, 43, 45, 97
minimalism
  ontological, 38
modality, 90, 96, 97, 112, 166
model
  of human nature, 152, 153, 154
modes, 37, 43, 44, 58, 68, 70, 94, 111–13,
    117, 121, 140, 141, 151, 159
  immediate infinite, 43
  infinite, 42, 111
  mediate infinite, 43
modifications of substance. See modes
monism, 24–60
  holistic, 26–8, 50
  Jamesian, 26, 27
  Spinoza's, 12, 32, 36, 41, 42, 49, 50, 52

Spinozistic, 12, 25, 26, 27, 50, 59
  Stoic, 12, 26, 36, 50, 100
moral progress, 13, 101, 119, 126, 127
mos geometricus. See method, geometrical
motion-and-rest, 42, 43, 124, 125

Natura naturans, 36–8, 97
Natura naturata, 36–8, 97
naturalism, 95, 99, 134, 138–9, 156, 167
Nature/nature
  as a whole, 35, 39, 52, 94, 163, 210
  laws of. See laws, of nature
  living in agreement with, 170, 194, 199,
    205, 206
  Spinoza's, 31, 33
  Stoic, 33, 57, 59
  universal, 28, 55, 107, 119, 163
necessitarianism, 165
normativity, 7, 12, 14, 20, 56, 83, 91, 116,
    154, 155, 156, 161, 165, 166
nous, 42, 222

oikeiosis, 100–43
ontology, 15, 31, 43, 44
  Spinoza's, 42
  Stoic, 31, 45, 63, 120, 121

parallelism, 34, 52, 68, 124, 136, 159,
    200, 207
passion, 5, 186, 192
passions, 4, 5, 21, 22, 129, 131–2, 186,
    205, 209
passivity, 36, 37, 39, 58
pathe, 62
perception, 50, 79, 81, 87, 91, 140, 159
phantasia, 12, 21, 61–99
physics, 17, 20, 27, 29, 30, 37, 38, 41, 45,
    47, 51, 57, 58, 95, 134–6, 171
Platonism, 38
pluralism, 25, 27, 28, 29, 44
pneuma, 22, 29, 42, 48, 50, 94, 129,
    134–6
power
  absolute, 6, 9, 149, 201
  human, 6, 9, 66, 89, 90, 95, 143, 149,
    153, 161, 193, 198, 201
  of acting, 131, 142, 151, 161
  of thinking, 97
properties
  intrinsic, 12, 25, 72
propositional attitudes, 67, 68, 74
providence. See teleology

Quellenforschung, 8

rationality
  divine, 44
reason, 4, 126, 127, 141–3, 148, 153,
    168, 176
  dictates of, 118, 197
representation, 71, 73
representationalism, 61
Rezeptionsgeschichte, 8

sagacity, 63, 126, 128, 129, 130, 136, 137
sage, 63, 64, 65, 66, 94, 104, 110,
    128–32, 136
self-esteem, 142
self-preservation. *See conatus*
semantics, 14, 113, 182, 195
soul, 1, 4, 22, 61, 62–3, 64, 65, 66, 71, 72,
    74, 76, 83, 87, 94, 97, 102, 121, 127,
    129, 134–6, 163, 174, 208, 217
Stoic principle
  active, 34, 35, 36
  passive, 34, 35, 36, 37, 39
striving. *See conatus*

substance
  theory of, 28–9
system, 11, 44, 100
  Spinoza's, 7, 8, 41, 46, 207, 209
  Stoic, 21, 45, 57, 100

techne, 128
teleology, 12, 13, 15, 16, 26, 39, 50–9, 115,
    117, 134, 164, 204, 207, 208
telos, 58, 75
theos, 42

utility, 4, 153, 159, 163

value, 144–69
  moral, 145, 146, 147, 151, 154–5,
    165, 166
  theory, 145–7

wisdom, 21, 127, 128, 137, 169,
    171, 191

Made in the USA
Coppell, TX
05 November 2020